The Future of Software

The Future of Software

edited by Derek Leebaert

The MIT Press
Cambridge, Massachusetts
London, England

Set in Sabon by Graphic Composition, Inc., Athens, Georgia.
Printed and bound in the United States of America.

Library of Congress Cataloging-in-Publication Data

The Future of software / edited by Derek Leebaert.
    p.   cm.
    Includes bibliographical references and index.
    ISBN 0-262-12184-0
    1. Computer software. I. Leebaert, Derek.
    QA76.754.F86 1995
    005.3—dc20   94-28458
                                                                  CIP

Contents

Foreword by Joshua Lederberg   ix

Acknowledgements   xiii

News from the Frontiers   1
Derek Leebaert

I Awakening Possibilities

The Evolving Resource   29
Denos C. Gazis

Is Any of This Relevant?   45
David Vaskevitch

The Keys to the Highway   77
Peter F. Conklin and Eric Newcomer

II New Kinds of Possibility

The Prairie School: The Future of Workgroup Computing   105
Deborah K. Louis and L. Alexander Morrow

Software without Borders: Applications That Collaborate   127
David Williams and Timothy O'Brien

The Fall of Software's Aristocracy: Realizing the Potential
of Development   157
Scott Brown

Naturalware: Natural-Language and Human-Intelligence
Capabilities   177
Gustave Essig

III On the Knowledge Frontier

Where's the "Walkman" in Japan's Software Future?   215
Edward A. Feigenbaum

Property of the Mind: Software and the Law   227
Jeffrey P. Cunard

Knowledge and the New Magnitudes of Connection   261
Derek Leebaert and William B. Welty

About the Authors   291
Index   295

Foreword

It seems close to a fact of technological life that the more powerful the instrument the less it can be put to use: the better the telescope, the vaster and more complex the universe it captures for us to make sense of. This has implications throughout human enterprise, from molecular biology to media interaction and from traffic control to oceanography.

At the hardware level, skills steadily *converge* to drive computer development at extraordinary speed, yet we find that we have failed to develop adequate *divergent* software capacities to put all this power to use. We build ever faster and better generators, but the light bulbs and the electric typewriters come fitfully in their wake.

The internal world of the computer is more astounding than we could have dreamed 30 years ago, but the capacity to give it an external world to mix with ours remains mostly unrealized. If the computer is to work with us to an extent approaching the capacities we have already given it, it must have direct contact with the things that we can see and touch; but the goal of giving it such sensoria, its own capacity to examine the universe, has been pretty much stalled by procedural (rather than technological) deficiencies. We have not been able to match our computers' analogies to the brain with adequate analogies to the incorporated mind: a *mens sana in corpore sano*.

Evolution is cultural as well as biological: every human instrument has its material history of insight, trial and error, and reapplication. The question is one of focus. Nature had a few hundred million years to colonize the land from the ocean. Do we have a century to fritter away the opportunities of the computer?

Each thousandfold multiplication of memory or division of speed will always find wonderful, not-really-anticipated uses, and we revel in the prospect that today's supercomputer will be tomorrow's personal computer. But we may also properly despair at how we will be able to harness that enormous power with the programming and knowledge-transfer tools now in hand.

For the first time, human material constructs have reached such a level of complexity, subtlety, and real-time reactive capacity that we are justified in analogizing them to the ultimate complexity of living systems. This being so, we can profit from studying how such systems learn from experience—indeed, how they develop ever more effective capacities of experiencing. In biological advance, reflex arcs become more complex, recruiting memory, which in turn potentiates conditioning. They elaborate a perceptual framework to integrate sensory data, and impose some coherence on the inputs that induce attraction or impel flight.

We are a long way from the construction of self-improving computer systems for natural language understanding akin to the child's learning of language. This is of course an intensely social as well as cognitive experience, and embedded in parents' and families' fascination with a child's every utterance. It would be an arduous task to impart to our computer systems the world's existing masses of knowledge without first providing computers with a natural language capability which would enable them to read and comprehend without intolerably costly and error-prone human mediation. So far we have only been able to accumulate stilted databases which heap up their own barriers to retrieval. Try telling your computer today: "I have this problem. . . . What do I need to know to solve it?"

To return to biological evolution: We encounter very little explicit programming in the most fundamental processes. What in DNA tells the *ur*-cell to evolve a brain capable of language, much less the rules of grammar? To call natural selection the survival of the fittest is tautological. Ever-changing environments, full of possibilities, impose destruction on the losers, not fitness on the survivors. Organisms of a certain complexity tend to replicate their own kind and are subject to some overarching variability for "experimental" diversification. Later in evolution, we see the incorporation of deep-seated motivational drives, pleasure and pain, to enforce these forms of behavior that contribute to survival in the long run.

Will we have any choice but to trust the further elaboration of software to such ends-driven modules? Then we can tell the computer: "I don't care how you do it, but I'll switch off your power unless you solve problem X. . . ." Such an approach is, of course, reminiscent of the nonlinear, complexly interactive approach of neural net programming. When it reaches back to the basic design of the machine, it will converge even more closely with organic evolution.

Achievement only rarely simplifies; usually it unveils or creates richer complexities. There is an ongoing and irresolvable tension between keeping a system receptive to such additions and controlling the system thus changed. Creation is a frontier activity, ahead of and almost necessarily apart from the integrating mechanisms that stabilize the system as a whole; however, it becomes necessary to assert some degree of control if the entire system is not to go random.

There may be no way, with finite human resources, to develop software that we can fully understand and control yet which meets the opportunities hardware presents to our appetite. I am not suggesting that we reject this Faustian bargain when, for instance, we are at the bare beginnings of trials of genetic algorithms. But, as the phylum *Automata* emerges from the ooze, we'd best keep a close eye on how faithfully that course merits "our" ends rather than an agenda of its own (which, just to meet our demands on it, it will have had to develop more than enough awareness to formulate). We will need to make full use of those very tools to achieve the requisite self-understanding to be capable of making—indeed, to be fit to make—such assessments. Derek Leebaert's *Technology 2001,* with its foreword by Arthur C. Clarke, helped paint a picture which sometimes seemed to outdistance science fiction; the present volume continues the quest to understand the antinomy between complexity and control, and to imagine the possibilities for enterprise.

Joshua Lederberg

Acknowledgements

Several people were indispensable in helping to address this vast, kaleido-scopic subject. Jeff Bellin of Bell Atlantic and Spencer Brittain Bradley of The Advisory Board Co. gave timely encouragement A. T. Kearney's General Counsel, David Webster, shared his faith and wisdom. Richard L. Veech, M.D., of the National Institutes of Health, opened up entirely new fields and perspectives for me. Don Rahmlow became both a friend and a business partner along the way. Carl Widell, Kevin Galloway, and Michael Black kept demonstrating software's startling commercial possibilities. Carol Welsh streamlined much of their work and mine.

Paul Marsh of Park City, Cynthia Tsai of MassTech, and Irene Rude of Germany's Ministry for Technology and Research contributed valuable criticism, as did my friend John Hauge.

Timothy Dickinson, of the *Paris Review* and innumerable consultancies in economics, remains a comrade in arms. As George Plimpton says, "I always come away from him keenly aware of the empty stretches in my brain." Mike Peterson, of MCI and Client Server Professional Inc., is both a renowned technologist and a patient tutor. Other lessons have been drawn from Bruce Marquardt, Bob Sevigny, and Ed Stephenson. Finally, at Georgetown University's Graduate School of Business, Dean Robert Parker and Director of Faculty Services Virginia Flavin have provided vibrant surroundings with unsurpassed colleagues.

Derek Leebaert
Washington, D.C.

The Future of Software

News from the Frontiers

Derek Leebaert

"What was victory but the ability to face larger problems without fear?" So reflects one of Lester Del Rey's remarkable science fiction heroes as he shores up his tottering world. This breathtaking Promethean assertion that imagination is the most vital element for transforming challenge into achievement might well be said to summarize the computer era.

Every now and again a civilization rises that shows what people can do if they dare. We have built incredible machines, yet so far we have won from them only a fraction of what they can do. The victories ahead will be at least as dramatic as those that have resulted in the immense multiplication of basic computing power. They will all the more be manifestations of imagination as such power is used to make it possible to undertake tasks of compounding complexity.

Asked what the most important long-term scientific quest was likely to be, Phil Anderson, a Nobel laureate in theoretical physics, raised a universal question of means rather than of any specific end: "Unless you solve the software problem, nothing else matters."

"Software" has come to mean almost any kind of interpretative or communicating routine employing some highly complex machine system—whether movie projector, book, or computer. But the term was coined to describe the intermediary organizations of knowledge that bridge the distance between individual human intelligence and the awesomely swift resources of computer power.

The astounding thing about software is the number of capacities we have awakened in the great cybernetic systems over less than half a century. The present juncture resembles the point in human evolution when language—the software of the brain—appeared and made possible cooperation, the transmission of knowledge and vision, and the lasting preservation of skills, thus enabling the brain to act on the world outside the skull in a manner reflecting its capacities.

Anderson's point is that computing power has greatly surpassed the development of the software that should enable us to turn such power into work. Computers still have few of the human capabilities that once made the dream of communicating disembodied intelligence both wondrous and frightening. Hardware—the built machine—is still far from nearing the complexity of the organic human brain. It could almost certainly perform much closer to brain-like capacities than it does. The constraint lies not in the computer's lack of adequate material connectedness but in the absence of software to provide it with even more startling uses.

The cost of software has generally followed the dramatic decline in the hardware unit cost of information, in line with Gordon Moore's famous statement that computer capacities would double roughly every 18 months. But overall, the advances in software have not kept pace with the increases in raw computing power. As computer use becomes pervasive, and as the number of new users and new programs increases dramatically, there is much discouragement with these practical limitations.

In spite of relentlessly mounting machine capacity and decades of extensive research and development, computers are still rather difficult not only to program but also to learn and to use. Idiot savants, they show extreme operational capacity in extremely limited domains. Otherwise their capabilities for intelligence and communication are poor—drawbacks that will become measurably greater as they are given more and more tasks and as their applications and capabilities are integrated.

The actual programs that run computers and allow them to perform are the commonest constraints on raising the performance to the level required. Power and keyboard skills are plentiful, but routinized judgment and organized imagination are not. (And surely we want better access than is offered by the keyboard!) What will quicker, cheaper, more comprehensible computer use—more widely applicable and more flexibly modifiable—be like as the machine offers ever more "intelligent" characteristics?

The great achievement of the last generation was the use of computers as information sources—basic processors of vast heaps of simple statements. Now what concerns us is the range of electronic capacities, ramifying into design, into all forms of visualization, and soon into biology. This is beginning to approach the more sophisticated neural processes— and at speeds much greater than the brain's. As we move into this great prairie of possibilities, the entire scope of human interaction will be affected—the new approaches to coordination in enterprise being the most obvious.

There are two dominant themes in these ten chapters. One is coordination; the other is the question as to what will be taken for granted.

The words "cooperation" and "collaboration" involve consciousness and reciprocity (i.e., willingness to work together). But "coordination" means working within the same relatively established system. It need imply no special level of awareness and no special intent. A car and a driver are coordinate, but it would be strange to say that they are collaborating, even when the car can feed back certain negative factors.

Today, software can facilitate the collaboration of scientists halfway around the world from one another who have never met, materially creating the Invisible College of which Francis Bacon dreamed. It may also facilitate the activities of a scientist acting upon a hundred automatic deep-sea research stations which she will never visit.

Ever more complex systems can talk to one another about ever more intricate matters; however, the initiative still lies outside such systems, in human hands. The collaboration of the systems takes place at a speed, and embraces a command of detail, beyond any possible human duplication, but the principles of such interaction are still embedded in the same level of non-conscious relationships as the feedback in a steam engine.

Actual coordination is always implicit when one is examining how technologies accelerate new combinations and ways of relating— particularly between individuals at work, but also in other areas of endeavor: in entertainment, education, between companies, internationally, and (inevitably) in the operations of the law. It is not a question of pushing straight lines of knowledge forward, of drawing out straight lines of single inquiry. Instead we need to draw three-dimensional nets through huge banks of knowledge. We insert structured learning—the equivalent of the "wisdom of the body"—into a million procedures.

To take something for granted, moreover, is to confer power upon ourselves—and to move closer to the Promethean ideal which Del Rey invokes.

Many of the achievements of applying knowledge technology to enterprise have rested on the programming and the deployment of human reasoning drawn from vast lateral storage. Few of them involve the complex approximations of judgment and perception. Most of us have become too familiar with the magnificent brute literalism of computers—their tireless idiot-savant capacities. The challenge is to imagine new uses for these tools and new ways of using them, and to figure out how to apply their power. The word "computer" is gaining an interactive sense beyond "hyper-abacus" and "super-file." Ironically, the term "electronic brain" has died out as some really brainlike qualities have begun to emerge.

How will we work all this into our lives? What new uses will enrich us? Ranges of issues arise, concerning not only operating software and software applications but also building, protecting, standardizing, producing, distributing, and educating people in the confident, creative, critical mastery of this next literacy.

It is difficult to anticipate the ways technology flows into culture, and how culture is then changed. Arthur C. Clarke not only envisioned communications satellites; he wrote a story about what would happen if the Soviet Union used them to bombard the United States with pornography. Few people have such an imagination. The personal-computer revolution was surprise enough; it thoroughly shook up all types of enterprise and authority, much as transistors and television had altered the family. What other revolutions are smoldering? And how do we prepare? What next will be taken for granted, as computer games now are, by five-year-olds around the world?

Clarke wrote the preface to this volume's predecessor, *Technology 2001* (MIT Press, 1991), a book that focused on the future of computers and communications. He confessed his amazement that slide rules and mathematical tables had become obsolete in the course of one decade, and that he now had the equivalent of several million vacuum tubes sitting on his office desk. Even he was taken by surprise.

This book assembles ten well-taken bearings on the country of the future. Such an effort cannot give us a map yet, but it can give us a sense of some of the characteristics of this strange land just over the horizon. Just as unexplored America exercised a magnetic force on the policies of the Old World, we feel this undiscovered country's pull on practical policies more and more strongly today.

Creative people are increasingly aware that they are eliciting only a fraction of the implications of their work—a fraction that probably gets smaller with each more powerful generation of technology. For instance, the most formidable computer scientists at the dawn of the computer era—even John von Neumann—were thinking about missile trajectories. Was anyone thinking about payrolls or cattle hybridizing—two of the countless uses to which computers would soon be applied? What are the unexamined opportunities as we ponder the future of software?

The Expert Dreamers

Software is the fastest-growing major industry in the United States. While the U.S. economy expanded by 30 percent in the years 1984–1994, the software sector proliferated by 269 percent, becoming larger than all but five manufacturing industries. It is one of America's foremost global competitors, holding a 75 percent share of the world market for prepackaged sales. Many of the major American software companies earn more than half of their revenues abroad (though this will change as other countries get into the act, as India is doing now).

There is a critical difference, however, between the way today's computer technologies have evolved and all previous technological development—a difference with immense significance for what might be called the Anderson Imperative.

In the past, a technology's pattern of advance could be broadly anticipated once it had started. New technologies usually emerged at the most basic levels. For example, the steam engine was a pumping device 100 years before it pulled the smallest truck. There followed a step-by-step climb up the ladder of combustion power to a vast, fairly predictable expansion. The steam locomotive—shocking in 1830—was a great but relatively manageable force by 1860.

With computers, however, we have had an explosion of deep and narrow devices, able to perform millions of transactions a second and to correlate the medical histories of entire cities but incapable of anything so broad as telling the difference between a cat and a dog. At this stage, computers show their power at two contrasting points on the spectrum: At the most basic, they perform the repetitive work—mind-numbing to us—of petty calculation and record-keeping, doing the work of 10,000

Bob Cratchits in less time than he would take to get on his stool. At the most complex, they attempt first approximations of the Arctic climate, the aging process, the world economy.

Everyday domestic and industrial operations appear pretty easy. But to enable electronic devices to, say, fold clothes, dust the house, or automatically fill a car's gas tank will involve vast inputs, very significant conceptual breakthroughs, and ultra-specialized instructions. When even routine housework becomes possible for these deceptively simple functionaries, so may many other things in our economy and our society. Imagine a disaster site with triage being performed for scores of victims at multiples of human speed.

So our path into the information era has been unprecedented, and not only in terms of accelerated change. Computers have let us tackle the high abstractions before addressing what (going by all previous human experience) *should be* the much more basic tasks of operational analogues to human physical activity. This retracing of steps—from highly intellectual repetitiveness to simple practicalities that would have been recognizable in the Bronze Age—is an increasingly important part of the current challenge to software.

Ironically, the information era *did* begin very much in the middle ground of industrial use. The Jacquard loom was, after all, a valued, practical weaving device for a century before it was applied to encode census data. With so much that is practical to be achieved, it is now timely to ask what new kinds of relations will be woven between man and machine—and, in particular, what new means of coordination will become routine and familiar.

The software problem—meaning the ongoing task of extending the "computational" competence of information machines into greater ranges of initiative, judgment, and subtlety—can also be compared to the problems raised by the semantic study of language. Here too, what we take for granted proves under serious examination to be enormously complex. Something as seemingly basic as the creation of this sentence is governed by laws far deeper than anything I'm aware of when I write. Just as the nineteenth century had to create an entire new logic to explore the processes of thought, we shall have to formalize large disciplines to enable entities (not human, but human-instrumented) to "do the obvious." And we are only just beginning to examine such puzzling obviousness.

Between 1000 and 1950 A.D. half the world learned to read, write, and cipher, but this was all done with fingers, paper, and a fraction of the human capacity. It was still incredibly constricting relative to the possibilities of the human brain.

Nearly 300 years ago, Jonathan Swift, mocking the aspirations of natural philosophy, unwittingly posed the problem I address here by imagining a sentence-generating machine. Being entirely random, Swift's machine produced little but reams of gibberish. His mad scientists at Lagado were probing the capacities of syntax, but the unasked question was how to impose conscious interrogation and creation upon the gigantic mindless powers of machines.

Then came the computer. Only then did we realize that the question was not only one of building a machine to match the brain's structural scope but also one of matching the operational intricacy thus conferred. To do this, it was necessary to employ the brain's own programming capacities. After all, these capacities had already shaped human endeavors from grammar through chess. To give them an autonomous role was the only way to give human imagination and flexibility adequate leverage upon the unimaginable powers of brute computation that were becoming available.

In less than a lifetime we have done this, passing through machine code to programming language. Immense achievement has only unveiled greater possibilities. Advances are being made at such a speed that we eagerly look to experts who can help outline our extraordinary future—not to mention that of our children.

The task is becoming one of creating *continua* of software out of the plethora of highly targeted programs now applied to separate machines or tasks. This entails the harmonization of standards and the harnessing of the highest communication capacities to computation. It also requires elaboration of the information processes so that ever subtler and more comprehensive activities can be taken as much for granted as are reading-mediated skills today.

An imminent step toward such a reality is the commercialization of software to create and dispatch "agents." John Markoff expects them soon to be coursing through the veins and arteries of the nation's data networks, intent on useful tasks as diverse as purchasing airline tickets or pizza.[1] Users issue requests—such as flying to Paris or ordering pepperoni—via computer networks and then go about their business while the task takes care of itself via phone circuits and databases. "As with biological microorganisms in the physical world," Markoff continues, "the interaction of countless teeming software agents seems certain to turn computer networks into artificial life forms whose evolution is impossible to predict."

One result of such evolution is that the narrow distinctions among kinds of inquiry are dissolving. So are the narrow and rigid frameworks we used to organize knowledge back when our best capacities were unassisted by the powerful surrogates of computation and programming. These surrogates are now endlessly being extended to "free up" information and turn it into knowledge. For instance, in biology we have passed from organizing huge amounts of discrete data to seeking to depict deep processes of interaction. This enlargement of vision applies yet more intensely to current information science.

We now take it for granted when a physicist, such as Philip Seiden of IBM, easily takes up new challenges on the frontiers of immunology after spending a career studying, say, the formation of spiral arms in galaxies. "Cellular automata"—chunks of computer code programmed to act like simple organisms—are used to simulate key parts of the human immune system in a mainframe computer. It is not too much of an exaggeration to call this artificial life, as self-contained chunks of software interact with their environment *in machina* much as organisms would *in vivo* or *in vitro*. These cellular automata fight for resources, reproduce, mutate, or flee. On the computer screen, they behave in ways that are eerily close to the behavior of biological life.

Such research is barely news in the mid 1990s. Discipline after discipline became transcendent once the basic processes were formulated: chess once the rules were established, calculation once zero was invented, poetry with the development of meter. But these older accomplishments, however powerful, tended to be formalist. Now information as well as pure reasoning lies at our command. We can all speak the language of the new world, and we can write our own scripts for work (whether physics, biology, or garbage collection) and for life. The boulders that once would have blocked the torrent of information are being bypassed. Before us lies not just an information highway but a wide-open information prairie.

In the 1950s, programming was the work of certified mathematical or economic geniuses, like Herbert Simon and John Strachey. Then just very clever people with a sense of form—from musicians to Sanskrit scholars—were able to play on the field. We now see (or we soon will see) a whole culture of software writers as well as one of users. These are simply competent people who have learned to apply fruitful principles. Two hundred years ago, educated people, from emperors down to squires, found it natural to compose music or write poems or contribute to science— sometimes very credibly. There is nothing new to this development but the instrument. This evolution is in the American grain of powerful amateurism (if that is the right word for a field that has yet, thank goodness, to evolve a professional qualification). "Language"—i.e., software—language—skills are being remade. The country of Edison, Stevens, the Wrights, and Ford is being true to itself. Using the possibilities offered by the computer is very much in the American style of addressing issues. This kind of inventiveness is classically matched to a wide-open culture in which talented individuals enjoy restating problems to more and more telling levels even more than they enjoy finding first-cut answers to them.

The authors here, however, are anything but amateurs.

Denos Gazis recalls the dawn of computing, when even the most sophisticated users—the scientists who pioneered the early applications— needed experts to help them access the computing power. Even with such demanding languages as FORTRAN, there was a population explosion in the community of users capable of communicating directly with computers. These languages made it possible for engineers to bypass the original middlemen, making the computer their personal assistant, albeit through a cumbersome process involving punch cards and batch processing.

Then came interactive computing (e.g., QUICKTRAN and BASIC), which cut turnaround time. A quantum leap in interactive capability was provided by APL, a marvelously compact way of talking to a computer. Although APL's intricacy confined it to a relatively small club of connoisseurs, it at last made the computer a true extension of a scientist's brain, permitting ideas to be checked immediately. Gazis asks "Where are we going from here?" His chapter and the ones that follow begin to answer that question.

David Vaskevitch provocatively asks whether software is even relevant to daily life. In so doing, he confronts the vexing problem of the two extremes of computer use. Because computers have not yet changed the lives of individuals and organizations nearly as much as was expected 25 years ago, when people spoke of "electronic brains," Vaskevitch finds them at best less than relevant. The search for relevancy will not succeed until technology is applied to the middle ground of practical use—to making the presence of a computer taken for granted in commonplace tasks. Some call this "information at one's fingertips"—getting the right information to the right people, quickly, regardless of where and how the information is stored. Efficiently controlling and distributing data throughout an organization can solve a range of familiar (and not so familiar) problems to enhance both routine administration and decision making at all levels. This underscores the twin themes of coordination and of a routinization that will enable us to draw on each complex achievement. The challenge of computer relevancy is quintessentially one of software. Vaskevitch explains how such interfacing will evolve while users try to protect their existing investments and routines. He specifies the modes by which access to data is advancing—timing, ease, availability, and interoperability—and illuminates the mixed blessings of automated or assisted decision making.

Conklin and Newcomer's discussion of common standards—or "open software"—lays out the prospects for further coordination of just about everything. Such standardization is implicit in the visions of Gazis and Vaskevitch. Standards shape the future of entertainment no less than that of work, and their vital role is yet another theme throughout this book. The business history of the computer era has increasingly been a shoving match as to who would define what—a scuffle far more portentous than that over AC and DC currents at the turn of the century.

A standard starts out as a working convenience. Almost any commonly agreed-upon measurement or procedure, however casual, is preferable to a wilderness of private reckonings, however sophisticated. A standard then becomes a prescription around which a new world is to be built. This usually painful, sometimes frightening passage exposes the power of momentum and inadvertence in daily life. What starts as a working vocabulary imperceptibly shades into a language of command.

The importance of "open software" goes beyond a focus on information technologies. If an organization is examined as a system, Carl Cargill of Sun Microsystems has noted, the sector actually dealing with information technologies (as opposed to operating through them) is rather small. The encouragement of an "open" organization in which any part of the enterprise can be changed without involving the whole is a way to the wider objective of "open systems." But such dynamism depends upon interchangeable software components which let any participant coordinate any relevant activity anyplace at any time. The ultimate business objective is to produce an undivided information ocean in which the users can steer like ships on the sea.

Having moved beyond building the amazing machine, information science now must find out how to get the most out of the amazing machine's implicit resources. The challenges of use still lie in computational potential and in interfacing (in the largest sense). All participants in a given activity must be able to tap into the flow of knowledge, just as various standardized appliances all run on the same electric power.

Although pursuing such a common objective seems like common sense, the fierce undertows beneath today's efforts offer a classic example of history being lived forward but made sense of backward. More than technological compatibility is at stake whenever standards are debated. Conklin and Newcomer remind us that today's corporate conflicts over standards are merely a subtler manifestation of competition. These efforts have long been beset by complicated and even contradictory battles over money and power. The Magna Carta, for instance, devoted a lot of space to establishing a standard bushel, in order to restrain arbitrary taxation. In the nineteenth century, weak countries used perverse rail gauges to obstruct invasion from adjacent strong countries, and the typewriter keyboard was standardized to keep nimble fingers from jamming the mechanisms of the day (as if today's personal computers would care).

The curiosities of technological standards span not only centuries but millennia. In Babylonia, for instance, the second was needed to measure a time unit no longer than a heartbeat or a word. It made sense for such a unit to be defined as the primitive average of a solar day divided by the primitive estimate of the days in a year (360) multiplied by any of its three pairs of most useful exact quotients (10, 24; 4, 60; 12, 20). This was almost pedantically exact for timing a foot race, but it raised serious arguments once the age of radio rolled around. In the end, the elusive time was happily equated to 9,191,631,770 times the quantum-level transition of the atom of cesium—an element unknown to the magi of Babylon.

Quarrels over standards arise from efforts to resist or bypass some awkward established system. One example was when the gold value of the dollar was adjusted, not to equilibrate with the gold value of world currencies, but to fit the convenience of dollars-and-cents accounting. A more recent example: a decade or so ago the Japanese threw their weight behind faxing because it saved them the mind-bending problems of sequentially transmitting *kanji, katakana,* and *hiragana.*

How are standards generated? This is not just a question of whether they have been established by a private initiative (as were typewriter keyboards) or whether they come from the scientific deliberations of some independent committee (as did the original metric standards of revolutionary France). How long is a standard likely to be rigidly self-renewing, like the keyboard, and to what extent is it subject to challenge in the marketplace? As with the keyboard, answers often arise from the short-term costs of turnover. Which corporate executive wants to be on deck when profits contract, even briefly, to offset the costs of standardization? And to whose short-term advantage is any standardization likely to redound? One organization or group of organizations is surely likely to have the most at stake. This fact doesn't discredit efforts at standardization, but it is all too likely to politicize them. Institutional shadows are still cast over software, personal computing, and overall coordination by historic constellations long since broken up. They raise intense challenges to the rationality and coherence of the next generation of the information order.

Only some serious attention at an early stage can prevent the casual adaptations of pioneers from becoming the monopoly principles of a mature system. And we are still at a very early stage of the computer. Our awareness of the benefits of standards too often comes only after a tangle of inefficiencies has been built into existing arrangements—like a company's *ad hoc* purchases of incompatible information systems. But the short-term costs of rationalizing the system have reached a forbidding level.

Barely a decade ago, in one encouraging example of standardization, the nations of the world decided to develop Airspeak and Seaspeak as consciously simplified and unambiguous forms of English for use in transportation, reducing British and American subtleties in the interests of universal comprehensibility and real-time clarity. At the same time, the metric system triumphed as an international standard (although France, its creator, receives no particular benefit).

The greatest issue facing information standardization is a corollary of what Gerard Piel calls "the acceleration of history." Knowledge passes from the small, highly personal world of a given cluster of innovations into a vastly larger planetary universe of discourse. Nowadays this happens within a few years rather than over decades, and things happen so fast that highly provisional conveniences solidify almost before most practitioners begin to notice.

It used to be said that equity was the length of the chancellor's foot, its scope altering randomly with each incumbent. Moving smoothly into the future requires coherence, foresight, codification, and reflection. These have to be at least proportionate to the almost exponential increase of technological complexity. Two things result from such rapid change: First, if something has reached a general working level, it is likely to be obsolete by the standards of the hot new stuff. Second, standards themselves are always just about to pass out of date—that is what makes them standards.

Deborah Louis and L. Alexander Morrow begin their chapter with an epigraph from H. G. Wells' *Food of the Gods,* and their story might be read as science fiction. Prediction, anticipation, and fictive imagination have always entwined. But the speed with which an amazing private vision now becomes the framework of the quotidian practical is unprecedented. Louis and Morrow's vignettes from a not-too-distant future show the software relevancy that Vaskevitch demands. In fact, their story about software and garbage collection is very much about the present.

When the old periodical *Astounding Science Fiction* ran an atomic-war story and was investigated by the FBI, which had been alerted by the managers of the Manhattan Project, the blurring of life spheres was well advanced. It is one thing to say that something will happen; it is quite another to tell how people will hitch their necessities, dislikes, and dreams to it. What is so unifyingly interesting in these chapters, and what unites the stories told by Louis and Morrow, is a concern for "the way we'll live then"—for the world that is being made, not for the laboratory possibilities.

Knowledge is the air and light of civilization. Transform it and you transform all else. A child born today arrives in the costume drama of his old age, and dies amid the science fiction of his babyhood. The greatest voyage has begun. We will soon enough be out of sight of the land we have lived on for all our recorded history. It is worthwhile to consult the first explorers' charts.

David Williams and Timothy O'Brien examine the future as it pertains to good old-fashioned work. What began with the personal-computer revolution and with the advent of networking has already opened into a third revolution, its progress characterized by radically new uses for computers and communications and certainly by their convergence. Today's revolution is energized by geographically unconstrained task groups (even the word "teams" may be too old-fashioned), which will use new capabilities to bridge time and distance in the service of operational effectiveness.

Computation will blend with communications and applications software to give such groups new capabilities and to increase their productivity. The once-disparate industries of computing and communication are blending to create the infrastructure for new leaps in collaboration. How will such collaboration (even coordination) affect the applications and system software required to exploit fully these new capabilities? And what might be the cultural implications of all this? Remember the "if it works it's obsolete" principle. We shall be lucky to get a fraction of the available potential before these capabilities go out of date—but that fraction may be sufficient for yet more revolution.

Soon after it became routine for corporations to appoint information-systems managers (and that was not long ago), those managers found that they had to do more than respond to the torrent of innovations. They had to administer a complete change of consciousness in the making, designing, applying, and using of hardware, software, and communications. The personal computer did not have to be around long for sensible people to intuit that there would be an upheaval in administration, access, procedures, and individual initiative. But only now, as the PC is at last being somewhat properly fitted into that matrix of administration, access, and initiative, are we beginning to fully realize the potential of new software applications and thus to start making the new knowledge world a way of life.

What Williams and O'Brien term CSC—the computer's becoming a gateway to the whole hardware-software universe—is the next, so far the subtlest, and one of the widest-ranging of cybernetics' contributions toward Norbert Wiener's great goal of the human use of human beings.

Such coordination works continuously along a broad spectrum. It enables us to relegate tasks that do not require humans to pure mechanical routine. It integrates innumerable necessary but time-consuming contacts into one vibrant web. This ability outflanks its human users' emotional barriers to circulating an appropriately intense level of conflicting ideas and criticisms, and it minimizes the complexities of conferring across large distances.

Such abilities figuratively raise the system's basic metabolic rate, extending the range of things to be taken for granted. What once had to be planned for consciously and anxiously can now robustly be called for, "just in time," at colossal savings to the previously inflexible overheads.

The leap in individual productivity first offered by the personal computer is now coming to the organism as a whole. The PC's separateness meant until recently that time series—so far practically unconnected—could at best add to but could not multiply its actual contributions.

To allude to the "organism" and not the "organization" is simply to recognize that such transcendent entities can be large or small, a fragment of one corporation or an alliance of the relevant aspects of several very different kinds of institutions. This will be a great prospect for original people, but possibly a still more beautiful one for anti-trust attorneys.

The ability to dynamize such previously passive entities as databases and electronic mail offers the possibility of transforming the nature of individual contributions to a large enterprise. Just as the city never sleeps, at the price of immense human watchfulness, our particular efforts can be made electronically wakeful and productive in ways hitherto impossible, requiring human attention only in emergencies.

Scott Brown speculates on how individuals may very soon and very naturally meet the ongoing demand for new software applications, a demand never yet satisfied because of the pace of development. This achievement has also been frustrated by the failure of many applications to achieve their potential, often due to poor rapport between the creator of a given software solution and its ultimate user. Within a decade, Brown argues, powerful tools will be developed to allow those in need of a particular software application to prototype the work without having to call in a professional programmer. (Today, as videotapes of software engineers demonstrate, developers spend about 70 to 85 percent of their time in thought. Software development remains one of the more complex activities of the human mind. How much software development really can be automated, and can end users who lack development skills successfully build systems?) The likely appearance of such tools presages an enormous extension of creativity in several rapidly changing industries—not least communications, where it will be possible to accelerate not only the prototyping but also the refining and the deployment of new services. Eventually the speed with which services can be introduced will be limited only by the ability of an organization to manage them (indeed, simply to handle them attitudinally), not by the complexity of the technologies. So when Brown talks about "revolution," he literally means an upheaval of classes. One can hope and believe that this will be brought about without guillotines and firing squads, but the change of power and authority will be as great.

Ideally, all these developments are heading toward some capacity to distill a form of artificial intelligence—at this moment toward voice interaction, and soon toward something as ambitious as the Very Large Knowledge Base. AI has reached middle age in the sense of artificial competence, not of artificial brilliance. While growing up it begat expert systems, knowledge bases, and software agents; now it is steadily passing its legacy on to these offspring.

The patterns we discern in the progress of AI and its progeny are likely to help us determine which of its offspring will be forerunners of the next powerful interaction. The original dreams, which once sounded like bad science fiction, are unfolding in such a way that they may produce several viable, real-world, practical functions early in the 21st century.

Inevitably, discussions of AI intensify the question "What is intelligence?" One at least partial criterion is the possession of certain "human" characteristics. But to what extent are such characteristics specifically "human"? To what extent are they the patterns of operation that *any* system has to evolve toward in order to be conscious and reasoning? Clearly, some of our own characteristics are embodied in our physiological nature, although whether by inescapable natural selection or by more particular paths is still a matter of debate. But since the 1950s it has been possible to demonstrate that certain patterns are pretty fundamental to inquiry. (Even before then, Boolean discourse could be regarded as a universal terminology of "the laws of thought" embodied in an algebraization of logic.)

Thus, it may be more fruitful to think of "the intelligences" when we examine AI and its agenda. We have all encountered both people and disciplines that reward great systematic learning much more highly than originality. Equally, there are disciplines (such as many branches of math) where a certain absence of complete knowledge (or perhaps I should say unconditionedness) appears to be a crucial impetus to the highest creativity. One rough but useful definition of intelligence is "IQ potentiated by character and temperament." And all of us who recall the homicidal HAL's soothing tones in the movie version of Clarke's *2001* find ourselves forced to think twice about a machine's temperament.

"Will HAL arrive on schedule?" Clarke asked in his memorable preface to *Technology 2001*. "No," he replied to himself, "but I'm damn sure he'll be here by 2100, which is only tomorrow in human history, and a millisecond away on the cosmic time scale." Even among us warm-bloods, the incapacity to be bored by such humanely horrifying repetition as that of the machine overseeing the spaceship in *2001* is no index of intelligence, and very often it is the reverse. Bring it down to computers and it is not even an index of character. The nearest human characteristic is the ability to review—in real time—the hundred thousand familiar sounds of the jungle and *still* single out the critical snapping twig.

Gustave Essig's approach to the subject reflects this book's twin themes, that of the ever-stronger coordination of knowledge and that of taking things for granted. Not incidentally, Essig argues that there is something fundamentally wrong with the way software is developed. Wrestling with definitions of knowledge, he presses the question of how we actually accomplish the things that we don't "think about." For instance, language is a system of signs. We respond to material questions in the external world and clothe them in sentences without conscious effort. (And some of us—some more admittedly than others—actually speak without thinking.) We constitute new information by forming new relationships in our minds. That is what creativity is. But how do we impart these approaches to machines?

We must now take such abilities for granted as parts of practical "civilized" life. Television was not a part of life for most of the parents of those born before 1950, but it certainly was to us. As children very few of us assumed that computers were part of the world, but they certainly are to Essig's nine-year-old son Kyle. They have not driven out other aspects of childhood; they have enlarged it. That is what high civilization is about. What will our grandchildren take for granted?

Children excel at responding *to* novelty *with* novelty, and nearly in real time. Almost by definition, such responses increase the chances of mistake as well as those of creative solution. In chemistry the carbon atom potentiates random novelties through mutation, unintentionally functioning as probes of the universe's overwhelming novelty. We must not forget that panic is one response to novelty, especially now that computer users can program a capacity for creative flight as a rich response to panic. But the fundamental challenge remains not merely responding *to* novelty but responding *with* it.

How do we set the computer to noticing not just correspondences but analogies, and to testing critical paths? How do we put zest into its well-stored but pedantic and unconfident mind? The chapters in part III of this volume examine more closely the political and managerial issues forced on us by the unprecedented onrush of capacity. For thousands of years after their invention, writing skills (and writing materials) were the possession of a largely self-selected few. But today the per-capita number of computers is already many times what that of cars was within the memory span of many people. The range of contact a child can now have on the Internet is vastly greater than that which even the most high-technology driven senior government official enjoyed a generation ago. But ordinary consumers do not think they have arrived in information paradise. Millions around the world are toiling to acquire much more information—and information that arrives faster, is more specific to the task at hand, is responsive to subtler questions, and is better ordered.

The international economy is integrated more in terms of services than of goods. The more impalpables there are in an economy, the more will be internationalized by default. International markets respond more clearly and efficiently to intellectual processes—American music, movies, and computer software, for instance. They minimize delay and up-front cost. One result is the business cliché of "globalization." Better to speak of *globalizations*—of technology (which is extraordinarily difficult to regulate behind national barriers), of attitude (the social bent of democratic revolution), and of consumption. "Globalization" is (partly) shorthand for information abundance and improved communication—the internationalization of information flow.

Edward Feigenbaum discusses why the United States holds the strategic high ground in such competition and dominates the world's software industry (America's last uncontested computer domain). Specifically, he examines why Japan—America's most formidable high-tech competitor—lags behind to such an extent that Tokyo claims it faces a "software crisis," including a shortfall of a million software engineers by the year 2000. Where are the Japanese—the people who successfully drove many U.S. companies out of consumer electronics and computer memory chips—when it comes to writing and marketing software for a mass market? And *why* are they in such a predicament?

A few years ago, many Americans were preoccupied with the challenge of Japan's software factories, expecting them to change the way the world's software is written just as Japan's automobile factories revolutionized manufacturing. After all, in every other industry Japan has first achieved high levels of production and then developed markedly better products. The trend toward industrywide standards would help the Japanese push their software as series of broad-market products, rather than leaving it tied to exclusive operating systems. But the global software agenda is being defined by American companies, because they are the ones setting the standards.

The basic concept of a "software factory" has been the same in Japan as in the United States, but the details vary. American companies are said to treat software as an art; the Japanese have tried to make it the product of rote processes. The Japanese are said to separate the conceptualizing from the subtle work of writing the concepts exactly and operationally as millions of lines of complex code. Hitachi, which built its first so-called software factory in 1969 and which in 1989 opened a 7000-employee plant that is as much like a factory as a white-collar office can be, is considered the pioneer.

Despite the dire predictions about the Japanese software threat, American companies remain the world's leaders as hardware prices spiral downward. In the United States there is clearly a strong trend toward software companies' setting the initiatives in the information-technology industry. In Japan, however, no major primarily software companies have emerged. In brief, Japan, with its fragmented personal-computer market, did not have a target to aim for in its software development. Japan had no prevailing standard, while the United States had DOS and the IBM PC. So the Japanese kept writing customized software for mainframes—a market in which a higher return on investment seemed a sure thing.

One pattern of technological innovation and demand was justifiably able to reward Japan's great consumer-electronics and (later) hardware efforts enormously from the 1960s through the 1980s. But the same changing world that gave the Japanese their chance has moved on, and the new pattern fits them much less well. In the mid 1990s the United States stands as the undisputed global leader in computing and communications, as well as in biotechnology—in every area of high technology that matters.

But high-tech leadership is famously fragile. The very term "high technology" begs the question: the steam engine was the awe-inspiring center of overall progress in 1830, the printing press in 1450. What is most salient about high technology is that its self-renewal is faster than can be assimilated by familiar approaches to management—not to mention education. High-tech competitiveness, after all, remains a worldwide competition for talent to produce products, to put them to work, and to adapt to them.

The U.S. Bureau of Labor Statistics anticipates a need for over 600,000 programmers and systems analysts through the year 2005—one of the country's five largest growth categories. But there is no particular reason for them to be American programmers—especially since many software applications are being created with standardized modules, and since the annual market for over-the-shelf software almost matches that for custom software. There is a great deal of talent—poorly paid talent, at that—only a plane ride or an international call away.

Again, it is a condition of modernity that at any given moment just about everyone is mostly out of date, even on matters that truly concern them. No one in the U.S. industry has reason to relax. American software companies are developing spreadsheets in Hungary and hiring crack Russian designers. Software is rapidly becoming a major Indian export, and as India's vast oversupply of engineering graduates enters the world fray their contribution is hardly confined to writing components for larger programs designed in the U.S.

The worldwide operational uses of all these innovations, not to mention international competition, require some rather specialized legal thinking. Jeffrey Cunard is the preeminent guide to the legal aspects of these mysteries, and his chapter helps us understand such matters without having to run up hours at a first-class law firm.

Software, like the first artificial satellite or Bach chorale, is something that genuinely did not exist before. A handbook of navigation, for instance, is subject to copyright. However complex in its original conception, it is really not likely to operate better than the navigator who uses it. The first software device to appear in mechanical form was M. Jacquard's loom-card, which emerged in the eighteenth century in a country governed by patent, not copyright.

There is a growing argument that software law may soon be seen as its own discipline—a discipline necessarily partaking of several forms of intellectual-property law, such as copyright and patent, and uniting them in its own powerful way, just as air law shook off admiralty law and as commercial law fought off its precedents to become a real discipline. Differences make differences.

The Hazakah joined a rabbinic guarantee of the accuracy of a text to a curse upon any scribe besides the editor who should copy it, creating an early precursor of general copyright law. But we may now be seeing the reverse: the dissimilation of law governing the outcomes of an unprecedented technology. Just as insurance and banking had to create their own branches of law by shaking off the taboos against gambling and usury, so we are likely to see attempts to formulate an information-science law that, while drawing upon its predecessors, will nevertheless be independent of them.

At the least, fundamental questions are raised. What happens to law in a world that innovates at such speed? Who wins when common approaches to intellectual problems emerge with such predictable near-simultaneity, and when much of the work is identical but honestly not derivative? And how do we, the sovereign people, structure such reward?

Will there be a policy of substantial lump-sum payments, amounting to purchase by the state or by the industry, with the inventor likely (and usually rightly) to have been treated as someone only very narrowly first past the post? Will an innovator of great originality have maximum access to consumers who in turn will encourage fast development? So unstatist an economist as Harry Johnson advocated in the 1950s that under some circumstances patents be bought by government to prevent their being employed as barriers to competition (as General Motors memorably did with locomotive patents). And Johnson was dealing with fields in which innovation was a good deal slower than it is in software. Modern science is characterized, even in areas conceptually much more abstruse than most high-level programming, by multiple discovery.

Thus, we must seek a balance between intense encouragement of the first achievement and a proper sense of how many people are capable of contributing (or have already contributed). Too rigorous a policy of intellectual property may too readily penalize creative involvement that does not move along the most economically rational, legally aware line.

In the final chapter, William Welty and I summarize what all this means for business, finance, and the economy. Management can be defined as skilled direction—at different times and in different degrees—that harmonizes action by demonstrating the simple need for binding decisions. It therefore embraces leadership, manipulation, and all the other ways of uniting human beings.

The problems to be managed are constantly moving and constitute a fit task for real administration. The only tasks that can be defined as "manageable" are those which are familiar: when we try to "manage" the new, we find ourselves white-water rafting. How can we hope to "skillfully direct" processes that are, in degree of specialization and speed of change, ever further beyond the capable administrator's skills?

Innovation—which, as it intensifies, accelerates the cycle of obsolescence—now comes splashing down upon us, bursting over our proprietary technologies and products, reshaping further our work environment, and demanding new assessments of the available workforce and other resources.

Nowadays, the peaks of innovation crowd much closer together, whereas the business cycle (largely because of improved inventory control—itself a software process) is flatter than it once was. The passive resources that were once considered as *stock,* such as skills and machinery, are steadily more subject to ceaseless reworking, which brings them into the organizational category of *flow.*

We all tend to feel defensive about the intensity of innovation. The awareness that we cannot stay up to date on everything that concerns us demands a reemphasis on the capacity to synthesize talents, skills, and leadership in an organization, and thus to redefine "authority"—a word with overtones of cumulative expertise and individual command.

Since everything is obsolescing at a much higher rate, we need to look with a historian's eye at current processes, and show a certain sardonic dissatisfaction with the way just about everything is done right now. The modern power to illuminate issues also throws harsh light on the complex choices that face us. There are always more choices than profitable decisions. All these technologies open a widening range of possibilities, while guaranteeing none of them.

As Knowledge Multiplies

"He who brings hence the wealth of the Indies," says the inscription over the U.S. Treasury Building, "must first bring the wealth of the Indies with him." There is no plunder of power; freedom is obligated to maintain its authority by creating. And so it is with computer power.

Computers can bring remote information wherever in the world it is needed, give voice to the world's dumb store of knowledge, and be the tireless, unerring eliminators of a billion harassed middlemen. But computers can do this only if they are told how. And telling how is much harder than telling that. For example, humans and their ancestors have been able to raise their arms for millions of years, but the work of understanding the physiological means by which we are able to raise our arms has been pursued for only two generations and is still poorly defined.

Huge tables of natural logarithms and of lunar periods have existed for centuries. Yet there is still no good book on something as seemingly simple as the process of assembling a car. A human being can watch a training film, but machines can't yet follow training films. Writing how-to books for machines, telling them how to do the things they could do effortlessly if only they understood, is the intellectual bottleneck of the late second millennium.

This bottleneck is not being alleviated by the American educational system. The role of education, and the need to bring up to speed the millions of average people who are ever more in positions to be users and creators of the new software forms, are only implicit in these chapters. Yet any country's possession of an adequate supply of appropriate talent and attitude cannot be taken for granted. The one thing the high-technology history of previous generations shows unequivocally is how fragile, conditional, and transient any nation's leadership may be. Software's potential to dynamize education, in the United States and around the world, may be its most exciting and central role. It may well bring achievements that will be beyond the imagining of any past generation.

One of the tragedies of baseball is what happens to many a kid who has been the best player in his whole world when he finds himself in a league where he is only ordinary. It is worse when most of the children in a nation are being encouraged to entertain delusions of adequacy. This country trusts its young to a school system that is taking them into a world where special relativity will be only a century old, the original ENIAC computer will be half that, and DNA will have been known to us for a mere 30 years. Yet the American education system confines itself to intellectual fingerpainting.

More than 40 percent of American workers are now using some form of computer on the job. In nearly all cases, their computer skills were learned outside the formal education system. In fact, from 10 to 15 percent of the $220 billion which U.S. companies spend on training is remedial—picking up after the failure of public education. There is a strong sense that public education has lost its nerve, with grave costs to those for whom it is responsible. America does not have endless time to remedy this, and the factory floor or the office is not the best place for emergency medicine anyway.

In the United States education and training consume about $630 billion annually, or 11 percent of the gross domestic product; 4 percent of the GDP goes for corporate training. Relative to that, spending on information technology to improve education is nearly nonexistent—troubling news at a time when a leading education theorist, L. J. Perelman, can say confidently that "over twenty years of research shows that computer-assisted instruction, properly employed, can produce at least 30 percent

more learning in 40 percent less time at 30 percent less cost than traditional classroom teaching." [2]

Business tasks, like all other tasks, are shifting and being redefined as
people try to meet them. Computer-aided instruction has therefore grown
to a point where $4 billion a year is spent on hardware, software, and
associated peripherals. Some 70 percent of trainees use computers to
learn. According to some studies, corporations spend about 30 percent
of their training budgets on these systems and software. Public education
commits only 0.2 percent of its spending to such resources, and the gap
is widening.

Recent leaps in software are bringing advances in multimedia and
compact disk technology that will let more and more children receive
education electronically, in the home and/or in the classroom. The opportunities offered by the coming learning technology will be colossal. Tens
of millions of people know they need to know more and feel cheated by
their teaching so far. The schools have to make the transition already
made by the corporate training industry. Only 2 percent of the nation's
education budget is spent on instructional materials—at a time when the
education system could be recast into a networked, high-bandwidth,
PC-using collaborative system.

One gleam of success in bringing the pressure of new possibilities to
bear on public education is the movement to allow or even to mandate
software as a direct substitute for textbooks. More than a quarter of the
states, including Texas and California, have now approved using textbook
funds to buy software, such as Optical Data Corporation's "Window on
Science." Integrated Learning Systems are being widely adopted, and new
generations of open-environment interactive multimedia systems are being introduced commercially. The vast majority of sales, however, are to
parents, not to schools. The rapid growth of the use of computers for
education in homes is slowly pressuring school districts to acquire technological solutions.

After all the spending on high-speed communication systems for corporate training and (slowly) for public education, this question remains:
Since all such attainments are tactical, by what processes do we seek to
transform individuals, industries, and professions? With most of the
world starting from the same line, the competitive implications are vast.

Think of how entertainment is being transformed. An old Broadway joke says that an audience should be able to decide on a new script even during the performance of a bad play. With full interaction, the fantasies of disappointed theatergoers are moving toward reality. Anyone can take part as one particular character, or we can change characters as the narrative unfolds. Drama came into existence ages ago as organized tales acted out to intensify an observer's emotions. Now we can acquire power over the drama, dissolving limiting patterns of expectation and barriers between different roles. The potential for transferring skills is virtually limitless.

Software, at this moment, has astonishingly wide-ranging potential. It can act upon huge reserve forces not yet adequately employed—underused material computing power and underchallenged human talent around the world. It moves rapidly and cheaply across national frontiers. It represents the broadest possible challenge to the huge range of problems—whose greatest common factor is their complexity—now facing the human race. How will we live up to our capacities, and how will we resolve the problems that we have been clever enough to pose?

The software problem is the unifying problem. Software's protean quality, which enables it to address a host of challenges, means that its full promise is unimaginable. What the authors have done here does not give us any final sense of the full promise of software creativity and use over even the next 20 years. Instead, it shows us the rewards that await those who come to the problem with daring and hope, and who can imagine even a fraction of the possibilities.

Notes

1. *New York Times,* January 6, 1994.
2. L. J. Perelman, Closing Education's Technology Gap. Briefing paper 111, Hudson Institute, Indianapolis, 1987.

I

Awakening Possibilities

The Evolving Resource

Denos C. Gazis

The real problem is not whether machines think, but whether men do.
—Burrhus Frederic Skinner, *Contingencies of Reinforcement*

Some 25 years ago I was asked to preview a short documentary movie intended to introduce the general public to the concept of software. The title of the movie was, appropriately enough, *They Call It Software*. The movie opens with a scene showing a beautiful young lady walking toward a handsome young man who offers her a drink and leads her to a piano. The young man opens the piano and looks at the young lady's eyes while bringing his glass to his lips. Suddenly, beautiful music emanates from the piano. As the camera pans toward the keyboard, it reveals the secret: the piano is a player piano activated by a punched paper roll. The movie goes on to explain that, just as the player piano comes to life through a punched paper roll, a computer performs its tasks when activated by software. I never saw the movie in its final form, and in fact I do not know if it was ever produced. From time to time I pondered about the appropriateness of the analogy it drew between pianos and computers.

At the risk of being labeled a boor, I must admit that I found the analogy somewhat strained. For one thing, player pianos were never known to reside in the range of high musical performance. One then might get the idea that software is only intended to bring to life the low end of computing devices, while the high end is brought to life manually by computing virtuosos, just as Paderewski may have brought to life a Steinway grand piano. A related implication might be that software could bring a computer to life but could never deliver the quality of performance that a human virtuoso could. However, the analogy was good enough to drive a distinction between a piece of hardware and something else, produced by humans and recorded on some medium, which activates the hardware and makes it deliver some useful function. In fact, over the past several years the term "software" has come to be used to describe other similar situations. For example, people refer to compact discs as the software of CD players.

Let us accept, then, such a definition of "software": the product of human labor, recorded on an appropriate medium, which activates a computer and makes it deliver a useful service. In what follows, I will go through a quick overview of the evolution of software since the early days of computing, take a look at its current state, and try to make some projections about its future.

The Varied Role of Software

From the early days of computing, software has served in at least two roles. One of them has been the activation of computing elements toward carrying out a specific task, be it a scientific computation or any other *application*. The other one has been the management of various computing and peripheral devices toward the execution of one or several tasks, either in sequence or simultaneously. The first role defines the domain of *application software,* and the second one defines the domain of *operating systems*. In recent years, we often talk separately about yet a third role of software: that of defining a *user interface*. It may be argued that such a definition is part of an operating system, and sometimes part of an application package, but it is an important enough topic to be listed separately.

Languages and Computing Environments

Underlying all forms and roles of software is the *language* we use to communicate with computers. At the dawn of computing, communication with computers required a detailed knowledge of a special language, the redoubtable *assembly language,* corresponding to step-by-step instructions to the computer for executing elemental tasks such as the addition of two numbers. In those days, even some of the most sophisticated users, the scientists who pioneered the early use of computers often needed an intermediary in order to access their computing power.

FORTRAN will go down in history as the most durable computer language. To this day, many scientists around the world speak only two languages, their native one and FORTRAN, although other more sophisticated "second-level languages," like PASCAL and C, are preferred by the computer cognoscenti. FORTRAN also gave birth to the first interactive computing environments, embodied in QUICKTRAN and BASIC, which cut down the turnaround time of man-machine interaction. Interactive computing meant that, instead of submitting a job to a computer by means of cards and waiting for the computer to execute it, with a time lag of hours or days, one could enter an instruction on a typewriter-like terminal and get an answer in seconds. Today the average user of personal computers knows no other way, but in the old days a lot of ground had to be broken. The resources of a large computer were shared through a kind of polling—a rotating pattern of service to individual users.

A quantum leap in interactive computing capability was provided by APL, a marvelously compact way of talking to a computer. I have a personal recollection of responding over the phone to a request of a scientific colleague regarding an algorithm in the domain of "0–1 integer programming." I was able to check an algorithm by writing a two-line APL program and testing it on the spot. Working in any other language would have required a lengthy program, and a sequence of steps, that would have precluded an immediate response. The problem with APL, however, is that often the programmer himself could not decipher his own marvelously compact programs after a lapse of a few days.

The dawn of interactive computing was also the first drastic change of the computing environment. Instead of lugging a deck of cards to a card reader in order to initiate a computing task, the user could initiate the task using a remote terminal, and receive the results in real time, if there was sufficient computing power available to deliver them.

The progression of languages moved on from the second level to the third, and then the fourth, although the demarcation lines between levels are as imprecise as they are uninteresting to most of us. What defines a high level for a language is its ability to convey a large number of instructions to a computer. For example, a language like PROLOGUE is used to create a "logical programming" sequence which commands a computer to carry out some fairly complex reasoning tasks, with every utterance of the language corresponding to a sizable subset of tasks.

An "Environmental" Movement in Programming

Programming has entered the environmentally correct age of recycling in recent years. There is a rush to reuse pieces of programs in order to increase the efficiency of programming. The increased emphasis on object-oriented programming is the ultimate in this environmental movement in computing. The idea is to create the capability of building programs the way we build physical objects, by connecting subassemblies rather than stringing along molecules. The future, as seen by computer scientists, will have some highly trained professionals build *objects* which can be assembled in various combinations by ordinary mortals in order to produce very sophisticated programs. This will be a giant step in the evolution of the programming environment. It promises to have a huge impact in correcting the imbalance of advances in hardware and software development which has encumbered progress since the beginning of computing.

The notion of recycling software has already been demonstrated and found to be a winner. A special case of such recycling has been associated with the advent of the development in computer architecture known as RISC, the *reduced instruction set computer.* The idea of this architecture has been to translate into hardware a basic set of instructions corresponding to the most common computing tasks, and build other more complex task in software (often reusable software corresponding to standard combinations of computing tasks). This led Martin Hopkins, one of the members of the IBM team that developed the software for the RISC machines, to quip that the term RISC should be best interpreted to mean "reusable instruction set computer." To Martin, the reduced property of the set is perhaps secondary.

"Two-Dimensional Programming" and "Agents"

Sometime in the 1970s, programming ceased to be exclusively a task involving line-by-line instructions and entered a two-dimensional domain of a sort. Moshe Zloof, the inventor of Query By Example (QBE), a relational database query system, was one of the first popularizers of this concept. Instead of issuing a string of instructions to a computer, a QBE user could call for a table or a diagram to be displayed on a screen and proceed to fill in the various entries in the diagram. The underlying QBE software would fill in the programming blanks and produce an executable program that would carry out the query. The notion of two-dimensional programming flourished with the introduction of "spreadsheet" software, such as the widely used Lotus 1-2-3. Today, users take it for granted that they can call for the execution of complex tasks by filling in the blanks in a table or a diagram. One might view this process as one supplying the inputs to a program, but it is more than that. Often the table-completion process involves establishing a functional relationship between entries, which entails embedding some short programs into the underlying spreadsheet or other program.

A recent development which promises to allow end users to carry out even more sophisticated programming tasks in a convenient, non-demanding fashion is the appearance of "agents." Agents have many of the properties of a scourge in computing, the infamous "viruses" and "worms" which have been used by mischievous hackers to invade computing systems and wreak havoc with users' files. Like viruses and worms, the agents are capable of wending their way into a network in order to interact with some files. However, unlike their destructive cousins, agents search for a particular file with which they interact in order to produce a useful result. A popular example is an agent used to make an airline reservation. A user issues an agent which travels through a network connected to airlines' reservation systems. When it finds a desirable flight, it contacts the airline's system, which then issues its own agent. The two agents carry out a transaction that produces a reservation. A third agent may be produced at this point which travels back to the user's system and brings a confirmation of the reservation. The original agent goes to sleep in the airline's system, standing watch over any changes that may take place because of such events as inclement weather. If any changes are required, the agent makes them and communicates them to the user. Finally, when the trip transaction is carried out, the agent gracefully bows out of the picture. Understandably, the advent of agents will have to come with adequate guarantees of system security, particularly in view of the notoriety of their destructive cousins. However, it appears that such guarantees are achievable, and so the agents are likely to provide a new dimension in the "programming" capability of the end user. At a minimum, local agents will be negotiating callbacks and other services from systems with which they interact. Traveling agents, on the other hand, involve security and accounting problems, as well as inefficiencies that may limit their usability.

The Agony and the Ecstasy of Operating Systems

The formal appearance of operating systems dates back to the mid 1960s, although previews of their onset appeared even earlier. The role of operating systems has been to schedule the execution of tasks by the central processing unit of a computer and the activation of the various peripheral devices of a computing system in support of the computing tasks.

The first operating systems were something of a setback for the average users. They meant that users had to learn yet another language, such as the abominable Job Control Language (JCL), in order to personally schedule the mobilization of the various peripheral devices needed for the execution of their programs. Some of us old-timers remember fondly the days when we were exchanging sets of JCL cards that "worked." Fred Brooks, one of the giants of computing in our times and one of those responsible for the creation of JCL, also reflects humorously and wistfully on those days. He admits that JCL was plagued by "a vision that was not high enough." Nevertheless, we survived JCL and went on to a progression of operating systems that is still evolving toward ever more powerful ones, ever more capable of serving the needs of users with diminishing agony and increasing ecstasy.

One of the great leaps in the development of operating systems was the invention of virtual machines, virtual storage, and the like. Virtual things are not real; but they seem real to users, who think they have the command of large computing resources all by themselves. This illusion is created by the intelligent management of computing resources by an operating system, which allocates such resources to build and destroy the virtual systems as the needs for them rise and ebb. A virtual system gives users control over their own computing regimes, but it also enhances the utilization of computing resources. Just as the impact of the money supply on individual wealth increases with its speed of circulation, individual wealth in computing resources increases with our ability to reconstitute virtual machines in response to users' changing requests.

Although virtual systems were originally used for the management of large systems, the same principles have been applied in creating *multitasking* environments for small systems, including personal computers. Multitasking means that a computer supports simultaneous running of several programs, with appropriate allocation of resources for each program.

The evolution of operating systems received a huge impetus from the advent of personal computers, which brought the operating systems closer to the end user than ever before. In addition, the large number of unit sales of operating systems led to warfare among the producers of operating systems vying for users' hearts and minds and for a share of their software budget. The competition has been very beneficial to the users, since it has stimulated progress and kept software prices low. It has also given the users a bewildering choice of operating systems software, with more yet to come. The detailed features of Windows, OS/2, NT, and UNIX, some of the leading contenders in the battle for supremacy among operating systems, are not the stuff of an absorbing story. Their efficiency in the use of hardware matters because it affects price, portability, and simplicity. For example, OS/2 and NT buy their success by using substantially more memory than earlier operating systems. The good news is that such relative inefficiencies become less and less important with advances in microcircuitry and with the concomitant decrease in the volume and price of hardware. Thus, what matters most about an operating system today is the total picture of convenience that it is capable of conveying to the user. To appreciate the challenges in the development of improved operating systems, it may be good to pause and look at one of the most recent developments: multimedia.

Perhaps it is excessive to speak of a revolution, but multimedia is certainly changing the computing scene. At least that is what my children must think, since they look with disdain on the perfectly good, powerful computer in their room and queue up to use the multimedia version I bought for my wife (well, for my wife and me) for Christmas. (I am forced to upgrade the kids' computer to multimedia capability immediately, by order of a higher authority.)

Multimedia has wrought an integration of audio, motion video, and a hierarchy of storage devices, together with one or more microprocessors, allowing a vast improvement in presentation quality for games and other serious computer applications. Incidentally, I feel compelled to show my respect for computer games publicly, even though I am not the least bit addicted to them. I am unaddicted mainly because I consider exploring the intricacies of an operating system a challenge at least equal to that of outwitting wizards, slaying dwarfs (games do not necessarily use politically correct language), crushing giant wasps, or eradicating zombies. But just as children's mechanical games prepare them for life, I think that computer games prepare children of all ages for the rigors of computing life.

It is certainly true that managing the relatively complex array of devices assembled around a personal computer requires a somewhat more sophisticated operating system than was needed up to now. No one has enough computing, storage, and input/output resources at his or her disposal all the time, and this means that these resources must be managed in order to deliver the expected services efficiently. Managing the flow of information across devices by issuing detailed instructions in an artificial language is not a task that appeals to an ordinary human being. This means that an operating system must provide means for the convenient management of these devices in a way only slightly more complicated than that of tuning a radio. In fact, the radio-tuning paradigm is mentioned repeatedly as the goal in personal computing: computers, it is said, will reach the general public, rather than just the computer enthusiasts, only when they can be handled as easily as a radio could when it graduated from the domain of "ham radio" to that of household entertainment devices. The name of the game is, and will continue to be in the foreseeable future, ease of use.

The multimedia revolution entered a new phase when it coupled to the client-server environment of the 1990s. Instead of relying simply on the multimedia library of an isolated system, a user could now have access to a virtually unlimited library of multimedia offerings by using "multimedia on demand." A server, which can be anything from a workstation to a large mainframe, can be accessed in order to ship information, in the form of text, data, sound, and video, over a high-speed communication link. This distributed multimedia concept can be used to enrich the capabilities of educational institutions, entertainment centers, etc. It blends nicely with the plans for information superhighways that began unfolding in the early 1990s. These information links will provide the transportation facility that will make multimedia a common feature of the user's computing environment in either a consumer or a business setting.

More on the Battle among Operating Systems

An article in the August 1993 *Electronic Design News* entitled "Showdown at the OS Corral" starts by listing some of the key requirements for a modern operating system:

real standards
true portability
easy networking
32-bit capabilities
consistent user interface.

The article goes on to describe the key features and the commercial prospects of some of the top contenders, including IBM's OS/2, Microsoft's Windows NT, NeXT's NextStep, and the various mutations of UNIX that dot the computing landscape. In addition to those listed above, the requirements for success of an operating system are use on different processor architectures (preferably over a range from large to small systems) and compatibility with existing applications.

Who is winning the battle of operating systems? At this stage, all that can be said is that more recent offerings are more likely to offer some critical advantages over older ones. For example, both OS/2 and Windows NT have superior multitasking capability, which allows them to compete with UNIX; at the same time, they provide excellent compatibility with existing applications. But the ultimate dominance of an operating system may also depend on some hardware considerations. Specifically, RISC (reduced instruction set computer) machines were used early after their development by UNIX enthusiasts because of their versatility. As a result, UNIX users drove the explosive growth in the use of RISC machines, and UNIX has been a dominant operating system for these machines. This is true of IBM's RS/6000 machines, including the derivative Power PC architecture. It may then be that some version of UNIX will emerge as a dominant operating system around the turn of the century, evolving together with hardware to serve the needs of a wide range of systems, from microsystems to large systems. There is some speculation that the increasing availability of parallel systems may dictate the development of some new operating systems that will be particularly suitable for parallel computer organizations.

Games, Applications, and Virtual Reality

An overly critical friend of mine once observed that IBM's personal computer division is very good at developing both things that save a lot of one's time and things that waste a lot of one's time. He was, of course, contrasting such things as the "productivity" series of PC software with computer games. I have already shown my respect for games, so I will not present yet another apology for them here. I shall only mention that, in many ways, games provide test beds for new computing paradigms. By generating income that supports an army of imaginative programmers, they may also strengthen the software-development infrastructure of the United States.

In the area of application software in general, in addition to the influence of languages and the concept of software reusability, some observations are in order with the regard to computing paradigms. In the early days of computing, most of the computer applications were for scientific computation. Computing was very intermittent as far as the humans were concerned, since it involved a considerable waiting period between submission of a job and obtaining the results. Interactive computing shortened considerably the turnaround time between submission and results. This was very exciting, particularly when it was observed that fast turnaround appeared to speed up people's thinking, thus producing an important second-order effect by increasing productivity. But the results still came out in strings of numbers and reams of paper. They were often difficult to unscramble, and they may have required interpretation into images involving intermediaries, meaning another communication delay. And then came virtual reality.

I do not hesitate to call the advent of virtual reality a revolution, insofar as scientific applications are concerned, because VR has really changed the way many scientists function. I am specifically referring to *visualization*, one of the earliest and most potent elements of VR to be developed. Visualization has given us the ability to immediately convert numerical output into convenient images and, even more important, into motion. Motion is a powerful tool that improves human understanding enormously. Today, a scientist pondering a theory is often able to make a confident judgement about a speculative feature of the theory on the basis of a visualization of the consequences of the feature, seen in color and in motion.

In the early 1990s, powerful special machines were developed for visualization, such as IBM's Power Visualization System (PVS). These machines combined special hardware and the software that orchestrated the use of this hardware to deliver the special functionality needed for visualization. The PVS was built as a platform for applications that required colorful 3-D graphics and high data bandwidths coupled with supercomputer-class computation. Some early uses of its capabilities were for the study of models of the human immune system, superfluid vortices, various surfaces provided by the scanning tunneling microscope, molecular models, cavities in metals, and holes in photoresist materials. Such applications often require more than the performance of traditional systems, which is constrained by limitations on their memory, computing power, disk storage, or input/output bandwidths.

The PVS comprised a computational server, an attached disk array, and a high-resolution video display controller. The server used 32 RISC processors operating in parallel to provide great computational ability. For applications requiring high-bandwidth or high-resolution display information, high-speed links from a PVS input/output processor could drive the PVS video controller to provide real-time video output. Users working on visualization of engineering or scientific data could use the PVS Data Explorer, an integrated software package, to quickly turn data into still or animated images using interactive visual programming. With special eyeglasses, or other devices that presented two distinct images to the two eyes, one could see a three-dimensional view of the visualized results.

The success of visualization is unquestionable. Early "static" applications in such areas as architecture have given way to "dynamic" ones that can be used to design automobiles or to create special effects for movies.

As visualization systems become more and more powerful, the realism of visualization is limited not by the capability of the system but by the accuracy of the physical model underlying the visualization. And in the final analysis, we can even improve on nature!

As the price of visualization machines decreases with increased market penetration, they are likely to revolutionize scientific exploration, just as laboratory automation revolutionized scientific experimentation a couple of decades ago. In fact, the analogy with laboratory automation is particularly apt. Visualization makes possible some form of experimentation that is carried out on a computer, instead of requiring the setting up of an expensive experiment. Computer visualization makes possible the elimination of many unfruitful alternative experiments, and thus speeds the scientific process substantially. For example, in 1993 NASA used VR systems to test planned repairs on the Hubble space telescope before approving and launching the repair mission.

Of course, there is more to VR than visualization. VR can address other senses besides the visual one. There is substantial experimentation with such forms of VR, and we cannot foretell how far they will carry us. At a minimum, they hold promise for new forms of entertainment. The movie industry, having already capitalized on the visualization capabilities of VR, is poised to capitalize on these new dimensions of VR.

User Interfaces

I have already touched on user interfaces, directly or indirectly, while talking about operating systems and about applications. I would like to add a few remarks about this most important facet of software.

Let us start with *hypertext*. Hypertext allows a user to navigate through text freely in search of useful information, instead of looking for such information serially by reading the text from top to bottom. The navigation is guided through "links" of text segments designed to correspond to individual preferences, or even to one's prior use of a computing system. For example, a computer may be taught to provide to a user links to text related to the destination of an air travel reservation made previously on the computer.

Hypertext has been described as a "generalized footnote" because it involves branching out to the reading of some text out of sequence with the main text, not unlike that involved in reading a footnote. But, of course, hypertext is much more than an organization of footnotes. It permits a selective compilation of reading material customized to suit individual tastes. In a very informative article on the subject, Nielsen observes that hypertext will give users access to a personalized newspaper, now available only to presidents and prime ministers.[4] Nielsen also quotes Gilbert Cockton of Glasgow University, who observes that hypertext is a very special, user-friendly task which can only be done on a computer, whereas most other computer tasks can also be done by hand, albeit somewhat more slowly. Hypertext certainly makes good use of computing power to improve a user's access to useful information. Hypertext has been extended to *hypermedia,* involving multimedia presentation of information.

Another important topic in the area of user interfaces is the symbolic form used for communicating with computers. It has been observed, with some degree of sarcasm, that mankind, having started communicating with hieroglyphic icons, has come full circle after thousands of years. We now use icons for most important computer communication functions, only now we speak of a *graphical user interface.* I confess that my first reaction to icons was less than resoundingly positive. (But then, I also confess that I was one of those people who liked APL). Perhaps I felt a little silly playing with icons instead of text and numbers. But it did not take me long to realize that it was not just the icon that was appealing; it was also the shorthand operation of clicking on an icon to access a piece of software. Icons and windows are two of the means by which computers surpass books in offering access to information. (But you still cannot cuddle up in bed with a computer—even a laptop.)

Graphical user interfaces are addressing the needs of both relatively unsophisticated users and programming professionals. Of course, there are GUIs that claim to be designed for ordinary people but fall far short of that objective. In any case, GUIs make good use of the abundance of computing power in order to make the life of the end user easy. At the "high end" of GUI use, professional programmers can develop applications without creating the masses of code that GUIs require. The code for the various GUI elements is selected from palettes and automatically added to the application. This gives the programmer a prototyping environment, plus the ability to add a GUI to every application, even the simplest one, without undue concern for the cost of the GUI.

GUIs are not, however, the only user interfaces, and they will not be the last. Speech has some distinct advantages over many other means of input and output of information, and it will dominate at least some application areas—particularly ones in which the user's hands and/or eyes are otherwise busy (as when one is driving an automobile while communicating with an *electronic back-seat driver* that provides step-by-step driving instructions). Pen-based systems are also being tried, if only to free us from being tied to a keyboard for alphanumeric input. Perhaps future user interfaces will be personalized to suit individual needs. There is absolutely no reason to be tied to any particular form of user interface. Rather, we will be able to switch from one interface to another to suit the needs of the moment or the limitations of the equipment we have at hand.

Some Economic Considerations

Who Pays for All These Things?
The justification of expenditures on information technology (IT) in general has been the topic of discussion for many years, particularly in connection with productivity issues in the service sector. For the first two or three decades of IT deployment, people talked about the productivity paradox—the fact that productivity did not rise at all in the service sector in spite of substantial investments in IT. A comprehensive study by a committee of the Computer Science and Telecommunications Board of the National Research Council[1] documents some of the facts in this case and provides some explanations. To some extent, the productivity paradox was due to our inability to measure productivity properly. But to a great extent it was also due to the fact that mere application of IT was not sufficient to improve productivity greatly. Such improvements materialized when enterprises were "reengineered" to take full advantage of the application of IT.

I believe it is fair to say that for many years companies viewed IT expenditures as the cost of staying in business. However, in recent years IT expenditures have been viewed as the cost of competitive advantage. This may seem a small difference, but it is an important one. Instead of routinely investing in IT for defensive reasons, companies now take a proactive role of investing selectively in order to improve productivity. We have also witnessed a decentralization of computing operations, from the "glass house" environment to a decentralized client-server environment, coupled with decentralized decisions for the purchase of IT equipment, including hardware and software. So, we have now reached the point when pure economic considerations alone may be sufficient to justify considerable investment in IT in general, and software development in particular, on the basis of expected productivity improvements. Moreover, as mentioned earlier, the consumer market (e.g. games) is fueling progress in the basic building blocks of software development, including GUIs, multimedia, and even VR.

It is very likely that the closer tie between IT expenditures and enterprise structure will influence the evolution of business much more in the future than it has in the past. For example, Malone et al.[2] argue that application of IT reduces the cost of coordination and thus leads to more coordination-intensive organizational forms, such as markets. Porter and Millar[3] discuss the application of IT in business and conclude that IT affects competition in three ways:

• It alters the industry/value-chain structure.
• It supports cost and differentiation strategics.
• It spawns entirely new businesses.

Once more, all these observations point out to a familiar refrain: the computer revolution in fact has just begun.

The last few years have seen continuing increases in the accessibility of computers to more and more end users. Much of the progress has been due to friendly operating systems and application programs which present a convenient interface to a user, requiring virtually no knowledge of the gory details that make computing possible. Today schoolchildren can carry out desktop publishing tasks that were in the domain of professionals just ten years ago. At the "high end," scientists (who remain the most demanding users of computers) can call on "virtual reality" systems to help them speed up their thinking and experimentation processes.

Where are we going from here? Computers will become accessible to *everybody*. The availability of inexpensive computing power will make using a computer as easy as turning a radio or a TV on, instead of requiring training and fortitude. More important, computers will continue to change how we live, work, and play. The multimedia revolution will couple the computer to familiar entertainment devices and make it a tool for education, business, and pleasure. Scientists have already achieved a productivity undreamed of by their predecessors by using computers as extensions of their intellectual power. The future will bring this capability to everyone. And it is software that will make the realization of this dream possible.

Acknowledgement

I am indebted to Marc Auslander, who read the manuscript and contributed many valuable suggestions.

Notes

1. Information Technology in the Service Society (Report of Committee to Study the Impact of Information Technology on the Performance of Service Activities, Computer Science and Telecommunications Board, Commission on Physical Sciences, Mathematics and Applications, National Research Council). National Academy Press, 1994.

2. Thomas W. Malone, Joanne Yates, and Robert I Benjamin, "Electronic Markets and Electronic Hierarchies," *Communications of the ACM* 30, June 1987.

3. Michael E. Porter and Victor E. Millar, "How Information Gives You Competitive Advantage," *Harvard Business Review,* July-August 1985.

4. J. Nielson, "Usability Considerations in Introducing Hypertext," in *Hypermedia, Hypertext, and Object-Oriented Databases,* ed. H. Brown. Chapman and Hall, 1991.

Is Any of This Relevant?

David Vaskevitch

What is relevant is what solves the problem. If people had thought real relevances through hard enough, we'd be on Sirius by now.
—attributed to Peter Medawar, Nobel laureate

What will software be like in the next century? The simplest answer to this question is "more of what we have today, but better." At one level such an answer is true. Software will be easier to use. New development tools and environment will make it possible for millions to build their own applications without ever learning a heavy-duty programming language. Networks will become transparent, and components really will allow systems to be constructed out of pre-built elements. All these things will undoubtedly come to pass. Still, this leaves two fundamental questions unanswered:

- Even if all of today's software trends continue to unfold, will it make any real difference to the world?
- What fundamentally new developments—complete new approaches—will be important that linear extrapolation can't really tell us about?

Another way of approaching the future of software is to try to imagine the computer of the next century—how it will look and what it will be used for. A large part of that guided meditation can easily be based on linear extrapolation. For instance, the personal version of that future computer is quite likely to be a lot like the Dynabook that Alan Kay proposed in *Technology 2001*. From a hardware perspective, the Dynabook is a personal computer with virtual no tradeoffs. Imagine a machine small and light enough to carry around all the time, perhaps weighing only a pound. This computer has batteries that last up to a week between charges. It has a display capable of showing two full-size, color, high-resolution pages. It interacts through pen, mouse, keyboard, and touch, as well as having more storage than an individual can use. Its radio-based connection keeps you constantly connected to networks, providing bandwidth unimaginable today even in a local network.

The problem with imagining the computer future of the next century is, in fact, not the hardware or the network, but the software. Without any doubt, hardware and networking advances of the next decade or two will make the computer just described not only possible but common. And we have no trouble at all imagining such a computer. What we have trouble imagining is what people will *do* with that computer.

Imagine taking 1995's inexpensive notebook computer running a graphical suite of applications and showing it to a computer user of 1985—or, even better, 1975. That a computer more than equal to a mainframe of the 1960s could be carried under one arm would be thought preposterous. The power of the graphical software would be even more amazing. Yet, are these computers changing the lives of individuals and organizations? Today, for the most part, the answer is "No."

I will set out in this chapter to trace how and why computers—hardware and software working together—will finally cause a truly profound change in people's lives in the next several decades. I will start by considering what is required to make computers and their applications really relevant. By "relevant" I mean "used in ways that directly change the way people play and work in at least small ways." I also mean "used in ways that can be justified in terms of value delivered." Finally, I mean "used in ways such that, if taken away, they would be really missed." The first step, then, will be to examine whether computers and the applications they run on are now relevant in this fashion.

Next, I will trace how things will change to make computers become more than just relevant. In fact, the primary theme of this chapter is that in the next few years computers will turn out to be fundamental agents of organizational and cultural change. The computers by themselves will not cause the changes, but they are fundamental elements in a larger shift—in business and even in society—toward decentralization and individual empowerment. That shift, it turns out, is directly linked to the idea of client/server systems.

Client/server systems: Isn't that a current trend? Isn't the whole point to avoid linear extrapolation? On the one hand, I am definitely talking about new ways of using computers that are more than just extrapolations of the present. On the other hand, it is very hard, if not impossible, to talk about the future without talking about how it is derived from the present.

Can Software Become Relevant?

Are personal computers really relevant? Is all the investment, at home and in the office, in ever faster, ever more powerful personal computers, networks, laser printers, CD-ROMs, and all the rest really worthwhile? Can the cost be justified? More important, are all the tens of millions of personal computers, networked or otherwise, truly delivering value to individuals and organizations?

The answer today is "No, personal computers are not highly relevant to people's lives and jobs." That is not the whole answer, though. Those same personal computers *will* be highly relevant, and soon. It is software that will make the difference, and the next generation of software will make those PCs not only relevant but indispensable. Consider a few scenarios.

• Your teenager has now had a carefully purchased personal computer for a little over a year. When you bought it, visions of well-crafted essays, meticulously researched papers, and spreadsheet-backed analyses danced through your mind. Your dreams, not your child's. As it turns out, the computer is indeed used heavily on a daily basis. It has become the center of social interaction, not only for your teenager and his or her friends, but for your younger children too. Has their homework come alive? No! For years, like many other parents, you steadfastly refused to buy them a $500 Nintendo, dreading electronic addiction. But now you find that your kids are addicted to a $2500 game machine, complete with a high-resolution color monitor, a double-speed CD-ROM, and stereo speakers. True, the machine does get used occasionally for academic work, but it's truly hard to tell if the work produced is any better than what other children produced before personal computers were invented. That home personal computer, while certainly fun and addictive, is hardly relevant to the purpose you originally imagined.

• The situation in the office, both for the individual and for the corporation, is hardly much better. Word processors, spreadsheets, and desktop databases virtually define the market for personal computer software. Yet most users of personal computers spend only a small fraction of their time producing memos, analyzing budgets, and building large lists. If their personal computers were to stop working, many users literally wouldn't notice for considerable periods of time—if it were not for electronic mail. Electronic mail, though not a huge category in the software market, is the one application used all day and every day. Yet, for all its ubiquity, email is the application that probably benefits least from the power contained in a personal computer. For most purposes, terminal-based electronic mail systems are just as useful as those based on graphical user interfaces. So why bother with PCs?

• The dilemma is most acute at the organizational level. Computers cost a lot of money. In the 1950s information processing was not even a budget item for most organizations. By the 1960s—still before the invention of permanent storage, databases, networks, and terminals—computers had come to represent a significant percent of the budget of most large companies. With the advent of networks and databases, computer costs continued to escalate as even senior managers came to realize that an organization without an effective electronic nervous system simply could not compete. By the late 1980s, even ignoring spending on personal computers, information technology had come to cost more than most companies could afford. Banks and insurance companies, for instance, found themselves spending from 10 to 15 percent of their budgets on mainframes, terminals, networks, and the operational infrastructure to keep it all running. Personal computers made that "cost crunch" far worse. Rather than replace mainframes and minicomputers, personal computers augmented them. At present, personal computers—even when networked—cannot handle the transaction-processing and batch-reporting jobs that mainframes are so adept at. Yet millions of users have come to view an easy-to-use personal computer as an entitlement. The result is a near doubling of the computer budget. Organizations are spending as much as ever on mainframes and minicomputers. At the same time, they are spending the same amount over again for personal computers.

Worst of all, the computers aren't doing the job. The expensive mainframes take forever to program. Application backlogs stretch out to months and years, while management continually worries about the organizational inflexibility caused by rigid applications. Personal computers can only be used for small tasks, extending at most to the workgroup. And the two types of computers, even after 15 years of trying, simply don't communicate well. "Mainframers" are always complaining about the amount of time spent feeding information to PCs, while individual end users feel that the information in the corporate mainframe might as well be locked in a vault.

In all three cases we can legitimately ask: Is the computer really relevant? If the computer were taken away, would life really be worse? In two of the three cases the answer would be "No." The personal computers used at home and in the office are still only marginally relevant at best. Yes, people have grown accustomed to personal computers, but their lives have yet to be truly changed. In the case of the mainframe, the answer is slightly more complex: the machine is highly relevant but also badly outclassed. While the mainframe fills an essential role, the tools and the technology it supplies are so far out of touch with users' true needs that the resulting solution is often almost as bad as the original problem.

Considering the home, the office desk, and the mainframe computer center can point us in the appropriate direction for computers to follow for the rest of the 1990s. In the past, a great deal that might be imagined about computers was highly constrained by hardware limitations. Today, though, computers have become so small, so fast, so capacious, and so inexpensive that applications are limited mostly by the imagination. And, with computer technology continuing to improve at an accelerating rate, the hardware of tomorrow will only be that much more amazing than what we have today. Thus, if computers are to shift from being interesting and mostly irrelevant to playing a central role in our lives, the software will have to change much more than the hardware.

What would it mean to have software that would make computers essential elements of our everyday lives? It can't be just a question of better interfaces, slightly better programming facilities, or the like. Surely some more qualitative change is required. What is the fundamental shift in the way software is thought about that will make computers truly relevant to us all?

While computers are continuing to get better at a frightening rate, another, perhaps even larger change is taking place in the organizations around us. It turns out that those two trends—the business revolution and the computer revolution—are directly related. Understanding that connection provides a straightforward answer to the question of how computers can become relevant.

Organization, Process, and Communication

Businesses around the world are downsizing. Downsizing involves much more than just having fewer employees; it also implies new organizational structures that provide better customer service and faster decision making in spite of having less staff to do all the work. At the core of the downsizing movement is a commitment to Business Process Reengineering, which calls for a focus on process instead of tasks. By rearranging jobs so that processes have single owners, organizations can function more effectively. Process orientation, in turn, depends on communication and information sharing, facilitated by computers. It is these concepts—organizational downsizing, process orientation, and the importance of communication—that really point the way to a new role for computers.

Hierarchical management has been the primary way of managing large organizations for most of this century. Hierarchical command and control is rooted in an assembly-line view of the world. As an organization grows, some way of dividing up the work is required. But in the past communication was slow and information sharing was minimal. Therefore, if an organization was to function in a coordinated fashion, with consistent policies and efficient sharing of scarce resources, decision making had to be centralized. Centralized decision makers could be depended on to adhere to the rules. In addition, a central decision maker could keep track of all the company's resources and allocate them in an efficient fashion.

The corollary of centralized decision making was the assembly line. Since most of the real decisions were made by middle or senior managers, the employees doing most of the work weren't empowered to make decisions, so they were given jobs that could be done without thinking. Thus the assembly line found its way into both the manufacturing plant and the office.

In too many ways the disconnected computer worlds we have today are a direct consequence of the historical task orientation of hierarchical command organizations. On the one hand, mainframes represent centralized decision making and resource allocation carried to its logical conclusion. In fact, to a large extent, the mainframe made it possible for centralized, bureaucratic organizational structures to last far longer than would otherwise have been possible. At the same time, personal computers catered to task-oriented individuals. The whole point of an assembly-line organizational design is to divide processes into tasks so small that they can be completed largely without thinking. Disconnected personal computers, lacking access to real, live data, fit into an assembly-line world very well.

If all this sounds cynical or negative, consider many of the examples in Hammer and Champy's recent best-seller *Re-Engineering the Corporation: A Manifesto for Business Revolution.* Time after time, a company analyzes its processes only to find out that dividing the work up into small tasks, each requiring no decision making, is a recipe for delay, inefficiency, and poor customer service. Yet building organizations around such tasks is the rule, not the exception.

How does this relate to computers and relevant software? Computers, for the most part, have been used to facilitate task-oriented organizations, both at the individual level and company-wide. Word processing and spreadsheets, for example, help with very individual-oriented tasks. Similarly, most large mainframe-based applications are built around transactions and transaction processing. The very word "transaction," aside from its highly specific technical definition, is a synonym for "task." Large computers are often measured and even characterized in terms of their ability to run hundreds of transactions—small tasks—per second. Thus, it is not surprising that the computer software we live with today is made in the image of our organizations. A large part of making software and computers more relevant turns out to involve focusing on tasks rather than on processes. When this is done, computers become at least as much tools for communication as tools for computing. To understand this, we have to delve deeper into process orientation.

A central goal of Business Process Reengineering is the elimination of queues. Queues arise because simple processes require many decision makers to be involved. For instance, a salesman takes an order, which has to be approved by the credit department; inventory is allocated in another department; shipping is scheduled in another part of the organization;

and so on. When information traveled at the speed of a horse, such an approach was inevitable. Today, with networks and computers, it should be possible to take the order, approve the credit, allocate the inventory, and schedule the shipment all in one step. Delays should occur only when unusual circumstances arise.

At first it might seem that universal access to a central database might be enough to facilitate the ownership of processes. In fact, a database *does* go a long way toward solving the problem. Not far enough, though. The problem arises from the number of questions that need to be answered to really solve customers' problems in a reengineered world.

Consider a salesman who has been told that he is now responsible for always solving the customers' problems. In the past, problems with credit were handled in one place, late shipments in another, defective product in yet another. Now, though, the individual salesman must be able to deal with all these problems and more. Such an approach is, of course, more efficient if implemented properly; it's more human, too. Nobody really likes to be told that his problem requires another phone call. In the past, however, there was no choice.

Now here's the rub. Reengineered business processes require empowered employees who can deal with many kinds of problems. Dealing with a wide variety of problems means asking lots of questions. And a centralized database can't keep up with that kind of demand.

The problem goes deeper, though. As more and more processes are reengineered, decision making keeps being pushed from the middle of the organization out to the periphery. And, as that happens, a desire to tailor not only the questions but also the processes starts to come to the surface. If the local sales office truly owns the satisfaction of its local customers, why shouldn't that sales office be able to tailor the company's procedures to meet local needs? Of course, many company-wide rules must be kept intact in the process—but is that a reason why some degree of customization can't be accommodated?

Local customization of procedures has been a standard request in large organizations since large organizations came into existence, and centralized information-technology organizations have been resisting requests for local enhancements since such organizations came to exist. Yet, in a world of empowerment and self-managed teams, making these local enhancements possible becomes an essential prerequisite to success.

The Role of the Server

In the past, the world of computers revolved around personal and corporate machines. The personal computers sit on people's desks; the mainframes sit in glass temples. With the advent of the local-area network, servers began to play an important role. Yet, servers have often been used in ways that have made their functions appear ill defined.

Personal computers run applications. Mainframes run applications. What do servers do? They act as intelligent switches providing intelligent sharing of resources for many users. The vast majority of the world's servers do no more than provide file and print sharing. Such a server is, in fact, acting like no more than a supersmart printer *cum* disk drive. Servers also play an important role in supporting databases; in this role they come closer to being true computers. Still, two facts are instructive about the role of database servers.

Most database servers are run in such a way that the applications which access the databases run everywhere but on the server. So, while the server is helping the database be faster, it's still hard to say how that server is acting a lot differently than a supersmart disk drive specially designed to support databases. Even as marketeers and salesmen run seminars touting the benefits of client/server applications, well over 85 percent of the world's production data continues to reside on mainframe databases. IMS, IDMS, VSAM, and RMS (all nonrelational and all non-server-based) continue to hold most of the data used to run large organizations around the world.

It is precisely the fact that so much data lives in the mainframe that makes the self-managed teams called for by Business Process Reengineering so hard to implement. Let the team ask lots of questions? Products like Paradox and Access certainly make it easy for nontechnical users to formulate complex queries graphically without knowing SQL or any other query language. Ask a mainframe operations manager about the very idea of ordinary users' running *ad hoc* queries against the mainframe database and watch him or her turn pale. Every such *ad hoc* query is highly likely to contain sums, averages, counts, and other aggregates that require going through the entire database. And every such traversal will drag the mainframe to its knees. Employees may be empowered to solve customer problems, but that empowerment is bereft of any ability to examine the sources and the implications of those problems.

Local customization? That is unlikely. All the real applications run in that single large mainframe. Keeping track of the dozens if not hundreds of modifications required to meet the needs of each local team is just unimaginable. The mainframe code would become so complex it would never run; even if it did run, no central staff could ever keep it running.

Thus, in a centralized environment, self-managed teams and empowered employees are essentially contradictory. But there is an alternative. Suppose the server could actually run applications. What would happen then?

A server—an inexpensive, shared computer that doesn't sit on a desk—can provide all the classical functions: databases can be shared, resource-allocation decisions can be made on behalf of groups, and so on. Because they are inexpensive, servers can be distributed widely. If a query brings a server to its knees, who cares? Only the users of that particular server. If those users complain, the answer is to buy another server. Can a mainframe be such a server? Yes, if it is inexpensive enough. For a mainframe to fill that role, it has to be possible for even the smallest team or department to buy another mainframe without flinching. If the cost of a mainframe is too high for that, then it can't be thought of as the primary server.

So, being shared and being inexpensive are two keys to the client/server world of the future. However, just as important is the fact that servers don't sit on desks. They can be secured; therefore, they can be used to enforce organizational business rules. If a local team wants to modify procedures to meet regional requirements, now it can do so. If those modifications violate company-wide rules, the server won't let the new application run. It is this last characteristic that really brings the server into perspective: the server, for the first time, is running serious applications.

Running applications on computers is hardly new. And in terms of fundamental architecture, the server is hardly a new type of computer. What is new is the ownership of the server. Mainframes are owned by the organization. Because they are expensive, they are few in number. Because they are few in number, they are easily overloaded. So, the central organization places serious limits on the ways in which those mainframes are used. Personal computers are individually owned. If necessary, individuals will buy the machines themselves just to have control over how they are used.

Servers are the first machines that are owned both by individuals or teams and by the organization.

A shared computer can hold shared data; that's the whole point of databases. With that sharing comes some loss of control; otherwise the shared data is guaranteed to be inconsistent. In the past, that loss of control was total. Not only could the shared data not be accessed and updated in flexible ways; it couldn't even be queried freely or with impunity.

A personal computer holds personal data. In fact, in the personal computer industry the same term—"database"—has come to stand for products that simplify query formulation, report generation, and application construction, all working with totally unshared information. How ironic: in the high-volume world of personal computers the very word that once virtually stood for data sharing isn't even associated with sharing. It is this conundrum that the server solves.

The core idea of Total Quality Management is that organizations need to shift their focus so that all internal processes become self-regulating. In a factory, products are built by individuals and teams each of whose job is large enough that the team or individual can manage the work so as to produce only perfect results. In the office, too, work gets rearranged so that all processes are self-regulating. Thus, orders don't pass from queue to queue; instead, the salesman who originally took the order becomes responsible for seeing that order through all the way to shipment and even collection of payment. Similarly, a bank officer needs to be able to answer all the questions a customer might have about accounts, financial products, etc. When a customer wants to initiate a transaction that involves many accounts, a variety of financial instruments, and a sequence of steps, that customer wants to be able to deal with just a single bank employee, and to set the whole transaction up without long delays. Let's stick with that example for a minute.

Banks sell a variety of financial products, all based on information. In fact, a bank's only product is information. In a bank, new products are generally built out of combinations of old ones: mortgage-backed securities, home equity construction loans, personally controlled retirement investment accounts, etc. The problem is that each of the bank's many products is typically handled through an application specifically built to make that product available to customers, and each of those applications has its own files and database tables. Customers, though, expect to be able to ask questions about arbitrary combinations of products, accounts, and services, and—imagine this—get answers to those questions all at once.

Computers are supposed to be good at combining information from lots of different sources. In a small or a medium-size bank, the combinations described in the previous paragraph often involve joining data from 20, 30, or 40 tables at one time. One developer of banking software estimates that the average query in even a smallish bank involves joining 25 tables.

In the past, even though customer service was important, banks revolved around specialists. One specialist dealt with stocks, another with credit cards, another with mortgages, another with bonds, and so forth. Today, though, Business Process Reengineering and the trend toward improved service have created a need to replace specialists with generalists who can handle arbitrary combinations of products. And those generalists need access to all the customer's records, no matter what kinds of products or transactions they involve, in order to do their jobs. In the banking industry, the creation of an environment in which employees have this kind of universal access to information is talked about in terms of the "uniform customer file."

Creating a uniform customer file is expensive. Providing general access to it is even more expensive. Customers frequently have complex requirements. The problem is that, once bank employees have access to all this information, they start creating complex queries all the time—and all those 25- and 30-table joins kill the mainframe. The implications of not providing that powerful query capability, though, run very deep.

A process can be self-regulating only if there is a direct feedback loop. A furnace can maintain a relatively steady temperature because it is directly connected to the thermostat that measures the results of the furnace's loop. The old bank environment, where relatively simple portfolio transactions involve the actions of many specialists, is the very opposite of closed feedback loops. The customer talks to a bank officer about rebalancing his portfolio. That officer can take down the request but can't act on it directly. The request then makes its way from queue to queue as the stock trader, the bond trader, the mortgage specialist, the trust specialist, and others act on it separately. Nobody in the process understands the larger goal except the customer. When a mistake happens, nobody is to blame, and the mess takes weeks to sort out.

Business Process Reengineering, which is based on Total Quality Management, virtually requires a focus on self-managing processes. Giving bank employees access to information systems built on uniform customer files produces three direct results:

• Things happen much faster, because the banking generalist can handle most banking transactions directly, on the spot, without depending on specialists.

• Since the bank employee handling the transaction understands the goal and how all the steps are related to one another, that employee can correct mistakes before they happen. This is what self-regulating processes are all about.

• Each bank employee now has enough access to information to be able to answer all customer questions, complete most financial transactions, and generally handle most customer problems. The employee can now solve most of the problems he or she encounters. Jobs become more interesting, and people feel like they have more control over their lives.

In a nutshell, then, a self-managed team is a team that is responsible for implementing processes that are under its control. A group of people all working toward a common goal (or a single empowered individual) has sufficient authority and sufficient access to information to be in control of its (or his, or her) own destiny. Where do servers fit into this picture?

Virtually without exception, self-managed teams require significant access to information. Several years' experience with Business Process Reengineering has shown that centrally based computers often inhibit the implementation of self-managed teams significantly. Servers, with the right applications running on them, provide the solution to that problem.

A server facilitates the transition to self-managed teams in two critical ways:

Information access.   Because servers are inexpensive, each team can have its own server or even several servers. Therefore, running *ad hoc* queries is not a problem, no matter how complex the queries are or how many files or tables they reach out and touch. Of course, personal computers encourage *ad hoc* queries too; the difference is that the data on the server is shared, live data representing the true, dynamic state of the organization and its customers.

Local flexibility.   The team can not only access data in the server; it can also write its own applications to change that data. Thus, local bank branches can mount their own marketing programs and use applications to track progress. Individual manufacturing teams can tailor inventory-management procedures to their own needs. In each case, because the server is owned by the team, it provides the team's members with an environment for writing their own applications. Yet, because that server is also owned by the organization, the server continues to enforce core business rules and to safeguard the fundamental consistency of the shared database.

Client/Server: What It's Really About

Most observers assume that the key computer revolution of the 1990s is about graphical user interfaces and the desktop. Certainly the impact of graphical applications is highly visible. And, of course, users, once they become accustomed to GUIs, insist that all their applications be written graphically. Central MIS departments, for example, would certainly characterize most of the pressures on them to rewrite applications as desktop- and GUI-driven. Yet GUI is only one part of the real client/server revolution, and perhaps the least important part.

In many ways, the 1990s can be characterized as the decade of downsizing. Companies are trimming thousands of positions, often permanently. At the same time, computer systems are being "downsized" as users attempt to shift applications from mainframes to smaller machines. In most ways those two trends are assumed to be relatively unrelated. Not so. And it is in searching for the link that we can most quickly see the limitations of the personal computer as a driving force.

The simplest way, conceptually, to get rid of a mainframe is to somehow convert most of the applications that run on it to run on networked personal computers. Such conversion is technically complex and quite often turns out to be just plain impossible. Instead, in order to get applications to run on networked workstations, rewriting is required. The problem that then arises is what to do with all those mainframe applications until rewriting becomes feasible. The obvious answer is to put a graphical veneer on the big old systems.

A variety of tools have been introduced in the last five years that make it easy to replace the terminal-based screens sitting in front of most mainframe applications with graphical equivalents. These tools allow those terminal screens to be effectively replaced without ever even touching the original application. Mechanically, the way this works is that an application running in a personal computer intercepts the terminal-bound screens and translates them on the fly. The end result is that the user sees a graphical application, complete with color, windows, mouse support, pull-down menus, radio buttons, and so on, while the mainframe continues to believe it is talking to terminals. Great . . . for a very short period of time.

Users, once introduced to such graphically transformed applications, start out excited but quickly become disillusioned. Though the application looks nicer and is somewhat easier to learn, the application is fundamentally unchanged. If users could not answer complex questions before, they still can't in the more graphical version of the application. If the old system couldn't solve many classes of customer problems before, the new version won't be any better.

Tools like PowerBuilder, Visual Basic, Access, and Microsoft Excel make it easy to prepare (or pre-process) applications in other ways. Yet, despite the fact that these tools allow very slick and powerful preprocessors to be written in hours or days instead of weeks and months, most organizations still depend on mainframes and still view personal computers as basically unrelated to the real work of running the business. All these things emphasize the limitations of the personal-computer-oriented view of the world.

If the personal computer is not at the center of the computer revolution of the 1990s, what is? The server! Understanding the role of the server brings downsizing into very sharp focus. Mainframes are too expensive. Simply converting applications is also too expensive. Rewriting complete applications costs a huge amount too. If the primary motivation for rewriting applications was either graphical ease of use or reduction of mainframe expenses, then the applications would never get rewritten; it would never be cost-justified. However, there is a much bigger revolution going on that justifies the cost of rewrites.

A phone company applied reengineering techniques to the process associated with activating new business telephone lines. This process, winding its way from queue to queue, from specialist to specialist, took 21 business days to complete—well over a calendar month. For decades customers had simply accepted the fact that new telephone lines took over a month to become available. On close examination, it turned out that more than 95 percent of the decisions being made by specialists could be made by appropriately trained generalists, with the right computer systems. For example, occasionally a customer would request a phone line only to find out that his local cable trunk was full. However, in more than 99 percent of these cases the cable trunk had spare pairs, and a computer could reserve a pair and make it available right away. In the end, by consolidating all the various decisions associated with line activation in this way, the phone company reduced activation time to under 4 hours. The savings were huge, and the competitive advantage was beyond measure. Over and over, such results of Business Process Reengineering create situations in which rewriting old applications is not only cost-justified but virtually mandatory. And, in almost all cases, the new systems revolve around the use of servers to provide hugely increased information access and local application customization.

The downsizing and client/server revolutions of the 1990s, then, revolve around three fundamental technological centers:

- distributed processing
- distributed data
- graphical user interfaces

Yes, GUI is on the list. Graphical applications simplify the processes of formulating queries, building applications, combining data of many types, and so on. Yet, although it is on this very short list, GUI is distinctly third in importance to the overall revolution. First and most important is the distribution of processing. Right behind it, though, is the distribution of data. It is the ability to distribute databases and the processing that goes with them that, in the end, makes self-managed teams and the Business Process Reengineering revolution possible. At a high level, those are the procedures we are faced with implementing over the next decade.

Distributed Systems: Myth or Possible Dream?

Computer scientists have talked about distributed databases since the mid 1970s. Many academics even believe that the most important problems associated with the building of distributed databases have been solved, and even that the topic is not interesting any more. At the same time, in the real world, where databases are built and used every day, distributed systems are few and far between. In fact, many MIS professionals believe that distributed databases are, in practice, just short of impossible to build and run. Where is the truth?

Distributed databases today are enormously hard to design, build, or run. Most commercial network and database management systems provide little or no support for true large-scale distribution of processing or data. The vast majority of organizations run around centralized systems. Even if an organization has many data-processing centers, they tend to run in a largely disconnected fashion. That's one end of the reality spectrum.

However, several examples of large-scale, commonly used, highly distributed systems exist as highly tangible proofs of concept. Probably the most compelling example is the worldwide point-of-sale transaction-processing system. The fact that a traveler can walk into a store anywhere in the world, proffer a credit card, purchase a product, and have the local inventory and his remote credit limit adjusted within a matter of seconds is nothing short of amazing. This is a distributed system, with millions of highly heterogeneous computing elements all interacting worldwide, and it works. That's the other end of the reality spectrum.

Why are distributed systems so hard to design, build, and run? Will the situation change in the next ten years? The answer turns out to be closely related to the very same task orientation that figured so prominently in the organizational design of the past.

The two primary factors that have made it hard to design and build distributed (database) systems are the following:

• Existing databases don't provide enough support, even though the key tools and techniques are now pretty well understood.
• The standard tools and techniques result in distributed systems that are just too fragile for widespread use.

As it turns out, these two reasons are interrelated. In the first place, certain standard mechanisms for building distributed systems have been understood quite well for more than a decade. Distributed query processors, two-phase commit for distributed synchronization, and so on are hardly new. Why haven't more database vendors simply built these facilities into their systems? Part of the answer revolves around simple self-protection. Any shift toward distributed systems is also a shift toward more open systems. As soon as companies start to design truly distributed databases, it is only natural that customers will want a variety of database types in the network. Thus, once a database vendor starts to implement distributed database support, it's only a matter of time before customers force the issue and insist that the distributed support facilities talk to databases from other vendors. While this answer (coupled with the technical complexity of distributed systems) offers part of the answer, it's only part. The rest revolves around a fundamental limitation of the industry's current view of the distributed environment.

Most current applications and business systems, like the organizations they support, are built around a highly task-oriented view of the world. The primary technique for designing the functional or behavioral aspect of large systems is called "functional decomposition." Like the assembly-line approach to organizational design, "functional decomposition" calls for the practitioner to take processes and tasks and chop them up finer and finer, decomposing them, until the designer is dealing with very small, atomic tasks. It is these sliced and diced tasks that are converted into application code.

Whenever these highly granular tasks affect the database, they are called "transactions." By definition, a transaction is the smallest task that can leave the database in a consistent state after it has been carried out. That is, the database starts out consistent (e.g., meaningful from a business perspective), then a transaction is applied to the database, and after the transaction the database is consistent again.

Today, large-scale application design revolves totally around either database design or transaction design. Typically, big application systems are even called "transaction processing systems." What's the matter with transactions, other than the fact that they are the computer equivalent of the unthinking tasks I talked about above? There are two standard things that supposedly prevent the large-scale deployment of distributed database systems: the problem of deciding which data go where and the limitations of two-phase commit.

Processes—Not Tasks or Transactions

"Two-phase commit" is a protocol (set of agreements) that allows a transaction to be completed in several locations at one time. For example, if one computer manages credit authorization and another manages order processing, a two-phase commit protocol would allow credit to be decreased if and only if a particular order was successfully processed to completion.

One problem with two-phase commit is getting enough database vendors to implement the protocol. At least one standard, promulgated by X/Open, provides a basis for heterogeneous databases to interoperate in a two-phrase commit environment. But, although the first version of that standard has been agreed to, database vendors have managed to block complete agreement on the next phase for some time now. Nonetheless, two-phase commit is sufficiently standard that developers can even find ways to make it work in heterogeneous database environments.

The "catch" is that, although two-phase commit always works, the resulting systems are fragile. Suppose the credit-authorization computer in the above example goes down in the middle of an order. That order remains suspended until the computer and the communication line leading to it come back up. Now imagine building a large distributed system with hundreds of thousands of servers supporting self-managed teams. Each time a server or a communications line goes down, some large part of the network grinds to a halt.

Two-phase commit is built to support a worldview in which transactions are of central importance. Transactions, in turn, are a highly real-time occurrence. And that, rather than two-phase commit itself, is the core of the problem.

Most organizations revolve around processes, not transactions or tasks. A transaction is a specific event that must either be completed all at once or not be completed at all. The whole point of a transaction-processing system is that it guarantees the "atomicity" of transactions; if a transaction can't be completed in its entirety, then the system rolls the incomplete transaction back so that the database looks as though none of it was ever done. Two-phase commit simply extends this discipline to many computers and sites working together.

Computers process dozens, hundreds, or even thousands of transactions per second. In order to guarantee the atomicity of a transaction, the computer locks up all the data affected by that transaction until it is done, so that if the transaction has to be undone nobody else is affected by the rollback. Clearly, then, transactions simply can't be allowed to drag on for very long; it wouldn't be fair or feasible to keep all the data locked away.

Transactions, although they are the key to running organizations, are on too small a scale. Consider for example, the most classical of business processes: order entry. A salesman enters an order. Credit is checked, inventory is allocated, shipments are scheduled, deliveries are made, invoices are printed and sent, payments are credited, commissions are paid, and so on. Transactions are completed in fractions of a second, but orders take days, weeks, months or even years to wind their way through these many steps. What is an order, then? Is it a transaction? Never. An order is a process, and a process is a sequence of transactions extended in time.

It is more important that distributed systems support "distributed processes" than that they support distributed transactions. The sequences of transactions usually define the process that is to be coordinated, but *not in real time*. Consider the scheduling of a shipment. A customer calls to place an order. We would like to tell him when the shipment will take place, but the warehouse computer is down. In a two-phase commit world, where transactions are all there is to work with, we would refuse to take the customer's order. From a business perspective, in most organizations, this makes no sense; the customer may *want* to know when his order will be shipped, but will he refuse to even place the order if that information is unavailable? Do we want to refuse to take the order just because we can't predict a shipment data? Not likely. What we need instead is a way for the order-entry application running in a server at the sales office to send a request to the warehouse, *knowing that that request will be processed soon*. In this case, "soon" is *real enough time*. And real enough time is all we need to build this system.

At a simple level, focusing on sequences of transactions instead of just individual transactions simplifies the process of designing distributed systems significantly. It allows us to design robust, resilient systems. In fact, at this level the new model corresponds with our intuition much better than the old model.

Intuitively most of us believe that distributed systems ought to be much more reliable and robust than centralized ones. After all, if every business location has its own server, shouldn't that location be able to keep operating even if some big computer located elsewhere stops working? In fact, shouldn't entire subnetworks be able to keep running, even when the headquarters' system is down for several days? Then, we learn about two-phase commit and grudgingly concede that our intuitions were wrong. It is true, then, that distributed systems are not more reliable? And are they in fact far less robust? Something is not right here.

A primary advantage of a centralized system, *when it is running,* is that all information is kept synchronized with all other information *all the time.* The centralized system seems to work entirely in real time. Of course, the real-time nature of that central system is actually fictitious too; it is the central computer that is synchronized. It is, though, only as synchronized as the information that has been fed into it. Nonetheless, a truly attractive aspect of central systems is their degree of synchronization. Attempting to maintain that same degree of synchronization in a distributed system leads to a design that just doesn't work. The distributed system, if it must be kept so synchronized, truly is less reliable than the central system. The point is that keeping it so synchronized is not only unfeasible; it's also undesirable.

In return for giving up some global synchronization, the distributed system offers vastly improved reliability, robustness, throughput, and local flexibility. And this is a tradeoff most organizations will gladly make, once the case is put this way. All of this focuses, though, only on the most mechanical aspects of the shift away from transactions. The philosophical aspect of this shift is more important.

Organizations are no more built around transactions than they are built around tasks. Organizations exist to implement processes. Actually, to be more correct, organizations exist to fulfill goals they set for themselves, and the processes that organizations implement exist to make those goals happen. Processes, by definition, extend through time. Transactions are the atomic steps that make the processes up. The database reflects the state of the organization between the steps defined by the transactions.

But the reason for all this to exist lies in the processes, not in the tasks, the transactions, or the databases.

There is a small irony here: The same shift to process orientation that is proving vital for large organizations is affecting the design of computer systems. Processes are indeed everywhere.

Where *Is* the Center of the World?

In the 1950s and the 1960s, the computer world was centered on programs, codes, and applications. In the 1970s, after the invention of the database, the data became central. Most modern application-design methodologies, for example, preach that good design focuses on the structure of the database first. Similarly, many frameworks for the strategic planning of information systems focus on the corporate data model, even to the point of recommending that senior management be encouraged to deal with data modeling. Even object-oriented design approaches have a firm foundation in data and database modeling.

All of this data-centrism creates serious difficulties when it comes to designing both process-oriented and distributed systems. In the distributed domain, it causes designers to focus on where the data go—the first of the two problems standing in the way of building distributed databases. In the process domain, it creates a focus on transactions instead of on sequences of transactions. The solution to both problems is to recognize a new center: the process.

Focusing on processes, including processes that extend over long periods of time, provides a simple and straightforward framework for designing *and* building distributed systems. More important, it provides a direct information-technology counterpart to the process orientation that lies behind business-process redesign.

After more than 40 years of increasing investment in information technology, senior managers are finally starting to do some real information-system strategy planning—without even necessarily realizing what they are doing. As they work with their favorite business consultants, and as they emphasize the core processes driving the enterprise, these executives eventually begin to focus on redesigning those core business processes. And, as they draw process diagrams on the board, they are effectively redesigning the organization's information systems.

How should the data in a distributed database be distributed? Where should the data go? Lots of data distributed across many locations? Keep them all centralized? Somewhere in the middle? In a database-centered world, with the data model as the primary tool for making these kinds of decisions, this question has remained unanswerable for almost 20 years. Try as they might, most database-centered organizations simply don't know how to begin deciding how to distribute their data.

How about deciding where the processes and their tasks should go? That's easy. In fact, senior managers will actually do a large part of that for us. As they draw the process-redesign diagrams, the creation of self-managed teams is a natural part of the conversation. They will talk about which processes and tasks should be "decentralized" or "distributed" to make the organization as a whole work better.

Distribute the processing and the data will follow. Credit authorization is to be decentralized? Tell me that and I'll tell you very quickly which parts of the database have to follow right along behind to support the credit-authorization decisions. Self-contained warehouses capable of making all their own inventory management and shipment scheduling decisions? That implies warehouses with self-sufficient local databases to support those inventory and shipment decisions.

By shifting to a process orientation, we have solved two big problems at once. First: We have involved senior managers in the strategic planning process. Perhaps even better, we have created an environment in which it is easy for them to involve us in their planning process. Business processes are going to be reengineered whether computer people are involved or not. However, if we computer people can directly support the process, perhaps we'll be invited to the party. For 20 years we have tried to get executives to understand our models; perhaps now it's time that we understood theirs. Second: When we are done, the problem of knowing how to distribute the distributed database will have been solved too.

Does this make the data model unimportant? Not at all. In all likelihood, it makes it a co-equal of the process model. The data model will always be somewhat more technical. Like architects, computer people will always work with many models and show only a few to their clients. The data model will, more than likely, be one that clients don't see very often. That doesn't decrease its importance a bit; it just acknowledges the facts.

No; rather than decrease the importance of the data model, what the client/server revolution does for the first time is give that model a true equal on the dynamic, behavioral side. The data model deals with the static, unchanging view of the computer world; now there is an equally rich model of the dynamic, constantly changing side of that same world. The good news is that that dynamic side can now be modeled at a high level instead of only at the granular, task- and transaction-oriented level forced on us by functional decomposition.

The Applications of the Future

At this point I am halfway through my story of the computer world of the next few decades. Computers in this new world will be highly distributed in support of self-managed teams. Each team will consist of individuals with powerful desktop computers, but all those personal machines will be connected to a server that is under control of both the team and the organization. The servers, all focused on supporting long-running business processes, will all talk to one another. Some of the interactions will occur in real time and will require protocols like two-phase commit, which by then will be broadly available and will support a broad variety of data-storage engines.

Most of the inter-server interactions, though, will not happen in real time. Instead they will consist of requests exchanged between servers in a fashion that will tolerate servers and communications lines that may be down without interrupting the flow of business except for users directly connected to them. In fact, the servers in this new world will be paralleling the operation of the organization they support. Just as offices, teams, and individuals are increasingly empowered and autonomous, so will be the servers that support them.

What will the applications in this new world look like? Many of the applications will be the same ones that companies run today: order entry, credit authorization, manufacturing planning, and so on. However, these applications will be transformed as they support new masters.

Today's order-entry application, for example, is owned by the central organization. In theory, the user runs the application; in practice, the application runs the user. To enter an order, the user is led through a sequence of screens and forms under the control of the central computer, which supplies information not dictated by the user. If a serious problem is encountered in the process of entering an order, the user can do little more than refer the customer to another department.

In the new world, there will be no order-entry clerks. They are specialists with very limited decision-making authority—exactly what reengineering is seeking to do away with. Instead, salespeople will not only talk to customers; they will also process their orders all the way through to completion. Imagine how that might go: Perhaps a salesman is visiting the customer's office. Working on his computer notebook, the salesman uses a spreadsheet and a database-analysis tool to analyze the customer's past order patterns and to suggest future orders. Massaging the simulation, the customer and the salesman agree on the orders for the next 3 weeks. At this point we notice the first few differences.

Today a salesman uses a spreadsheet only when necessary. After all, the spreadsheet only runs on a desktop computer, and it has no direct access to real data. Besides, the best a salesman can do with the results of a spreadsheet is print them up for a formal presentation, and such presentations happen only three or four times a year. In the new world, the spreadsheet is directly connected to the real data, and it allows the salesman and the customer to directly make business decisions. No wonder the salesman uses that tool all day every day.

Next we notice that the order-entry application, *per se,* has disappeared. Instead, once the order profile is finalized in the spreadsheet, that updates the database in the computer notebook. The order has now been generated. Best of all, the spreadsheet model is one developed by that salesman *for himself*—a unique presentation suited to his customers, his territory, and his style. Talk about local customization!

Once the order is finalized, the computer responds immediately with the observation that one of the parts is out of stock. Then it proposes a replacement. Exploring the local bulletin-board system, the salesman and his customer find an application note from another country about the use of that replacement in a very similar situation and decide to accept the substitution. The graphical interface has made the process of flipping between all the different system components involved in that exploration totally seamless.

As the computer continues through the order validation process, two problems arise: the customer appears to have slightly exceeded his credit limit, and the substitute part is available only from a warehouse which is too far for the order to arrive in time. Dealing with the first problem, the salesman explores the customer's recent payment history and discovers several late payments. Reviewing the situation, the customer and the salesman agree that in the future payments will be accelerated.

The salesman authorizes the shipment. After checking its rule base, the team's server decides that the salesman has the authority to make this decision. Next, the salesman reviews his team's territory profitability model and determines that he can easily afford to cover express shipment of the substitute part, even though the shipment charge for such a heavy and large part will be substantial. In this case, the server processes that request provisionally, subject to review by the team manager, and makes a note in the salesman's calendar to double-check the expected approval the following day.

Finally, the order, subject to the shipment confirmation, is scheduled, and the relevant information is passed on to the customer's computer for processing.

The Office of the Future

Let us reconsider the three scenarios at the beginning of this chapter to see the software of the future from a slightly different perspective.

Starting with the office computer and its relationship to the mainframe, the changes should be fairly obvious at this point. By the turn of the century, many of the applications that previously ran on mainframes will have moved to servers and desktops running in local offices. The implications of this change are somewhat subtle in terms of market dynamics, but let's put that aside for a moment. The distributed applications of the future will be strikingly different in form and even function from those we are used to today, and this justifies the huge conversion costs.

The simple scenario presented above implies a very smooth merger of a wide variety of applications, including classical order entry, credit authorization, customer forecasting, part substitution, shipping, bulletin board, and spreadsheet. Such a merger gives a new meaning to the term "component." It is popular to talk about objects and components as the tools that will eliminate programming altogether. Yet, the amount of new functionality required to make tomorrow's applications real is so large that programming is unlikely to go away. Instead, tomorrow's applications—still written by professional programmers—will be structured entirely in terms of components that encourage a high degree of inter-operability, not so much among programmers as among users. When the salesman of the future combines parts of fifteen or twenty different applications, as described above, it is component technology that makes that combination possible. As a result, applications as we know them today disappear. Software vendors may still sell packages called "order entry" or "purchase-order management"; however, that packaging will be purely for marketing and sales purposes. Once installed, those applications will all seamlessly merge into the larger component pool.

Much of the processing now carried out by mainframes will be shifted to local servers and personal computers supporting self-managed teams. The cost of the rewritten applications required to make this possible will be large, but it will be tiny in comparison to the benefits that emerge from the reengineering of business processes.

Management will finally see computer costs come into a reasonable relationship with the benefits delivered. Personal computers may still provide personal productivity, but they will also be directly involved in running the business. Best of all, the organization will finally be able to customize applications locally without compromising organization-wide business rules.

Just to put this need for customization into final perspective, let's consider banks again. Many banks roll out changes to their fundamental business applications *every business day*. Banks need this kind of flexibility to react to local competition. A neighborhood bank is offering a special on mortgage refinancing? Add the same deal yourself. Interest rates are changing more rapidly than expected and a new kind of interest based hedge is invented? Roll it out. Sometimes these changes are organization-wide, sometimes local. A system that allows the applications to be customized on a day's notice is the prescription for success in the future, and that is what the distributed graphical systems described above make possible.

So much for the office as a whole. What about the individual and the workgroup? Recall that today's use of personal computers is defined by word processing, spreadsheets, database, and some electronic mail. Ironically, it is the electronic mail, the smallest of those categories, that really points the way to the future.

Individuals in the future are likely to use their personal computers throughout the day because they are more likely to be generalists than today's individuals and also because using a computer and its server is the way to tap into the organization's procedures. However, the role of the server goes further than that in supporting the workgroup.

Today, electronic mail is the one application that people use day in and day out. Anybody connected to an email system tends to check his or her email first thing in the day, last thing before leaving, and periodically throughout the day. If email goes down, Operations hears about it in moments. Email changes the organizational culture in ways that other personal computer applications don't come close to. It silences the telephone, eliminates memos, and creates new, more democratic communication patterns throughout an organization.

Email is not enough, though. In spite of the proliferation of computers and software, most people still manage their priorities, their schedules, their goals, and their planning using paper and pencil. Secretaries, even in heavily computerized organizations, still report scheduling meetings to be among their most time-consuming activities. As computers continue to evolve and software gets better, these activities too will benefit from the coordination capabilities only a server can provide.

Consider directories. Wouldn't it be great if a sales team could automatically share the customer contact list? What about tracking contacts—not just contacts with a prospect, but all the various interactions with customers? Lotus Notes is a harbinger of the future in this area. Precisely through its ability to provide a shared information space for tracking unstructured information about products, customers, contacts, and the like, it becomes, like email, an indispensable, culture-changing application. Notes is weak at many personal and time management tasks, but it is not hard to imagine a future where the software is finally right for managing time as well as data.

Underneath these scenarios lies a fundamental concept relating to the importance of process to the software of the future. The concept of process is often confused with the concept of processing, perhaps because the words are similar. Processing is the work done to complete a task. It is the programming, the code, that makes individual transactions and tasks happen. Process, on the other hand, is about sequences of tasks, each involving processing. Processing is about computation; process is about communication.

Communication can take place in two ways: direct and indirect. Direct communication is the exchange of messages between two parties. Indirect communication relies on the sharing of information, typically in a database. Either way, communication, unlike processing, is typically extended in time. Communication is the glue that holds processes together. Processes are sequences of tasks, each involving computation, that are chained together by communication, either direct or indirect.

The key point is that a great deal of the software that will most change our lives both at work and in the home revolves around process and communication rather than computation and processing. Yes, spreadsheets and word processors will continue to be important. However, email, bulletin boards, databases, and process managers will be even more important. Perhaps all this makes sense in the context of the office, but what about the home?

Imagine a typical night in a home of the next century. While everyone is asleep, your daughter receives an invitation to a party. The home server notes that the invitation conflicts with a dental appointment. Consulting its rule base, the server quickly determines that, because the person throwing the party is a close friend, the party is more important than the dental appointment; it decides to change the appointment. Your server contacts the dentist's server. A new appointment time is found and confirmed, and the party invitation is accepted and put on all the relevant calendars. Finally, a notation is placed in the appropriate tickler file.

Here again the server is managing a process. In this case the process is ongoing and relates to your personal calendar as well as the calendars of your family members. The key to making the above scenario work is the combination of server, database, and communication. Without the communications, the server would never hear about the party and could not deal with the dentist's server; the whole thing would not work. Again, though, without the shared databases in each location, none of the servers could do its job. The server itself, always on and always acting on your behalf (and on the dentist's behalf) is crucial too.

As we have already seen, process is about communication, which in turn is about time. Not having enough time is a standard complaint these days. Servers and the software that will allow us to really take advantage of them promise to finally give us some time back, both at home and in the office.

How Big Is the Change? How Relevant Will Software and Computers Be?

Today there are about 30,000 mainframes in the world, probably as many as there will ever be. In addition, 300,000 super minicomputers play a major role in running organizations. About half a million largish computers run medium and large companies. The function and form of those computers and the terminals that talk to them haven't changed much in 20 years. Even when personal computers replace terminals, they still emulate them. Worst of all, those half-million computers have not truly changed their host organizations. Yes, banks can have more branches, credit cards have become possible, and bureaucracies operate somewhat more efficiently. But the basic model for running big organizations has not really changed much since computers became commercially available. In fact, if anything, computers and their software have helped to keep companies in their original form by making obsolescent systems last longer.

The nearly 100 million personal computers in the world today have introduced the idea of software on a scale not previously imaginable. Yet personal computers have hardly changed our organizations. And many large companies are now struggling to determine how to afford all the personal computers that employees now believe they are entitled to. Not a pretty picture. Unless things change, it's hard to imagine where the computer industry will continue to find its potential for growth. Many observers believe that the computer market may be close to saturation. Fortunately, the answer is in sight, and the implications are that most of the growth is still ahead.

Suppose the distributed systems described here really are built? How many servers will there be several decades from now? The answer is pretty simple. In the United States, for example, there are somewhat more than 11 million locations to which one or more individuals report each working day: corporate headquarters, car rental booths, sales offices, stores, restaurants, warehouses, garages, churches, schools, gas stations, churches, synagogues, airports, police stations, fire stations, and on and on. Why wouldn't each of these locations have at least one server, running around the clock? How else can your home server change your appointments with the doctor, the dentist, or the veterinarian? How else can a retail store order products from the distributor's warehouse during the middle of the night?

If one is the minimum number of servers in each office, what is the maximum number of servers? And what about the rest of the world? Realistically and pragmatically, we are talking about a world with tens or even hundreds of millions of servers in workplaces alone. Let's explore the implications of that number.

Today, server software in particular and computer software in general is complex, hard to install, and not very self-repairing. Yet, the scenario we are now picturing says that even server software has to become totally self-installing, self-adjusting, and deliverable through completely conventional channels of distribution. Is it even possible?

Consider the automobile industry. Tens of millions of cars are sold every year, each at least as complex as any server we can imagine. Furthermore, those cars are repaired by individuals with (typically) limited education. So, clearly, it ought to be possible to develop software that makes servers just as salable as cars. The hardware, for the most part, is actually already there. The challenge is almost entirely in the software.

In many ways, applications really haven't changed much over the last 20 years. Computers have gotten cheaper and faster. Concepts have been refined. Still, as early as the late 1960s, Doug Engelbart, Don Bitzer, and others were demonstrating highly graphical word processors, electronic mail, shared bulletin boards, and other facilities which today are still considered new. The fact that this kind of software can now live in a machine that fits under your arm is new. And some fundamental breakthroughs have occurred. Spreadsheets, for instance, made computer-based financial planning accessible to millions. Still, for the most part, watching a user at either a mainframe-hosted terminal application or a personal-computer-based personal productivity tool reveals how little things have changed.

In this chapter I have focused on how computers can change our organizations and our lives by supporting individual empowerment and self-managed teams. But how about the actual look of the applications that run on those computers? As a closing note, let's consider how that look will also be fundamentally different. The trick is to understand what direction the differences will come from.

Consider the two extremes of the computer world: big databases and children's games. Is there a relationship between them? Surprisingly, perhaps, there is. Games, whether running on a Nintendo or on a graphical IBM PC, have the appealing characteristic of being highly graphical, very interactive, and supremely easy to use in sophisticated ways. Databases have the advantage of offering access to shared data. A problem with games is that the interfaces they offer can't, today, be used in the context of workaday applications. The problem with databases is that the information they contain is so structured that it can be used only in very limited and boring applications. Imagine an alternative.

A saleswoman is visiting a new city, picking up a territory from a colleague. As the plane lands, she uses a computer notebook and its database to explore her new sales region. As she plays with the numbers in her spreadsheets, a few graphs quickly help her zero in on a set of accounts to visit. The problem lies in developing an appropriate driving plan. Her notebook computer contains street maps for the entire country. Even today, Delorme, one of the leading cartography companies, sells such a database, and it fits on a single CD-ROM. Calling up the city map, the saleswoman asks to see where the prospects are. Her computer, using information about traffic patterns and so on, suggests a detailed itinerary and provides driving directions. The implications of this scenario stretch our definitions of "application," "database," and the rest. The same database and the same tools that deal so well with structured tables have to be able to deal equally well with streets and with spatial relationships. And the user interface will start to look amazingly game-like as we shift from working with only graphs, numbers, and letters to working with streets, buildings, and faces as well.

The changes that lie ahead of us, both in the characteristics of software and in the number of people who will use it, will be vast in scale. Imagine the richness of a world where computers finally help people manage their too-complex lives. Software can be relevant.

The Keys to the Highway

Peter F. Conklin
Eric Newcomer

I've got the key to the highway. . . .
—Big Bill Broonzy

Open software components are the keys to the information highway and
to a multitude of emerging business services: video on demand, global
charge cards, electronic funds transfers, international automatic tellers,
wireless fax, videoconferencing, home shopping, interactive television,
and so on. The companies building the new computer-based services, are,
like any other enterprise, finding that they need multiple sources for their
software components. They are pressuring their suppliers for open software standards, and this is creating a force that will change the entire
software industry.

Open protocols will be used to build the information highway, and
open interfaces will be used to build the services that access the highway.
Open software is crucial in reducing the costs of the highway and the
services that use it. The daily costs of doing business without software
standards are quickly becoming greater than the cost of imposing them
would be. Without software standards, the information highway's construction and access costs will be too great.

Over time, all commonly used products must be standardized to be
used efficiently—and today almost nothing is more commonly used than
computer software.

We hardly think about standards in other parts of life. Time zones are
standard, of course, but about a century ago each community kept its
own time. A bronze plaque on Chicago's LaSalle Street commemorates
the establishment of the standard time zones, which greatly simplified
railroad scheduling and reduced the costs of transportation. Nor do we

worry about matching the manufacturer of staples to the manufacturer of a stapler, or worry about buying film from the manufacturer of a 35-millimeter camera—any film manufacturer will do. And film costs much less than it would if each camera required its own manufacturer's proprietary film type.

Standards allow us to buy things without worrying about which manufacturer made them. We compare quality, performance, and price against a common standard, rather than bother to measure every manufacturer's product. By the time this is true of all computer software, the industry will be vastly different.

Good software standards specify interfaces and protocols, not the underlying technology of the software. Programming languages such as COBOL, C, and SQL are examples of interfaces. The way computer programs are connected to one another is defined by an interface, as is the layout or appearance by which a program is visible to the computer user. Protocols define how computers communicate with other computers, specifying the rules of greeting and responding in much the same way that diplomatic protocol specifies the rules for formal communications between countries.

Having agreed on the rules of communication, the software suppliers have great leeway in choosing among implementation alternatives to realize a standard in more effective ways, while retaining the customer's flexibility to mix and match components from multiple suppliers.

In the future, adherence to software standards will allow freedom of choice among competing suppliers while encouraging innovation. "Standards of interoperability . . . give users the freedom to change vendors and technologies," writes William R. Johnson.[1] "Standards will also accelerate the rate at which organizations adopt new technologies" by laying a foundation of technology upon which to build the new networks and services.

The benefits of software standardization will become apparent in the information highway's ability to provide access to any of the new services, anywhere, at any time, and to connect them all to a common network. Software standards identify the point of separation between the underlying platform, which can flexibly be supplied by any computer manufacturer, and the service itself, as shown in figure 1. Many personal-computer

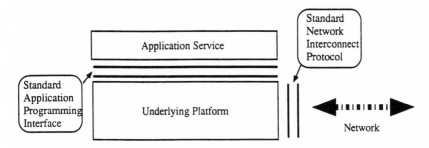

Figure 1
Interchangeable applications and open network access.

applications run on a variety of platforms, such as a Macintosh, an IBM PC, or a UNIX workstation. Standard programming interfaces and network protocols are required to let the software run without worrying about the hardware platform, and to ensure that the software application is easily connected to the network. An application built using a standard programming interface can be easily moved to another computer. An application that supports a standard network protocol can be easily connected to the network. Once the key standards are established, software can be moved to another computer at any time to take advantage of better prices and performance, and can then be reconnected to the network. Eventually, connections to the network will allow us to load spreadsheets with information from almost any source in the world.

Bill Gates, the president of Microsoft, has a widely discussed vision of a "highway" in which personal computers are connected to a variety of information sources, including media, art, literature, and music, in a global network. David Stone, former president of AT&T's Network Systems Operation business, has a similar vision, which he calls the "information utility." In Stone's vision, personal computers are appliances plugged into an equally vast global network, consuming information services the way electric and telephone services are consumed today. A standard interface between the "appliance" and the network is therefore critical, as is one between the network and the information services at the other end. Mitchell Kapor and Daniel Weitzner, who lead the Electronic Frontier Foundation, see tremendous potential for enhancing health care and education, as well as cultural and political dialogues, and for providing new kinds of entertainment, all based on a national communication and information infrastructure.[2] Officials at Boeing Corporation expect airline passengers to soon have access to a laptop computer in each seatback, connected via a wireless network to ground systems.

AT&T's recent television advertisements highlight imminent services such as video telephones, wireless fax machines, and expanded capacity for portable telephones and computer modems. Nippon Telegraph and Telephone, the Japanese telecommunications giant, calls its own vision "visual, intelligent, and personal" (VIP) communications. The slogan is "You are there," which is intended to capitalize on the growing demand for international personal and business communications. The new services which the telecommunications corporations plan to offer are beginning to signal a tremendous race for shares of the rapidly expanding global information market.

Financial institutions have already put their own "highways" in place to provide worldwide credit authorization and bank card withdrawals, capitalizing on foreign currency exchange rates. Along the way, the travel industry will benefit from faster confirmation of reservations, better capacity planning, and associated bookings for rental cars and hotel rooms from travelers participating in frequent-flyer incentive programs. Nor is it surprising that the U.S. real estate industry is creating a national network of property listings so that potential buyers can shop with a minimum of travel.

The telecommunications industry is undergoing a period of acquisition and merger among communication providers, entertainment suppliers, and information services. Obtaining the information and entertainment products is only half the battle. The big problem will be delivering the new products and services reliably and accounting and billing appropriately for their consumption.

Developing New Services and Standards

Developing new services, new networks, and the applications that run on them will require a definition of open standards for protocols and interfaces so that everything can fit together—unless, of course, all the software is supplied by a single company. In that case, open systems will be unnecessary. But a single supplier will not exist, in view of the huge amount of hardware and software that will be required and in view of anti-trust concerns about such a vital resource as a national or international computer network.

There is no widely recognized single definition of "open systems"; it is one of the most consistently misunderstood terms, and one of the most commonly used. Yet the building of global network services dictates that an essential requirement for open systems is to provide standard interfaces and protocols that will eliminate fundamental incompatibilities among multiple computer companies' software products.

One clear requirement is a regime that allows products supplied by many companies to work together in an integrated fashion. Different efforts are underway to create and promote such open systems, either through standards bodies or through broad-based market acceptance. Different efforts follow different paths to the same basic objective: an environment in which it is cost-effective to implement such huge software applications as are required by the information highway or by global bank and telephone cards.

The information technology industry is thus at a critical stage. (The IT industry comprises computers, network technology, and distributed processing, which includes software for information highway applications.) "The single most important factor in these changes may be the development and implementation of IT standards. . . . Standards can be seen as the key to the widespread and successful use of information systems, and the interoperability and portability standards known as 'open systems' standards are especially important." [3] Without open systems standards, it would be impossible to build and support the applications of the future at reasonable cost.

Who will control and manage the global networks once they are developed? Principles of free trade dictate that no single corporation can be allowed to control something so vital. Yet international law is lacking in this area, although initiatives are coming into place which may ensure that global electronic trade remains open to equal access. Regulations are likely to be required to prohibit predatory business practices, as they are for other utilities, and to ensure that everyone is guaranteed access to the network. Service or product quality may suffer, however, if regulation results in a significant decrease of open competition among manufacturers.

Secure and regulated access to information highway services will also require a standard answer.

The leading formal standards body is the International Standards Organization (ISO), an amalgamation of the national standards bodies of the world's industrial countries. The ISO is a voluntary group whose results depend on building slow, careful agreements among a variety of participants. Its annual output of standards, covers everything from soup containers to nuts and bolts, is staggering. The process is slow, and businesses are impatient. ISO standards are developed in public forums and are based on input from the membership, and all of the activities are carried out in public. ISO standards are typically adopted by the national standards bodies of the member countries.

The ISO's major contribution to computer standards has been the definition of the Open Systems Interconnection (OSI) group of communication protocols for open networking. This group of standards represents a significant 10-year effort, but the OSI specifications are anticipatory standards—that is, the specifications are written first, and the software is supposed to be developed later. Anticipatory standards can be error-prone because of problems that show up during implementation, such as incompatible interpretations of ambiguous specification wording. OSI products consequently have been slow getting to market, and are not yet widely used.

Another major force in creating open networking standards is the Internet Activities Board (IAB). The IAB oversees the architecture and specifications of the Internet—the closest thing in existence to an information highway, already connecting more than a million computers and rapidly approaching its capacity. The Internet is based on a core network technology originally developed by the U.S. Department of Defense in 1969. Its predecessor, ARPANET (Advanced Research Projects Network), consisted of four computers connected via an experimental wide-area packet-switched network. The project, funded by the Defense Advanced Research Projects Agency (DARPA), continued until the IAB was established in 1983.

The IAB's primary responsibility is to maintain the transmission control and internet protocol (TCP/IP) specifications, which define an open network protocol, the practical application of which in the worldwide Internet has established it as a standard to rival (and likely overtake) OSI.

The IAB and ISO approaches to open system standards are very different. The Internet was already working before its specifications were published. The interfaces and protocols were developed as working code, rather than as paper specifications first (as was the case with OSI). This is called the *reference implementation* approach because the software is developed at the same time as the specifications, eliminating potential problems and bugs such as those caused by ambiguous wording. The specifications can therefore be proven to work before they are published and adopted as standards.

Because the U.S. government is a member of the ISO, Washington at first said it would adopt the OSI protocols as its networking standard. The Department of Defense was put in an awkward position because its Internet initiative had emerged as a rival to the OSI standard, but the decision was consistent with the way the world's governments had agreed to develop and adopt standards. After agonizing over its decision, the U.S. government finally decided that it would allow the use of both the Internet and the OSI standards in its information highway initiative, which shows that there can be room for more than one standard in a particular area of technology.

Another standards body, the Institute of Electrical and Electronic Engineers (IEEE), was founded in 1890 to develop standards for the emerging electric industry. Its most significant contribution to open computer systems is POSIX (Portable Operating System interface based on UNIX), a standardization of the UNIX operating system interfaces. POSIX is widely accepted, implemented on many platforms, and required to be used in procurement by government agencies and many large corporations. The IEEE's definition of open systems is as follows.

A system that implements sufficient open specifications for interfaces, services, and supporting formats to enable properly engineered applications software:
• To be ported across a wide range of systems with minimal changes
• To interoperate with other applications on local and remote systems
• To interact with users in a style which facilitates user portability.[4]

This definition may seem like an unreachable ideal. Many people would settle for open software systems that run on multiple hardware platforms, or that run on some variant of the UNIX operating system. Some would even settle for a standard based on a single product that runs on multiple platforms. But large corporate users, such as the telecommunications industry giants (who have been crippled by proprietary systems in the past), must avoid being locked in to any single supplier in the future. It does not matter whether the supplier is a hardware or a software company. Users are taking the necessary steps to ensure that the IEEE's definition of open systems becomes reality. Then they will be able to buy the software they need from multiple sources in a competitive environment.

For these large corporate users, the standards bodies have made some progress but not enough. Open systems today are lacking in many areas. Standards developed separately by independent bodies are not integrated, and ensuring the identical conformance to specifications implemented by different manufacturers creates a whole series of unresolved problems. These users are responding by creating consortia to pressure suppliers to implement common interfaces and protocols. In some cases, an agreement forged among manufacturers by a user consortium can also become an industry standard. This represents yet another approach to open systems.

The question of the acceptance of the user-driven standards work in the general marketplace remains. Ultimately, all standards are de facto— if a standard is not accepted in the marketplace, it isn't a standard, no matter how many *de jure* standards bodies or user consortia endorse it. Many of the ISO's 8000 de jure standards are not known or accepted, for example.

For a de facto standard, the process of standardization basically involves a fight for control of a market segment. An example is the MS-DOS operating system, which through market acceptance, rather than through the action of a standards board, became the standard for IBM-compatible personal computers, defeating the CP/M operating system. (It should be noted that MS-DOS is a "proprietary" standard; that is, it is under the control of a single, profitable corporation—Microsoft.) VHS is another example of a de facto standard, having beaten Beta in the VCR market.

For a typical de jure standard, the process of standardization involves a controlled or moderated discussion within a recognized industry group, such as the American National Standards Institute (ANSI) or the ISO. Representatives from companies in a particular industry propose solutions, formulate agreements, then work out detailed specifications that everyone can agree to implement. No single company controls a de jure standard; rather, a de jure standard is under the control of an independent standards body or consortium that ensures open competition.

One problem with de jure standards, in particular with anticipatory ones, is that testing for conforming implementations is not always practical or reliable, and thus the efforts toward a standard for portability or interoperability often fall short. There is often no established means of enforcing conformance to the standard, or of ensuring that the standard meets its goals.

De jure standards therefore do not always produce the best results, and they are often not accepted by the marketplace—especially when a superior alternative exists. Manufacturer-dominated standards bodies tend to aim for the common denominator and must avoid objections from manufacturers who might find it too costly to change their current products to meet a proposed standard, all of which may defeat the development of the one necessary characteristic of a standard: usefulness.

One approach is to base standards on existing products as much as possible, thereby avoiding the time-consuming chore of creating a new specification not overly favorable to one manufacturer over another. "The injustice in favor of the chosen vendor is a small price to pay in comparison to the alternative, which is that proprietary products win the race." [5]

The Process of Standardization

The COBOL (Common Business-Oriented Language) standard has been successfully used for more than 30 years. Initially put in place by the American National Standards Institute, it is evolving with changes in the industry.

Because most people bought software from a single supplier until the late 1980s, issues such as application portability and interoperability were often overlooked. This defeated one of the main purposes of standardization. The ANSI COBOL specification was a result of voluntary agreement among software manufacturers at the request of the U.S. government, which believed that a standard programming language would reduce the cost of computing. The COBOL specification contains much ambiguous language, however, and numerous optional sections which a manufacturer can choose to implement or not. ANSI compliance alone does not guarantee the portability of COBOL programs from one computer to another. One reason for this may be that software users did not insist upon portable source code, focusing instead on establishing a relationship with one supplier. Many of the large applications were single-supplier solutions or customized multi-supplier solutions, incorporating the proprietary system's advantages best suited for the particular application.

While standards have been effective at establishing a common syntax for COBOL, they have not been as effective at establishing a common interpretation of the syntax. In other words, the language may have been successfully specified, but the behavior of the language was not successfully specified.

COBOL—originally developed for batch, sequential processing—has been reworked every 5 or 10 years to adapt to changing technology, such as terminal display management capabilities for online or timesharing processing. Recently an ANSI subcommittee has begun adapting COBOL for object-oriented technology. COBOL's advantages over other programming languages are its readability and its ease of program maintenance and change, say the ANSI committee members.

The C programming language is newer than COBOL and was developed in a different way. C, created in 1978 by Kernighan and Ritchie at AT&T Bell Labs, began as the language of UNIX (also developed by AT&T). It has an economy of expression, modern control flow and data structures, a rich set of operators, and few restrictions.

For many years, the standard definition of C was Kernighan and Ritchie's book *The C Programming Language*.[9] Because of C's popularity, and because of the need to more precisely define its behavior, ANSI started work on a formal C standard in 1983. The ANSI C standard was finally completed in 1988, but of course by then the original C was in widespread use. People have made careers out of the problems involved in porting original C to standard C, which might have been avoided if C were developed originally by a rigorous standards committee. There are many books on the subject, and great pain has been endured by programmers converting from the original to the standard versions of C (which, of course, are not entirely compatible).

The original idea of C was not only to support operating-system programming for UNIX but also to provide a potentially computer-independent language with great power and flexibility. The basis of the disagreement between COBOL advocates and C advocates boils down to a difference of opinion over the merits of great power and flexibility versus readability and ease of maintenance.

ANSI C has been followed by C++ (also developed at AT&T) and Visual C++ (popular among PC programmers). But today, these various implementations of C have a lot of incompatibilities and are not truly portable, especially as a result of the differences among the various C++ class libraries that the software manufacturers provide for typical programming functions.

It is ironic that one of the reasons why C++ has become so popular—its huge class libraries—is also the biggest obstacle to standardizing it. ANSI is currently working on a standard version of C++, but it will be interesting to see how closely the standard version of C++ matches current implementations.

Some of the first standards activities were voluntary activities among software manufacturers, who in effect created voluntary agreements for controlling market segments. The first standards often fell short of their goals, primarily because their practical benefit was not obviously superior to the proprietary alternatives.

The personal computer revolution has spurred the need for formal standards and has illustrated by stark contrast the lack of effective standards for larger computers in such areas as user interface, floppy disks, operating systems, utilities, printer connections, and applications. It remains to be seen whether standards committees and consortia can reach effective agreements before the proprietary solutions become established.

Windowing is an example of a computer interface for the nontechnical user that has become a standard because of superior design rather than through any formal agreement. Many manufacturers have produced versions of windowing software. The fundamental principles of the icon/object-based interface can be traced from Xerox PARC's Alto research machine through the Apple Macintosh, the Massachusetts Institute of Technology's X-Windows system, IBM's OS/2, and finally into Microsoft's MS-Windows. Once users learn how to use any one of these windowing systems, they can interact with any other.

MS-Windows, because of its market dominance, is currently the de facto windowing standard. If any one company essentially owns such a standard and can control its changes, there is a danger that it can manipulate the standard to the disadvantage of competitors.

X-Windows was brought out of MIT and licensed to the computer manufacturers who support MIT's Project Athena. X-Windows began as a UNIX-based standard and followed the UNIX standardization process, which means that an implementation of the software was developed as part of the specification process to prove the viability of the standard. While Motif was originally developed for the UNIX operating system, it can also run on other operating systems. This has helped its acceptance as a realistic alternative to MS-Windows.

The Common Operating System Environment (COSE) and similar recent initiatives have focused an attack on the Microsoft windowing standard using a commonly specified version of Motif. The Common Desktop Environment (CDE) from COSE has yet to deliver a successful counterpunch, and whether Microsoft can be convinced to "open" its interface to an independent body and make a committee standard out of it remains to be seen.

The *reference implementation* approach to standards (that is, implementing the software as part of the standardization process) may provide the approach the standards bodies need to ensure the success of their standards. However, getting a large agency such as the International Standards Organization to change may be very difficult. The effectiveness of this approach is better than the older process of developing the specification first and then developing the software to match the specification. Standards bodies are under increasing pressure to speed up their efforts, and creating a reference implementation is one good way to do that, as proven by Motif. The reference implementation approach is likely to also better address the issues that have plagued committee standards.

The world is big enough for multiple standards, especially when there is a way to convert from one to the other or to merge them. Metric and American tooling standards are easy to move between because the principles are the same, even though the measuring systems are different. For many years computer data was stored using either the EBCDIC or the ASCII standard, and these encodings can be converted to and fro by many utilities now in place. Most popular personal computer software runs on both the Mac and the IBM PC, and conversion programs allow data to be easily moved between them.

Thus, the software industry will likely not end up with a single standard, or even a single set of standards, for a given functional area, such as networking, application programming, or human interface. The result of the open-systems efforts now underway will probably be multiple standards with requirements to convert back and forth among them.

In today's market, most computer manufacturers expect customers to insist on products that are immediately useful and require little or no training. But this requires a change in how software is developed. An expert on user interactions must be involved in the planning of the product not as an afterthought. If the operation of a particular piece of software can be so obvious as to require no training or explanation in order to use it, there is no need for formal standards or specifications.

Ease of use will have to be added to the list of goals in each step of a project's life cycle. This cannot be added at the end of the software-development cycle, after the majority of the code is already written, without incurring prohibitive costs and delays. Improving usability can increase profit for a computer manufacturer by ensuring quick acceptance of the new product and by creating early demand. Consumers vote with their pocketbooks, and can make a product succeed whether or not it implements a standard or becomes one.

Once a common set of principles of operation, setup, and routine use is accepted by the market, the job of the computer manufacturer becomes different. Instead of seeking to find a competitive advantage by making their interface the easiest to use, the manufacturers of the future will concentrate on the time it takes to bring to market, on quality, and on acceptance.

Some items are too specialized for standardization. They cannot be commodities, because the demand for them is not great enough. A giant high-speed stapler used in magazine or newspaper production, or a stereo camera, does not require standardization. For other items, good design is enough. In the automobile industry, formal standards do not exist for the shape and size of a steering wheel or for foot pedals. Common principles of design and operation, enforced by consumers' preference, are sufficient.

According to these principles, the end user of a computer should not have to be aware of the manufacturer, any more than the user of a telephone or a television needs to be. End users must be able to rely on a predictable interaction with a machine, as the driver of a car relies on the existence of a steering wheel (instead of a steering lever), foot pedals, and hand-operated gearshifts. Each car may be a little different, but the principle of operation is the same. Likewise, users of windowing systems recognize buttons, bars, pull-down menus, and icons used in conjunction with a mouse. Whether the mouse has one, two, or three buttons is much less important than the fact that a mouse tracks a pointer across the screen to perform some operation on an object on the screen to which it points. Once we understand the purpose of a mouse, we can use any manufacturer's mouse with little or no additional training.

For those who build these applications, however, there is a different requirement. For the more specialized computer user, the term "standard" has a specific meaning. The interaction between a technical professional and a computer is often formally standardized, because this kind of user expects to be trained in the technology at hand. He or she is expected to meet the technology halfway, or at some other structured point, such as learning a standard programming interface. An interesting result is that the training of technical professionals can be standardized as can the software, providing for interchangeable people who assemble interchangeable parts. Open standards allow the professional to train on any computer and then work on any other computer. Personnel costs associated with computer application development are lowered by eliminating specialized training for each manufacturer's computer.

Probably the most significant benefit of open software is the standardization of knowledge about computers. The interaction between a technical professional and a computer can be the same, no matter who built the computer. The savings can be great, especially since personnel costs are constant or rising while computer costs are falling.

Challenges for Users

Even though standardization in information technology has been increasing in response to the demands of users, what results is poorly integrated and difficult to use in the development of multivendor systems. Specific applications such as enterprise-wide electronic publishing and electronic mail have not really been put into place, never mind the far-reaching applications needed to drive the information highway and other global network services such as international mobile telephones.

Users will continue to need standards, but the voluntary standards process that has been in effect for many years is too slow and does not respond well to users' requirements. Nor has this process taken a coherent view of systems and applications. This is especially true in distributed computing, which requires distributed management and which cuts across traditional boundaries between suppliers.

Large computer manufacturers that once bore the costs of voluntary standards are scaling back and laying off employees. Users have to begin investing in the development of the standards, identify additional needs for them, and enforce procurement policies based on standards. Truly achieving open standards means that users will have to break their traditional reliance on computer manufacturers to identify solutions to their problems.

Because standards are often incomplete, and are not integrated, users may have to complement the standards with additional specifications of their own. Users are forming consortia for this purpose and are cooperating in developing prototype implementations of the specifications. "The commitment to buy products based on widely implemented vendor-neutral standards can be communicated on a collective basis to vendors and others. Users could negotiate agreements to continue to buy the products of vendors who agree to meet user needs for interoperability and portability."[6]

One such large user, the Nippon Telegraph and Telephone Corporation (NTT) of Japan, did form such a consortium, create specifications, and purchase software for portable, interoperable applications from its suppliers. To reach its vision of competing in the coming information age, NTT knew that the costs of information technology would have to be reduced significantly. Perhaps more than any other company, NTT has been burned by proprietary computer systems. Its 25-year-old procurement specifications resulted in specialized hardware and operating systems built specifically for NTT, according to its unique specifications.

When it came time to update procurement specifications, NTT decided to go with open systems only. Existing standards alone would not fulfill company needs, so it established a joint research project. Together with IBM, Digital, Hitachi, Fujitsu, and NEC, it created standards-based specifications for application software that would run on any manufacturer's platform and would interoperate. This joint research project is called the

Multivendor Integration Architecture (MIA) Consortium. The first results of its work (eleven volumes of open software specifications) were published in the early 1990s.

Early on, NTT's scientists decided they needed such an architecture as MIA in order to specify how the open systems standards would work together to solve business problems such as directory maintenance and customer billing with independently developed standards. When NTT discovered insufficiencies in standards, the company asked the manufacturers participating in the MIA Consortium to propose solutions that could be implemented by all of them. NTT not only worked with manufacturers to create specifications for multivendor software; the company also purchased what it specified, enforcing its will with a tremendous pocketbook.

Computer systems, once simple, have spread widely to become the "brains" of a company, generating management information vital to determining corporate strategy. Because a system must provide a broad range of services, "it is desirable to construct such a computer system flexibly enough to include different computers, each of which covers the area of business in which the vendor's model is the most powerful." [7] It is first necessary to solve three major problems, according to NTT:

duplicated development of application programs
difficulties in resource sharing
differences in operating methods.

The solutions are portability, interoperability, and a common user interface—in other words, software interfaces and protocols implemented by different suppliers using the same specifications. Programmers and end users no longer have to be trained separately for each manufacturer's products, and computer-to-computer interfaces are standardized to allow proper network communications.

NTT's architecture specified a full set of services for general-purpose computing, not just a list of standards. However, by matching current software standards to the architecture, NTT discovered that the computer industry is lacking in standards for transaction processing (TP)—a functionality that is a requirement for almost any business. A transaction is a group of operations on data that succeed as a unit or not at all, and the software guarantees the integrity of data regardless of hardware failure or other system failure. With computer transactions, a business can be confident that its electronic records remain consistent and protected.

Most of us are familiar with transaction-processing applications through experience with automatic teller machines, airline ticket processing, and car rental. Telecommunication corporations such as NTT also have many transactions that need to be processed, such as customer service orders, problem tracking, and changes in the telecommunication network. Transactions provide the means of reliable delivery, accounting, and billing for the information highway.

Software for transaction processing is usually produced and packaged into a product called a TP monitor, although the definition of a TP monitor is unclear. "The many transaction processing monitors . . . differ widely in functionality and scope. Each evolved to provide either essential services absent from the host system, or services the host performed so poorly that a new implementation was required. Consequently, each TP monitor is a Swiss Army knife of tools reflecting the particular holes in the surrounding system: in a contest for the least well-defined software term, TP monitor would be a tough contender." [8]

When the MIA Consortium was established in the late 1980s, TP monitors were so incompatible that transactions could not flow from one monitor to another, nor could a single application be written to run on more than one manufacturer's TP monitor. "The important concepts to remember are that one mechanism, a FAP, is needed for interoperation, and a second mechanism, an API, is needed for portability." [9] (FAP stands for "formats and protocols"; API stands for "application programming interface." In other words, as in any type of software, TP needed standardized interfaces and protocols to achieve portability and interoperation for applications built using software from multiple suppliers.)

Because of the importance of the business applications covered by TP and the need to standardize corporate business systems, NTT posed the problem of harmonizing the disparate TP monitor products to the membership of the MIA Consortium. The Digital Equipment Corporation responded by creating two specifications for open TP software that all consortium members reviewed and agreed upon for implementation: the Remote Task Invocation (RTI) protocol and the Structured Transaction Definition Language (STDL). Together these specifications solved NTT's problems of interoperability and portability for TP applications. Both specifications were based on Digital's TP monitor, which provided the reference implementation for the specifications.

NTT chose Digital's TP monitor because it wanted portable client/ server TP applications. Digital's TP monitor was the first client/server TP monitor in widespread use, and it also contained a TP programming language from which STDL could be derived. A programming language such as STDL was the only practical way to unify the manufacturers' widely different TP monitors, providing a thin layer that would fit on top of all of them (as SQL has been used to unify existing manufacturers' database products).

The protocol specification created for the MIA Consortium was later adopted by X/Open as its TxRPC (Transactional Remote Procedure Call) specification, thereby validating the approach to open software followed by MIA.

MIA specifies a client/server architecture in which any manufacturer's system can be a client and any manufacturer's system can be a server, as shown in figure 2. The MIA specifications spell out exactly what each manufacturer must implement in order to achieve NTT's goals. The specifications are divided into different categories of function, comprising the complete application architecture. The major divisions are the following:

• HUI

  Human Interface—Motif, OpenLook, or CUA (selectable options)

  In the area of human interface, MIA achieves a common look and feel with a style guide that describes exactly how the application program-

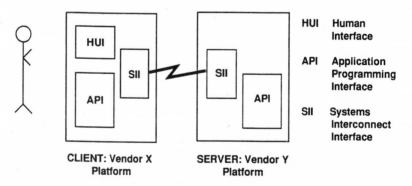

Figure 2
Results of MIA Consortium joint research project.

mers create the graphical user interface using any one of the selectable options.

· API

Application Programming Interface—C, COBOL, FORTRAN, SQL, and STDL

These specifications delete optional parts of established standards and list the parts that each manufacturer agrees to implement in order to ensure portability. The Structured Transaction Definition Language is the new language developed by the MIA Consortium to achieve portability for TP applications.

· SII

Systems Interconnect Interface—OSI and TCP/IP (selectable options)

These specifications detail the network protocols for local area networks, wide-area networks, Ethernet, and token-ring configurations, and include the RTI protocol for client/server TP applications.

NTT recently demonstrated the portability achieved by MIA by transferring an application between IBM and Digital implementations, and demonstrated the interoperability achieved by MIA by performing remote procedure calls between IBM, Hitachi, NEC, Hewlett-Packard, Fujitsu, and DEC implementations. By using the MIA specifications when procuring systems, NTT can now be assured of achieving its goals for open systems.

MIA represents a significant accomplishment in the world of open systems, but wider acceptance is needed to ensure the company can purchase compliant products off the shelf, without computer manufacturers' creating specialized or customized versions. This would defeat the purpose of open systems, because specialized products are more expensive.

The Network Management Forum recently sponsored a user consortium called the Service Providers Integrated Requirements for Information Technology (SPIRIT), which had the same goal as MIA: to produce common, general-purpose platform specifications to lower the costs of information technology. (The Forum is an international consortium created to promote international standards for network management.) The members of SPIRIT include the Japanese, European, and American telephone companies and the world's largest computer companies. These other telecommunications companies, like NTT, have a need for off-the-shelf products based on open software specifications. SPIRIT is attempting to bring together the open systems work of the telecommunication service providers. The world's largest telecommunications corporations have thus joined forces to influence computer manufacturers in the implementation of open systems by cooperating on the development of procurement requirements.

SPIRIT defines a general-purpose platform as follows: "a set of software specifications that is not aligned with a specific application type. The desired qualities of the general purpose computing platform are portability, interoperability and modularity." [10]

The first SPIRIT publication[11] describes the common ground of the member companies' existing procurement specifications for open systems, including NTT's Multivendor Integration Architecture, BT's Open Systems Standards Guide, European Telecommunications Information Services' Open Systems Components Guide, Bellcore's UNIX Standard Operating Environment and related documents, the Network Management Forum's network management specifications, and AT&T's corporate architecture documents. The publication is significant because it demonstrates that these separately developed specifications have a lot in common and that the member companies will cooperate to achieve open software. It remains to be seen whether this powerful group of users will be successful in speeding up the process for standardizing information technology.

One way to think about the user-driven standardization process is to recall the early days of the automobile industry. Each manufacturer once had its own specifications for the threading and tooling of bolts, screws, bumpers, axles, cylinder heads, and other parts. When a customer placed an order, he specified the exact kind of car to be built and contracted for it, the way someone today might specify and contract for a customized house to be built. Henry Ford is famous for revolutionizing the auto industry with mass production, but he couldn't have done it without establishing standards for interchangeable parts. "The key to mass production wasn't—as many people then and now believe—the moving, or continuous, assembly line. Rather, it was the complete and consistent interchangeability of parts and the simplicity of attaching them to each other." [12] After establishing standards, Ford could buy parts from one manufacturer that were interchangeable with parts from another one. Getting his suppliers to build parts to standard specifications was a long and difficult process, but it allowed him to establish assembly lines and cut expenses. (At first, Ford established assembly stations—only later, as a further efficiency, did he establish the moving assembly line.) The effects of mass production produced a downward price spiral that continued to cut the per-unit price as economies of scale increased. Ford's huge investment paid off. The automobile manufacturers who could not adapt to these standards were put out of business. Ford also achieved a division of labor by standardizing the job of each worker, eliminating the need for highly skilled assemblers. Not only were his parts interchangeable, his workers were too. Another benefit of standardization is eliminating the need for specialized training so that professional training can then be used throughout the industry.

Today, software and software systems essentially remain a craft industry in need of standardization to allow the efficient mass production of advanced applications such as the information highway. In the computer industry, this move toward Ford-style mass production is just beginning. Personal computers and their software have extended the capability of consumers to buy computing and place it everywhere. And as prices drop lower and lower, demand continues to grow.

Also growing is the demand for connecting personal computers to a network. The Integrated Services Digital Network (ISDN) standard for digital communications is a fundamental enabling technology, allowing communications services to reach sufficient speed and capacity. Telecommunications corporations are thus on the edge of a broad-band revolution, both in terms of network capacity and in terms of variety of possible services. "The convergence of telecommunications, networks, and service is imminently feasible, since, for the first time, today's communications capabilities match the internal speed of computers." [13]

New technology is often available before telecommunications companies can bring the new services to market. One obstacle is often the information-systems applications to process bills for the new services. The telecommunications companies that are members of SPIRIT realize that they cannot bear the costs of proprietary software any longer, and they know that they need reasonable cost solutions in order to make their network investments pay off. They need to efficiently account for their equipment, their customers, and their cash transactions. Applications will have to be built to handle all this. These huge software users are paying attention to standards and helping to drive the standardization process forward like never before. They cannot wait for the manufacturers to solve the problem.

Thus, the telecommunications corporations may be the ones to drive the standardization of the computer software industry, the way the automobile companies were the ones to drive the standardization of the mass production manufacturing process. The world telecommunications market is before them the way the mass market was then in front of the automobile companies. The telecommunications giants know they need reasonably priced information technology to successfully roll out the wave of new services. It remains to be seen whether they succeed. If they do, the future will be very different for everyone.

Adapting to the New

During the period of intense technological change that followed Ford's introduction of mass production, the corporate landscape changed dramatically. The same trend is apparent in today's computer industry. Companies that do not adapt to the demands for open systems risk becoming extinct. They will have to see themselves primarily as suppliers to other industries, such as the information highway industry, global banking, or retail chains, and they will have to establish long-term relationships with network and application builders.

The market for computer systems will keep shifting toward competition on services and systems integration rather than on differences in functionality. Companies will be forced to supply standard software protocols and interfaces. Competition will be based on which company best implements a standard and which provides the best service.

Computer software and hardware manufacturers will face consolidation and annexation. Some will go out of business, unable to adapt to the sweeping changes from proprietary to open software. Manufacturers must identify and focus on particular skills—"core competencies"—and establish outsourcing networks based on them. One manufacturer may be good at spreadsheets or document processing, for example, while another may provide leadership in networking, database software, or distributed transaction processing. Future competition will increasingly require companies to cooperate in order to produce finished products quickly and effectively.

Economies of scale will also change. As software standards produce a commodity market for software as well as for hardware, software sales volumes will have to increase dramatically to ensure a manufacturer's profit on a decreasing margin. The software industry will end up with only two or three manufacturers of a given component. Many manufacturers will do nothing but integrate the components produced by other companies.

Management of computer applications, especially large projects, also will change. Reorganizing an enterprise to accommodate the requirements of each new project is not feasible, especially in view of the heavy time pressures caused by rapidly changing technology and the demand for new services.

Digital's Alpha program, for example, had to coordinate dozens of departments for hardware, software, and systems engineering to bring a new generation of computer hardware and software to market. A program office was formed especially for the Alpha project. The program office enrolled Digital's various departments into the vision of the program and coordinated the pieces without having to reorganize the engineering departments.

Periodically the state of the art in computing takes a significant leap forward. The new computing systems will include large amounts of parallelism. The levels of performance and connectivity will finally allow the "anything, anytime, anywhere" computing that will boost productivity and connect the globe in a network of information systems and information utilities. By the end of the 1990s we will very likely see chip-based parallel processing, shared memory interconnects among separate computers, and new applications designed to take advantage of the new speed and parallelism. One application of the new Alpha AXP technology will be efficiently managing the vast amounts of storage required to process digitized video.

The combination of underlying technological advancement and open software standards will create a different business environment.

Imagine that at the FluffRite Seat Fabric Company, in the not-too-distant future, the sales department is examining a better way to receive and process orders. If customers could use the public "Information Utility" to directly place orders themselves, the sales manager argues, the company could save on the cost of sales and could integrate its shipping systems with its ordering, delivery, and billing systems.

FluffRite's order-entry system, in place about five years, relies on a sales representative to contact a customer, fill in a specialized order form on a portable PC, and upload the information to a remote database server for update. The sales representative has the responsibility of finding customers, helping them decide what kind of seat fabric they need (color, weight, finish, etc.), and estimating how much they need.

When the new online Order Information Clearinghouse (OIC) service is introduced by BNT (Big National Telephone), the FluffRite sales department is convinced that the customers would rather use the new utility than rely on a sales representative. The company evaluates the cost of the new service and decides it will be better than maintaining the current system. Jeanne, the sales manager, calls Henry in the information services department and tells him about her plan to convert to a direct customer order system. He mentions that they might as well incorporate a direct customer billing system, since the utility can be used for that purpose too.

Then Henry uses the OIC utility to search for the software he needs to build the new application. He finds packaged software to fill most of the requirements, such as accepting order information from the utility and generating electronic billing. However, part of the application must be built from scratch and integrated with the packaged software—the part that helps customers estimate the amount of seat fabric they need and helps them pick from the various options. Standard software allows Henry to easily integrate the built-from-scratch part with the purchased part of the new order-entry application. He gets the software and the documentation (delivered electronically via the OIC utility) for the application parts he needs and starts building the system for Jeanne. Later on, after the application has been built and tested, FluffRite will decide on the platform or platforms on which to put the application into production, and how to securely control access to the application.

In the past, such a company would have spent weeks evaluating the various proprietary offerings of different computer manufacturers to see which one was the best fit for the application. The amount of time it would have taken to actually start building an application like this new order-entry system may have made Jeanne think twice about even suggesting it. And by the time they got through evaluating the myriad hardware and software options, estimating the cost of the project, finding or training technical personnel, and balancing the priority of this new request with a hundred other requests for maintaining and enhancing existing applications, Jeanne and Henry might have just given up altogether.

Before this future can be realized, however, the agonizing and costly process of defining, specifying, and creating open software standards will have to be completed. Among the various approaches to creating standards, one or more may emerge as the most effective. The great contest will be between proprietary standards created by one company dominating the market and the more independent standards created by cooperative groups. Currently, the independent standards bodies are losing ground. A formal standardization process of any kind is slow relative to a single company's efforts to develop its own software. More and more, the future belongs to those entities which are fast and flexible and which allow themselves literally to be open to collaboration. In the future, Adam Smith's dictum will be proved ever more correct: competition is disguised cooperation.

Notes

1. William R. Johnson, Jr., "Anything, anytime, anywhere," in *Technology 2001: The Future of Computing and Communications,* ed. D. Leebaert (MIT Press, 1991).

2. Mitchell Kapor and Daniel J. Weitzner, "Developing the national communications and information infrastructure," *Internet Research,* summer 1993.

3. Peter Judge, *Guide to IT Standards Makers and Their Standards* (Technology Appraisals Ltd., 1991).

4. *Guide to POSIX Open Systems Environment,* IEEE P1003.0. ("Formats" are the same as "protocols.")

5. Bengt Asker, "Information technology standards, a scarce resource," *Computer Standards and Interfaces* 14 (1992).

6. James H. Burrows, "Information technology standards in a changing world: The role of the users," *Computer Standards and Interfaces* 15 (1993).

7. Multivendor Integration Architecture: Concepts and Design Philosophy, Nippon Telegraph and Telephone Corporation, 1989.

8. Jim Gray and Andreas Reuter, *Transaction Processing: Concepts and Techniques* (Morgan Kaufmann, 1993).

9. Ibid.

10. Service Providers Integrated Requirements for Information Technology, Issue 1.0, Network Management Forum, September 1993.

11. Ibid.

12. James Womack, Daniel Jones, and Daniel Roos, *The Machine That Changed the World* (Macmillan, 1990).

13. "Broadband-ISDN, Personal Connections to Global Resources," *Internet Research,* summer 1993.

II

New Kinds of Possibility

The Prairie School: The Future of Workgroup Computing

Deborah K. Louis
L. Alexander Morrow

"What's it all for?"
—H. G. Wells, *The Food of the Gods*

The year was 2005. Stretching out in his comfortable auditorium seat at last, John had to admit even he was impressed. John had come to Las Vegas to hear Merwin Williams, president and chairman of the board of Ouija, Inc., describe his vision of the industry he had bounded. Ouija clearly saw this event as the culmination of their decade-long rise to the top of the Omni/Fortune 500. They had re-created, as a set piece for their chairman's talk, the 1995 edition of the giant computer trade show COMDEX.

Enjoying the re-creation on his way to the speech, John had felt a pang of nostalgia for COMDEX. He remembered how he had enjoyed taking part in that twentieth-century version of the *Canterbury Tales,* a tapestry of the thinkers, ideas and marvels of his age. He'd been impressed how well Ouija had recaptured the medieval pageantry of COMDEX. Because of the location, there was no lack of kings and other royalty. His hotel had a Knights of the Round Table theme and boasted hourly jousting tournaments. As he walked from the cab stand to the convention center, he passed open-air grilles where first-time conference attendees, like Chaucer's simple country folk on their first pilgrimage, ate at long wooden tables while studying thick conference proceedings that described thousands of exhibitors. Hurrying on, he fell in with a collection of high priests, engineers in chinos and knit shirts, laughing and arguing about the mysteries of instantiation, magic numbers, and zombie processes as they walked with him toward the hall. As he neared the hall he came upon the merchants, professionals wearing summer weight suits, who ignored the crowds as they warily discussed business conditions and property rights.

Inside the exhibition hall was a city like Canterbury on a festival day, complete with neighborhoods. Just inside the doors was a commercial zone of gray-curtained booths where small businesses displayed bar-code readers, vaporproof keyboards, and other no-nonsense business devices. Nearby, cyberspace dwellers on an annual visit to reality formed a noisy arcade of flashing, plinking, and plonking computer games. Farther on, people were queued up waiting for an amusement-park ride through a giant personal computer. And uptown, at the sides of the hall farthest from the doors, the major hardware and software vendors of the time had formed a spotlit theater district. Here, two- and three-story structures housed ticket booths, information desks, demonstration stations, and fully equipped multimedia stages. In each of these little theaters, live salesmen and women used karaoke mikes to talk to video characters projected on screens behind them. This year, it seemed like all these advertisements featured know-it-all teenagers hanging around on giant user interfaces. The salesperson, playing mom or dad, would ask Henry or Martha to get started on his or her homework because it was going to take a long time. The on-screen child would respond "don't you know *anything?*" and proceed to perform the task in three or four clicks of the mouse by means of a new product feature. Naive questions from salesmom or salesdad were greeted with teenage contempt. John noticed that audiences asked few questions at the end of the show.

It was an impressive re-creation, but John had to admit he was glad things had changed since then. He hoped that Merwin would help the audience grasp the extent of the change. For one thing, of course, Last-ComdexEverHurrah! had been held in 1997, ending the middle ages of computerdom. This current lecture was John's first NVM—non-virtual meeting—since 2001. He wasn't all that happy to be away from his family, but he was certainly looking forward to the keynote speech.

The auditorium lights dimmed and the familiar image of Merwin appeared sitting in benevolent Lotus fashion on a small, soft, somewhat unruly cloud.

"It is now five years after the millennium," Merwin began, "and we are living in a world that has changed profoundly from the one you've just passed through. As we have agreed, we are going to spend an hour or so taking stock of what those changes are and what they have meant, not just to us and our businesses, but to the whole relationship between business, technology, and civilization.

"First, let me help you tie our re-creation of COMDEX to this talk. Ten years ago we at Ouija realized that there was a new use for computing, one that changed its role in society. We referred to this new use as Workgroup Computing in 1995. Few realized how wide-ranging the change would become. No one realized this new way of using computers would define this twenty-first century as fundamentally as global mass production had defined the twentieth.

"What occurred, of course, was a second advent of humanism, fully the equal of the renaissance that ended feudalism in Europe.

"Most people didn't see this change coming. We can see now that the two perspectives from which the future was predicted almost made it inevitable that the change would be missed. Beleaguered liberal arts graduates who might have seen the change in broad perspective were not familiar enough with the emerging technologies to see how they differed in fundamental ways from existing televisions and personal computers. Science and engineering specialists focused on the hard business of making incremental improvements in their specialties, and were very wary of sweeping statements. This left the future in the hands of the science fiction writers, who, as it turns out, are all closet medievalists.

"In any case, the change was in the way organizations were run—generally not a subject of deep contemplation. Educational institutions generally took comfort in the fact that their operational traditions, such as the gowned academic processions at commencement, had obvious medieval roots. In this they were not alone. Most institutions at the end of the twentieth century still operated as hierarchical bureaucracies, an organizational design that had evolved from the government, ecclesiastic, and military organizations of the middle ages. These organizational techniques were based on written rules and centralized decision making. Cases not covered by existing rules were escalated up the hierarchy, where judgments were made and written up as new rules for the operation of the institution. Decisions that had been rendered provided a corpus of standard corporate responses. This type of organization was clearly suitable to the unchanging medieval world. It had grown increasingly inappropriate for the changing world of the twentieth century.

"Let's discuss intelligent communications.

"It's not hard to argue that the renaissance world of the last millennium began with Gutenberg and moveable type. The resultant widespread literacy, a skill previously reserved to the estates, became the primary tool for the scientific revolution and its vastly widened world view. After Gutenberg, it became easy for a single writer's musings to be reproduced widely and, in effect, broadcast to an audience. Interestingly, this technology and its descendants were also based on a centralized organizational model— even as technology reached its peak at the end of the last century, when satellite technology permitted ideas to reach the entire world.

"The problem was, of course, that the process of selecting what was broadcast was biased toward the broadcaster, rather than the listener, because the broadcaster controlled the medium and effectively set the agenda for what could be discussed. While most of you probably found the video theaters in the exhibit hall annoying by the standards of 2005, they were quite normal for that time. I'm sure some of you are old enough to remember being interrupted during dinner by a sales call from an automatic dialer. You may even recall trying to think of ways to effectively insult the voice on the other end of the line.

"Many psychologists today believe that the strange emphasis on hopelessness and victimization at the end of the last decade was at least partly due to the lack of control people felt over a pervasive broadcast communications system they could not talk back to. Some feel that the success of the shopping channels were partly due to the early excitement viewers felt at their ability to talk back. It certainly wasn't the merchandise.

"Initially, computing had little impact on the organization. Economics dictated that early computers, expensive to obtain and operate, would be centralized in organizations. This central place in the organization and the subsequent attempts to unify all corporate data into databases made computers seem a natural adjunct to centralized decision-making. Computers, in this role, did not change institutions in a major way. Personal computers, on the other hand, were justified as improved versions of simple office equipment like typewriters and desk calculators. Personal-computer networks were initially just a means to trade files and share expensive laser printers. Communications devices, such as telephones and fax machines, were not seen as having much to do with computers. Televisions, stereo systems, and CD players were for the home.

"The sudden broad availability of hardware systems that brought together central computers, personal computers, engineering workstations, telephones, television, stereo systems, and CD players in 1994 and 1995 was amazing, of course, but most people didn't know why they needed such a device, except perhaps for playing fancier games. The equally sudden availability of telephone and cable services that could deliver and charge for exactly the required capacity, from a single character to several television channels, permitted interconnecting the games. But what was the catalyst that caused this so-called convergence of hardware technologies to throw open the celestory windows and clear out the medieval cobwebs in every organization almost overnight?"

Merwin looked over the audience and waited a moment. Then he continued:

"If I had been asked this question back in 1995, it would have been hard to give an answer that didn't cause a groan. I would have been forced to give the answer to this question a neutral name and then proceed to spend some time defining and giving examples of what I meant by that name.

"Fortunately for us, we have such a name—a term coined by the authors of an article about the future of technology published about that time. The name is, of course, the Prairie School."

Another short pause, and Merwin continued.

"The Prairie School was an initiative to provide software that would make the converged technologies available to absolutely everyone with a purpose. The purpose was, as a final act of medieval magic, to make the technologies themselves disappear and give way to a new type of communication, the technological equivalent of the Gutenberg press. The difference, though, is that this initiative suddenly made mass communications available to everyone. Not only could grandmother see the kids; if the kids wanted to, they could put on a show that all their friends—or for that matter, the entire eastern seaboard—could watch.

"The Prairie School separated the technology, which it dubbed *intelligent communications,* from the effect of the technology on society. The

effect, which it didn't give another name to because it was already familiar, was to provide a system that permitted all organizations to gain the
benefits of participative constitutional democracy.

"What is especially interesting about the success of the Prairie School
was the change in people's attitude toward technology that paralleled the
Renaissance's new attitudes toward literacy. The Prairie School required
real standards for computing, just as Gutenberg had required interchang-
able type. This domesticated computing. Because it has been domesticated, people find it friendly and a great help to understanding many
other aspects of science and technology, the literacy of our era.

"In 1995, most executives associated business reengineering with improving productivity by amplifying a smaller number of workers with
fixed-function robots, like the video salesperson. It is obvious now that
what was meant was the opposite—not amplifying the work of one individual, but establishing new methods for communication and decision
making in companies. The tools were not robots but computer technology to support courtesy, active listening, effective decision making, and
responsiveness to change in an organization.

"Further, these new ideas for exploiting technology went well beyond
productivity improvements. They fundamentally redefined what business
and government were. Where before the technology involved selecting the
message or product that was least offensive to the largest number of
people and then using broadcasting to alter attitudes to favor the selection, the new technology emphasized better decision making through diversity of opinions and flexibility."

John was impressed. He had heard some of this speech before and had
found it about as relevant to him as his calculus class had seemed long
ago. He was beginning to get glimmers of the idea now. He was getting
ready to listen.

"Let's jump from math to social studies for a moment," said Merwin.
"Think about the relationship between customers and businesses. By the
end of the last century, we had trained the whole world to be good consumers—and we were getting exactly what we deserved. Customers knew
what they wanted and were generally unresponsive to brand names and
glossy ads. People were starting to be very analytical in their buying decisions. The racks at corner newsstands of the time provided proof that the
press—which has always fed on change—saw product evaluation as a

business opportunity. Interactive catalogs and consumer-driven buying clubs were just in their infancy then. Who could have imagined the changes communications would bring to consumer buying power, such as the dishwasher and coffee table boycotts of 1996 or the wholesale replacement of the U.S. Congress in 1998? The answer, of course, is 'anyone who was listening.'

"We've always known that business thrives on innovation. The innovation of the Prairie School, though, was not primarily in internal business processes, but in the way companies relate to their customers and to one another."

Merwin stopped, removed his glasses, and looked directly at John. "Now, I know that many of you are in this audience because you still don't quite get the idea. I have brought along some virtual reality segments that I think of as a lesson plan for the Prairie School. We'll be using the standard year indicator and reality beacon, which you'll be able to see from the corner of your eye. A green beacon indicates reenactment of actual occurrences in the indicated year, a yellow beacon indicates occurrences that could easily have happened in the indicated year, and the red beacon, which we won't be using in this talk, indicates an infomercial.

"Let's look at the impact of Prairie School technology from three viewpoints: that of employees, that of teams, and that of the enterprise. We'll start at the beginning. What was that voice command? Oh, yes, 'PrestoChangoSelector!'"

Self-Reliant Employees

John found himself seated on the passenger side of a huge truck cab hurtling along the Loop in Chicago. From the corner of his eye he could see the reality beacon. It was green and read "1993," indicating that this virtual reality segment was based on actual reality for that time. John noticed he was wearing thick gloves. In front of him was a touch-screen computer displaying large icons. "Appropriate," thought John, "for pressing with my gloved hand." He looked at the driver, who was wearing a frayed leather jacket with "R. Norton, WMX" embossed on the upper arms. The truck slowed and turned down an approach road. John saw a large dumpster looming in front of him. "Good gravy stain," he thought to himself, "I'm in a garbage truck."

"Hit the arrival button, Jumpster!" the driver commanded. Although he didn't like his nickname much, John pushed the screen button that showed a truck arriving at a dumpster. He noticed that a flashing arrow appeared to the left of "Art Institute, 55 Cambridge Parkway," one of the entries in what appeared to be a list of destinations for the truck. Looking down from the high cab, John could see that the dumpster ahead of them was full of paintings of Madonna holding Campbell's Soup cans. "Pop tart school," said the driver. "Never got off the ground."

The driver positioned the truck in front of the dumpster, set the parking brake, and hopped out. John jumped out too, to watch the driver maneuver the truck's giant hydraulic arms around the dumpster, then lift it, tip it into the yawning truck bed, and lower it gently back to the ground. As he got back into the cab, John noticed that the arm must have been instrumented to measure the weight. The screen read "0.16 tons." "Stop daydreaming, Jumpster, and hit the button," barked the cheerful driver. John did so, and noticed that the computer immediately calculated the time it had taken to load the new additions to the Trash Can School into the truck.

John figured he'd better say something. "You know, I've been wondering," he yelled over the engine noise, "what do you think about the computer system?" Norton snorted, then yelled back, "Hey, Jumpster, punch up a blocked container on the Merc." Sure enough, there were two stretch limos blocking the container in back of the Mercantile Exchange. John pushed the "Arrival" button for the Merc, then pushed the "Exception" button. A second panel appeared on the computer screen. He selected "Blocked Container" and the computer hummed to life, obviously connecting itself by radio modem to a remote server machine. "To answer your question, Jumpster," said the driver, "I've got two things to say. It's pretty obvious that the entire route is clocked, so we don't have much opportunity to lollygag. The technos were worried we'd find the computer too invasive and try to junk it. Just the opposite has happened. We love it. First, look at how it changes the way I look at my job. Before, I was just picking up the trash. Now, I'm running my part of the business from my truck. Second, it's a lot more useful than most of the helpers I've had." Here he shot a look at John. "Before we had the computer, a blocked container meant a call back to the dispatcher, who would then try to call the company. It never worked. Now, the blocked container message gets sent directly to the security office of the client and they have an hour to fix the situation or get charged extra for a skipped pickup. It always works. You watch. These limos will be long gone when we get back."

After a few more stops, including a final stop at the now unblocked Merc container, the driver hopped onto the Loop for the drive to the transfer station. From somewhere over the rear-view mirror John heard a soft "PrestoChangoSelector" and found himself back in the auditorium.

Merwin looked around, adjusted himself on the sulking cloud a bit and continued: "It should be clear that employee empowerment through technology was already in full swing at WMX Corporation in Chicago in the early 1990s. It is not hard to argue that if mobile computer technology could be useful on garbage trucks, it was very likely to be useful everywhere to employees in the field.

"Now we're going to try a before-and-after experience. We'll play this next segment first in the 1990s mode, then in the 1995 mode. PrestoChangoSelector!"

Customers as Partners

John found himself seated in a cubicle decorated with family prints and a 1990 calendar featuring the L. L. Bean happy hunting dogs. He—no; in this simulation he was a she—was wearing a telephone headset and facing a mainframe terminal screen entitled "L. L. Bean Order Entry." Fields on the screen were arranged into orderly rows and columns, and she felt pretty sure that she could handle order taking. The phone rang, and John, whose VR name seemed to be June from all the "L. L. Bean Means Service" award plaques on the cubicle wall, found the Answer button, pushed it, and said, in her second friendliest voice, "Hello. I'm June, and you've reached L. L. Bean. How can I help you?"

She heard, "Hi, June. My name is Amy. I've just found out I'm going to be an aunt for the first time, and my sister Pat is a real L. L. Bean fan. I've been looking through your catalogs, though, and I don't see any maternity clothes. Do I have the right catalogs?"

June answered, "It's great about your sister, but we just don't carry maternity clothes. If it's any comfort, you're the fourth call I've had this month asking for them. How about some extra-extra-large turtlenecks?"

Amy said, "No thanks. I'm really disappointed. I thought you'd have something embroidered with cute little wading booties or LLBean-Sprouts." "Those are great ideas, Amy," said June, "but we never see the folks who make those decisions except at the Christmas party. Would your sister like an oversized thermometer with a nice picture of a cardinal?"

The click on the other end of the phone line was her only answer. June quickly scanned the terminal screen for places to put new product ideas. There weren't any, and her phone was ringing again with what she hoped would be a real order.

The reality beacon began to flash, and the date changed to 1995. Now the calendar was on screen, along with a little home movie of the twins decorating June's hunting dog with chocolate frosting. This time the phone blinked on the screen and June simply said "Answer" into her headset.

The screen icon changed to a small picture of the caller and a tiny dossier. Scanning it quickly, June found she remembered the caller and could say, with all sincerity, "Hi, Amy, thanks for calling. I'm June. We spoke about two months ago about presents for your sister Pat's birthday. Did she like them?" Amy answered, "She loved them, and I just got the greatest news! I'm going to be an aunt! How can I get your maternity catalog?" "Uh, oh," thought June. "Here's the thing, Amy," said June. "We don't have one, but we'd really like your ideas. Would it be OK with you if I recorded this for our idea department?"

"I guess so," said Amy.

June clicked on the Record icon. A little tape recorder appeared on the screen, where it was shortly joined by a picture of an envelope with Amy's name and address on it. "You said your sister Pat is expecting, Amy. When is she due?"

"April," said Amy. "And I've got to say, this is the first time L. L. Bean has let me down. I was hoping for jumpers with LLBeanies on them and smocks with tumbling hunting puppies. And maybe a little pink LLBeanie or a tartan crib cover. Sniff."

June said, "Amy, I'm going to forward your comments right along to our idea department. We'll call you back and let you know what happens. Would you like anything else today?" "No thanks," came the answer, "but thanks for listening, June. Bye."

June added a few comments of her own to the tape and submitted the result as a customer need workflow to Skip Tracer, the head of product research. She thought: "This would have been a missed opportunity for change only four years ago, before we realized that non-orders were far more valuable in some ways than orders."

The twins on screen finished decorating the dog, turned to the screen, and chorused "PrestoChangoSelector."

In the auditorium once more, John looked up at Merwin beaming from his cloud. He could obviously detect that people in the audience were seeing the light. "You can understand," said the gleeful Merwin, "how early workgroup computing caught fire with individual employees. They suddenly found themselves with the tools to participate in business and to drive decision making. Seen in the aggregate, this meant that companies were learning to listen. The interesting thing was how quickly customers caught on, and how effective they were at favoring companies that listened with business and information. Once again, it's obvious to us now that the change is exciting if you are a participant, and frightening only if you have no control. Essentially, workgroup computing—and the operational principles of the Prairie School—gave people, both employees and customers, the control they needed to feel comfortable with change. As the technology advanced, with coaxial and copper infrastructure replaced by high-capacity fiber-optic channels and mainframes replaced by huge networks of powerful workstations, it was the companies (and government agencies) that had provided and used the first workgroup tools that benefited the most. They saw early on that the real revolution in communications was not in creating 483 more broadcast networks but in the millions of small discussions and interactions that joined diverse viewpoints together for much better decision making, and in the building of trust and the sharing of pride of authorship that resulted.

Let's get back to how we succeeded in getting the computer to help people work in groups, so they could eventually recognize and learn to solve these problems.

"As you've probably guessed," said Merwin, "the big change in the use of computers occurred in the 1990s, when we learned to use them to help business people work together in groups, not just more efficiently but better. Let's examine this change through another before-and-after comparison."

Groups without Meetings

Things shimmered around him and John found himself walking down the hall of an office building, carrying a black leather 1990 FiloFax datebook bristling with multicolored pens and section tabs. He noticed it was labeled in French, and that his name seemed to be Jean. Turning a corner, he entered a conference room that had clearly been set aside for managing a crisis. Summaries and action plans written on big sheets of flip-chart paper lined the walls. It was early in the morning, and people were settling in for an hour-long status meeting. They were armed with status reports, attitudes, and cups of coffee. A facilitator called the room to order and started the rounds of the conference table with Jean.

"Hey, mon gar! How's the Australian survey coming along? Are those guys in Perth tout fini?" Jean consulted his Filofax and answered, "Well, Al, they were shipped Federal Express yesterday night, they should be arriving tomorrow morning." "Sacre bleu," said Al, "that means we'll have to push the design freeze out until next week's status meeting. Manufacturing will have to work over the Halloween weekend if we're going to meet the holiday deadline."

After an hour of similar reports, about three of which were relevant to his responsibilities, Jean began to wonder how great this notion of superpowered employees really was. If it meant sipping another styrofoam cup of coffee-flavored water and trying to squeeze daily assignments, names, and status reports into 20 square centimeters of FiloFax paper, he was ready to find a mildly despotic barbarian and go back to work.

Walking back to his office, Jean passed another small conference room where people were managing the crisis of allocating conference rooms to situation management. The tentmakers were discussing a potential alliance with the maternity wear designers in a power play for a room with dual whiteboards and a view of the hills. The outdoor-thermometer-with-cardinals group was looking for allies in the compass and bird feeder divisions. Jean found himself wondering if the company would still be in business in a few years if the top priority for teamwork became allocating the time and space to engage in it.

The reality beacon blinked in pause mode, and Merwin spoke. "As you've seen, even the fundamentals of computer-assisted-collaboration science were largely unknown at the beginning of the last decade of the 1900s. If we go forward just five years, though, to 1995, things have improved significantly. Prestissimo-de-Changissimo!"

With a green reality beacon and a 1995 copy of *World Commerce* on his desk, Jean (John) found himself sitting in a pleasant office near the Seine, scanning the latest communiqué of the Parisian focus team in his WhitherEuropeWear Notes database. As he already guessed, the hiker/biker/kayaker crowd he had grown up with in Europe felt wholly at home with the ChezEux line of LLLegume clothing, but were now finding themselves wanting dark flannel maternity jumpsuits, backpacks with fold-out changing pads, and "Place de l'Enfant" pullovers. A quick check of the production plans reassured Jean that these results had already been picked up by design shops in Valbonne and Chartres, and that places were reserved in the autumn printing of the catalog and in the flannel and Gore-Tex production lines in Rennes.

Scanning the marketing database, his eye caught a tag line on a proposed mailing from the CuddlyAnimalSwimsuits Division that he thought might be offensive to parents with one or more canoes. He selected Compose from the menu, chose Response Document, and quickly typed up a sharp note that flatly informed the writers (and anyone scanning the database later) that "Paddle your own gnu" might sound original and apt to them but was 30 years old and probably offensive to children's-rights advocates through most of the civilized world. "Probably beyond France, too," he thought. As usual, he looked the response document over and changed it to open-ended questions ("Does anyone else find this somewhat offensive?") addressed to members of the committee on marketing communications. He then posted it on the wall of the virtual conference room, next to the offending brochure, to invite comments. How much nicer, he thought, than waiting through an hour-long status meeting for a chance to bring up the same question. He spent another half-hour reading his mail and scanning the *Le Monde, Le Canard Enchainé,* and *Women's Wear Daily* newsfeed databases for mentions of LLLegume, Finisterra, and eddie bauerhaus before returning for a final review of the collateral database. He was surprised to find attached to his observations eleven supporting responses and two proposals of marriage. Lifting his espresso and turning to look out over the Seine through the gray afternoon drizzle, he mused aloud: "And they said a liberal arts education would be wasted on a software engineer!" The intercom icon on his screen buzzed, and a pleasant-sounding French voice said "PrestidigitationSelecteur."

John shook his tête. These VR shifts could be really tough if you weren't ready for the changes. He was trying to remember where on his new PentiMillenium server the Notes database on marketing collateral was cataloged when Merwin reappeared on his wan cloud and started in again.

"You've just seen how things improved for end users in the five years after the first real workgroup computing systems came into use. I realize that most of you use intelligent communications every day, but just in case our experimental Internet link to 1995 works I'd like to point out a few things. First, people prefer communication to transportation. Many business roles, from customer support to order taking, are both cheaper to provide and more effectively done from the home. Even some face-to-face discussions can be accomplished in shared virtual reality conference rooms. Actually, although you can buy simple virtual classrooms and conference rooms, most companies have an active repertoire of situation rooms that address ongoing projects, plus a suite of ready rooms that contain instructions and datafeeds for managing various crises, from hostile takeover bids to natural disasters.

"Customers are, if anything, far more demanding; on the other hand, uniqueness has come back into style. The number of changes that have been generated by listening and trying to reduce problems to human scale is staggering. Self-recrimination has advanced from "why didn't I think of that?" to "why wasn't I listening?" We all remember the e-mail about wooden tomatoes ignored by a supermarket giant. The supermarket sysop took the writer's observation that typical use of heated basements in Massachusetts left plenty of room for computer-controlled hydroponics gardens, and formed the international Winter Garden chain.

"Let's go to Japan to describe how the relationships between businesses changed based on the Prairie School initiatives. Presto Chango."

Partners with Shared Goals

In the next VR sequence, John (Masao), out of breath and with aching calves, found himself dressed in running gear at the door of a chic townhouse whose brass doorbell plate read Masao O. Bento. The door opened and two young children emerged. They bowed to him and said, in polite Japanese, "Papa-san! We will be back in time to go to the Fujiokas' dinner. Mom's taking a special rice cake for your birthday. Ato de!" Masao shook his head. He had completely forgotten about the dinner, and he had a fair amount of work to finish for Ike's Bikes in the two hours before they had to leave. Entering his home office, he noticed he had several updates and priority flags highlighted in red on the computer screen. He touched the kanji character for Channel Inventory and listened to his first message, a phone-mail note: "Hi, Masao. Fred calling from Harley-Davidson in Milwaukee. Could you please double check the forecast for the MachoRider line you're planning to ship to Rome next week? I think that the numbers should be cut about in half, since we'll be doing a big product announcement for the IGetIt line of bikes for the unthreatened male, and we anticipate a fallback in volumes on the Macho line. Gloria says hi. She really liked the rice cookies your wife sent. She said to ask Sueko if they really have negative calories." Masao quickly scanned the MachoRider inventory at each distribution site in Italy and noticed that the weeks on hand could easily cover the forecast. His only concern was Naples. The number of bikes sold there had increased by ten units since he first sat down to work. He pulled up the Mondo Napoli feed and saw an article about how people who didn't like mufflers on their bikes should buy Machissimos before they were replaced next month under a noise-control ordinance. If he could reroute the new Macho shipment to Naples, Ike's Bikes could cash in on this last stand of the anti-ordinance Boys Will Make Noise crowd by taking the whole lot and about forty more. Masao touched the kanji character for Logistics on the screen, scanned the list, and highlighted "Harley-Davidson Global Logistics Office." A set of shipping manifests appeared on the screen. He roped them all with a quick mouse drag, then spoke into the microphone: "Hi, Mark. Could you take all these and reroute the whole lot to Naples? Thanks!" As soon as he finished saying thanks, the screen copies of the manifests folded up and sailed into a box, along with a little tape cassette labeled REROUTE. A voice from the computer said "What's the authorization code?" When Masao replied "4077 Mash," the box on the screen was sealed with a stamp and sent to Mark Walling of Harley-Davidson's shipping department for processing. Masao rearranged the production schedule for the collateral video in Milwaukee to put IGetIt Bikes first by pressing a few keys and sent the new one off to Fred, forwarding a ScreenCam copy of the session he'd had so far and an automatic "Thanks, old buddy" voice note by way of explanation. Meanwhile he noticed that Mark had OKed the request to reroute the MachoRiders to Naples. Only one more item to take care of before he turned his attention to the next message. Masao read through Harley-Davidson's schedule for parts deliveries from its suppliers and spoke into the microphone: "Contact Rose at LogiFab Steel Works." The screen changed to video conference mode. Rose answered, looked up from her work, and smiled at Masao. "Hi, Masao! What's up?" "Hi, Rose. Listen, we've just changed the production schedule for the final week of MachoRiders at Harley Davidson's in Milwaukee. It's well inside their production envelope as they ramp down, so it shouldn't cause a capacity problem there. They won't be in until tomorrow morning their time, and I'm afraid this will mean they need more high handlebars delivered to the Milwaukee Harley plant tomorrow. I can't authorize a delivery change, since this is happening within the next 24 hours. Can you help me out here? I'd hate to see them leave money on the table." Rose turned to her keyboard and typed a few keys as Logifab's delivery schedule appeared on the bottom half of Masao's computer screen. "Well, you're in luck! We just had a cancellation on high handlebars for Volvo sidecars, so we can ship this to Milwaukee. OK?" Masao nodded. Rose typed a few characters and said: "Great, Masao. I'm sure Harley-Davidson will be quite happy with its suppliers and customers for getting together to help their bottom line." After thinking for a second, Masao said: "You know, Rose, we should run a quick environmental impact report on this, just to be sure." He brought up an official-looking form and dragged the transaction she'd been working on over to it. The answer came back within seconds of his dragging the filled-in form to the UN/EPA window: "MachoRiders are now considered collector's items and will receive little street use at this point. The impact is judged insignificant. The wisdom of making the purchase, of course, is up to the purchaser." "Wow," thought Masao. "I still can't get over having responsive government agencies."

Rose filed the form with the new order and sent the resultant folder on its way. She turned to Masao and said "Now for the payoff." "Uh, oh," thought Masao. Rose continued: "I understand Sueko makes fantastic rice cakes. How about having her send over the recipe?" Relieved, Masao laughed and said: "Well, she's the copyright owner, and I'll have to negotiate that with her, but I'll see what I can do. Thanks, Rose. I'll conference you in when we review this tomorrow with Harley. Cheers!" Masao hung up and began working his way through a prioritized list of his remaining work. He had just about finished when his wife leaned over his shoulder and touched the keyboard. An animated birthday card appeared. It started with a video of his children and gradually became a gathering of his entire extended family singing "Happy Presto."

With this VR segment now over, John could see that Merwin was nearing the end of his lecture and was looking quite encouraged. Merwin summarized the last vignette: "With the new hardware and software technology, doing business changed, not because of a mandate, but because it made better business sense. Businesses could help one another, permitting decision making to span corporate boundaries. This is, of course, a part of the Prairie School philosophy of self-reliant individuals who understand how to work toward shared goals. Since businesses could now easily protect and regulate exactly what information was shared, they were more willing to share information with one another. Businesses that took advantage of this change in relationships prospered. Companies that preferred to keep all operational data from one another, and used lack of information as a bargaining tool, found that they did not do as well. Increasingly, they learned to take advantage of the ability to share information and began sharing decision making. It's clear that the decisions required to implement the last vignette would have taken days or weeks in the early 1990s, not because they couldn't have been done by phone and fax, but because business relationships were different. Once competition required companies to become faster at decision making, it didn't take long for these new ways of working together to develop. Businesses quickly realized the opportunity this offered to improve flexibility, customer service, and profit margins. It just made much more sense to work as a global team once the changes in technology initiated by the Prairie School made that feasible.

"So much for the past," Merwin said. "Let's now take a quick look at the future. I think we all agree that the future lies in our classrooms, so let's visit one. Prrrresto. . . ."

A View of the Future

Johnny found himself standing in a fourth grade classroom somewhere in Ohio talking to Mary, a classmate, about the project they were working together on. "What are you doing now, Mary?" he heard himself say. "I'm starting up *All The World*," was her response. "What is that?" "Well," said Mary, "basically, it's a stage. You use this (pointing to a computer-like device) to tell it what to show. What we're going to do with it now is finish the class project so we can get on the air in an hour with it." "What do you mean, on the air?" John said. "Well," Mary replied, "it used to be that you had things called, I think it was, channels that played tapes over and over, and you could pick which tape you wanted to listen to. Then there was a change, and a Prairie School thing happened, and now you just tell people that you want to show them something, and if they want to see it they put in your name and they can see what you want to show them. Do you understand?" "Um, I think so," said Johnny, who sort of understood. "Anyway," said Mary, "we've told people that Miss Bloom's class will be putting its pageant on in two hours, so let's get going." "What are you doing?" asked John. "Oh," said Mary, "we're going to take these actor and prop objects over here," pointing with a stylus to an display that displayed what looked like excellent color photographs of children and props such as television sets and microphones, "and arrange them in the order we want them to play on this timetracker." She pointed to a child's photograph with the stylus and dragged it onto what looked like a strip of 35-millimeter film. The photograph appeared in the first frame she touched. She then dragged out the first frame, producing a whirl of images on the next frame until she saw the final image she liked. "That's where he finished the first part, just before he forgot his lines again," she said. She then reached over to a puppet-theater icon and dragged it in place the same way. "That's the cartoon we did yesterday," she said. After a few more of these edits, she pushed an on-screen Rewind button and started playing the pageant, which consisted of a flying title, the anchorchild, several cartoons, some original songs, some fourth grade humor, and a rolling list of credits. She looked pretty pleased with herself as she saved the session.

John was interested in how Mary was able to put the whole program together. "My daddy told me," she said "that before the Prairie School, um, thing, you had to know a lot about how the equipment was built in order to use it. My daddy says he lost most of his hair during that time. People really liked the Prairie School because they said the things were stupid, not the people. My daddy said he once had a neighbor he didn't know come to his house and ask for help with his computer, which he was using to pay bills. The man was very embarrassed that he had used the computer the wrong way, so that it had lost six months of checks. My daddy went to the man's house and fixed as much as he could, then started talking. It turned out that the man had won a Nobel Prize three years before. My daddy said this pretty much convinced him that the people who thought that computer problems were caused by dumb users were wrong. He says the problem was always always dumb programs. Anyway, the Prairie School said specifically that people used computers to talk to each other, not to talk to computers, and that most of the problems in computers were that computer people talked too much to their computers and not to other people. Now we can take things like cartoons and videos and put them together ourselves, and they always work. I don't understand why anyone thought the other way was right. But I'm only in fourth grade."

It was air time. John looked at the monitor to see the entire fourth grade class singing "The cowboys and the farmers should be friends." Then a giant logo spun in from the distance to form the words "Hey kids! It's time for PrestoChangoSelector!"

Merwin reappeared and continued his tale:

"It's hard to believe, but if you referred to a concept as simple as the first derivative in most business or government settings in the mid 1990s you would be met with blank stares. Yet today, a mere decade later, every schoolchild understands that the calculus is just a handy formalism for dealing with the simplest types of change. Any child can also relate, in technical detail that amazes us all, the ways in which the infinitely more human, helpful, and accessible ideas of the Prairie School bloomed almost overnight into the world as we know it in 2005—from decent arugula in western Massachusetts in November to international virtual conferences with auto-translation—precisely because the school wholly rejected the goal of finding the single truth that could be represented in a database or captured in some AI program and replaced it with the goal of supporting in every conceivable way intelligent communication and cooperation among human beings.

"The odd thing was that the more sophisticated the technology became, the more it seemed to disappear as a separate object of contemplation. Today, Colombian children think nothing about screen chats with distant Chinese and Kenyan pals, unaware of Avery Auto-translation, ATM-5 routing, or X.5E6 directory services. To them, the little computer they use, which is as powerful as any supercomputer of the 1990s, is about as interesting in itself as a video player was to tots in the 1990s. The difference is that parents feel good about their children's use of the intelligent communications box, because it strengthens their social skills. We had no idea in the 1990s how constant replaying of Barney and Friends videos would lead to a generation averse to real interactions. Fortunately, the Prairie School changed that almost overnight."

"And now," said Merwin, "let's see whether you've been listening effectively. Presto . . ."

Graduation: You're in Charge

". . . ChangoSelector," John heard in a familiar voice. The reality beacon was changing from chartreuse to sunset pink and back to ochre. If that were not disorienting enough, John couldn't really see very much else because a brilliant light was shining in his face. From somewhere deep in his unconscious, a certain thought crossed his mind. "Either I'm about to meet my great-grandmother or the audience is going to appear before me as soon as my eyes adjust to the dark," John thought. His eyes adjusted to the dark. "Gee, I was hoping to finally meet granmama," he thought wistfully as 3000 faces appeared, looking expectantly up at him.

Then John stood up, rising to the occasion. He smiled at the audience and said: "Let me tell you what I think we have experienced this morning. In general, we have set out to find a shift in the operation of institutions from a sort of updated feudalism to participative constitutional democracy brought about by what have come to be known as Prairie School methods.

"As Jumpster, we experienced some of the early experiments in this new way of doing business. The surprise was that the new technologies, which could have been perceived as invasive, in fact gave people the tools they needed to be squarely in control of their part of a business. Second, as June, we saw how intelligent use of these technologies changed the relationship between customer and business from a monologue in which the customer was an abstraction to a dialogue in which the customer who didn't place an order provided other value—feedback—to the business. Third, as Jean, we experienced the impact the Prairie School technologies had on work groups in business, saving time by using intelligent communications to replace international meetings. Fourth, as Masao we experienced how the Prairie School technologies changed the relationship between business partners, making it possible for partners to take actions such as controlling production schedules in order to help both companies. Finally, we asked where these technologies are leading by having Johnny visit a contemporary school and asking a classmate."

"It's clear that the Prairie School premise has been correct—by deemphasizing the technology and focusing on human communications, it has changed the way information is handled. The simplest way to put this is that the rule-driven systems of a decade ago have been replaced by systems that reward innovation and good judgement. The resultant flow of new ideas has provided solutions for the many of the problems that plagued us at the end of the last century. In short, by following the Prairie School direction of purposefully subordinating technology to the role of assisting communication between intelligent human beings, we are on our way to creating—or re-creating—a world of intelligent, self-reliant individuals who feel fully capable of finding solutions to the problems that plagued us at the end of the last century."

"Thanks, and good afternoon."

The audience exploded into the type of applause John knew was an indication he had gotten it right. He removed his headset and settled back into the armchair. "That," he thought to himself, "was the toughest game they've come out with this decade." His two-year-old toddled by and asked "Daddy get COMDEX 2005?" "Yup," said John, "finally won, honey." "Good," she said. "let's take a walk." And they did.

Note from the authors: We chose the term "Prairie School" to reflect first of all Frank Lloyd Wright's architecture, which produced without compromise contemporary and beautiful buildings that were scaled for human use. Laura Ingalls Wilder's sense of community in the wide-open spaces and just a splash of Rogers and Hammerstein and Aaron Copland were thrown in for good measure. Here's hoping the cowboys and the farmers become friends.

Software without Borders: Applications That Collaborate

David Williams
Timothy O'Brien

Is it possible for ideas to compete in the marketplace if no form for their presentation is provided or available?
—Thomas Mann

Over the past 10 years, increasing access to information has accelerated changes in business, entertainment, and education all over the world. Computers, networks, phone systems, and global television broadcasting have given individuals and entire populations the chance to use information as a tool in redefining the ways in which they live, communicate, and work.

Now another fundamental shift is underway. No longer is it enough to simply increase access to the information sources that exist as important yet "outside" ingredients of a business process. In today's society, information has become the oxygen of the whole process of interaction. By necessity, business has become virtual, dissolving many archaic forms and structures. Information unites all the processes and components of real-time, cooperative work. Information and the tools of technology are now reinventing the world's business infrastructure.

Organizations used to be relatively rich in work hours and poor in information—whether in looking up cases for a law firm, monitoring sales for a car company, or transmitting and comparing revised blueprints in an engineering office. With information more abundant and accessible, many labor-intensive tasks can now be done in real time, with the digital realm as a medium for learning, communicating, and conducting all forms of business.

This shift toward greater use of information technology reverses the ratio of work hour to information and fills the huge, wasteful gaps of human contact within individual lives and groups of people working together. Organizations have evolved to take advantage of this increased access to information despite having to struggle against the pressures of a global economy and a lingering worldwide recession. Businesses, schools, and cultural institutions are all finding the need to restructure in order to survive and become more effective.

Organizations are attempting to adapt to this transformation amid upheaval in most industrial democracies. Many countries have already been affected by the international implications of the previous stage of global electronic interconnection. Now, restructuring and the formation of global alliances are imperative. Yet many fear the consequences of restructuring.

In many of these organizations, software technology is being used to reengineer the very processes and procedures of work. This organizational restructuring is enabled not just by the creation of digital communications infrastructures but also by software that dramatically increases access to information and collaboration among workers throughout the network.

Computer-supported collaboration (CSC) allows a user of a networked personal computer or personal digital assistant, regardless of his or her geographic location, to access and manage information, to communicate and collaborate with co-workers, and to automate many processes in the business that had previously been done manually.

By utilizing underlying network and application services, such as electronic mail or databases, CSC leverages the investment in existing technologies but, at the same time, combines them in new ways with collaborative and interactive software to offer greater levels of application integration and functionality.

Insomuch as technological innovations have facilitated this higher mode of information sharing and collaboration, CSC has also brought about changes in the global business climate. The pace of change in business is accelerating around the world. Today, businesses of all kinds—be they industrial, technical, financial, or service-oriented—are critically dependent on information resources just to keep up, let alone get ahead.

This capability to take the initiative and respond to rapidly changing business conditions is increasingly being referred to as "just-in-time business." The term CSC describes the use of computers and information systems to enhance collaboration within and among teams of knowledge workers. Yet applying the term "just-in-time" to the processes of the information age can be as misleading as referring to a well-managed railroad as practicing "just-in-time scheduling." The flow is understood clearly enough without the label.

As the notion of "just-in-time business" evolves into "real-time" applications, business processes will operate with a high degree of information connectivity, both for forward planning and for feedback. In defining the next generation of cooperative applications, CSC combines enhanced networking capabilities with cross-platform messaging-enabled software technologies to make possible a widespread restructuring of interaction through real-time information sharing.

The goal of real-time information sharing will be achieved through creating applications that rely on CSC, since greater technological efficiencies and productivity will be required to keep up with business challenges.

The Roots of Computer-Supported Collaboration

The proliferation of personal computers and the growth of networking have forever changed the role of computing in institutions of all forms. Now, instead of building on host-based, centralized computing roots, organizations are seeking to maximize their effectiveness by making the information needed to manage and run operations much more accessible to a growing base of interconnected personal computer users.

Whether for business, educational, or cultural purposes, the possible benefits resulting from information sharing and access outweigh the penalties for neglecting it. In fact, information is now the catalyst enabling organizational and business-process restructuring to be done at unprecedented speeds.

To lower costs, get products to market faster, and respond to changing market conditions, many organizations have turned to a flexible form of computing that supports the use of personal computers as "clients" accessing data and programs from various back-end "servers." The migration from mainframes to client/server computing has resulted largely from the emergence of the widespread use of personal computers and software, several standard graphical user interfaces, better networking, and increasingly capable and inexpensive servers.

At the same time, slower economic growth, increased competition, and a greater realization of the benefits of fast, flexible access to information are contributing to the broader acceptance of client/server technology in corporate computing environments. All in all, as more companies downsize to smaller, less expensive platforms and commit to organizational restructuring, the benefits of client/server technology are becoming much more widely accepted but are still difficult to measure.

Although such organizational changes as the elimination of now-irrelevant bureaucratic hierarchies have driven the technological shift to personal computers, it has been the flexibility and cost-savings achieved through networking and downsizing that has facilitated much organizational restructuring. Technology has been both the means and the end in fulfilling key organizational objectives.

Since users no longer settle for one type of hardware or operating system, market pressures are forcing computer and software companies to provide interfaces that allow a common way to share either front-end applications or back-end services. These emerging standards enable people to achieve mix-and-match functionality with different types of hardware and software in client/server computing. Additionally, client/server computing means that users can run the most efficient software and hardware that will support the application.

Companies involved in intense global competition have begun "flattening" their organizations to avoid unnecessary layers of hierarchy. With the use of decentralized computing resources, management is able to give users more authority for local decision making, eliminate bureaucratic positions, and tap into the innovative talents of more members of the organization. Although CSC applications built around a client/server model closely simulate the way organizations now function and conduct operations, the wider use of advanced communications technologies is also facilitating the evolution of collaborative computing.

Very soon, anyone owning a telephone and a computer will be able to do any type of desk or library work anywhere. The concept of the "virtual corporation," with workers "telecommuting" from anywhere, may mean that many people will move away from cities. People will be able to live and work where they want and still perform tasks that would have in the past required being present at a physical location.

Deregulation has enabled new telecommunications services to be introduced. When AT&T was first broken up, the seven Regional Bell Operating Companies were still closely regulated, but in the past few years many of these regulations have been removed. At the same time, television networks, media conglomerates, and cable providers have been given greater freedom to enter new markets.

Along with deregulation, technological advances in networking are bringing these industries into convergence. Wide-area networking technologies, such as the Asynchronous Transfer Mode (ATM) and the Integrated Services Digital Network (ISDN), are enabling any combination of voice, sound, graphics, or data to be digitally communicated at ultrahigh speeds. ATM offers phone companies, computer networking companies, and even cable providers a standard format in which to carry multimedia information; ISDN is based on upgrading the basic phone company network from analog to digital. As these services become more widely available and cost-effective, new CSC applications that encompass multimedia will be used in businesses, schools, and eventually homes.

By using new technologies to unite workers over great distances, it is now possible to deploy CSC applications in many offices to facilitate the cooperative design, development, and production of products and services. For instance, Ford Motor Company is linking design and engineering workstations in its centers around the world so that different teams of designers can work simultaneously rather than sequentially.

Along with communications, the whole role of messaging in organizations is being transformed. Electronic mail is no longer simply a convenience, it is a necessity. As a result, software systems are now required that can enhance messaging. For instance, a messaging server should be able to support person-to-person, person-to-server-process, or even server-process-to-server-process forms of messaging built with distributed database-like facilities, such as stored procedures, triggers, or event alerts.

To address the needs of all the users who have been keeping host systems simply for scheduling, an enterprise messaging environment must offer integrated messaging, scheduling, and directories. Messaging should also be integrated with desktop applications, powerful database server applications, or legacy applications. Enterprise messaging must work with leading tools, front ends, and operating environments and must support an open application programming interface.

As an example, a corporation still depending on host-based enterprise scheduling using IBM's Office Vision would also want to integrate this scheduling information with various personal-computer-based electronic mail programs. Gateways providing batch updates between the two environments were sufficient in the past, but users now want to rely on graphical user interfaces to immediately and transparently provide messaging access to and from multiple environments or applications.

In the future, electronic mail functionality or features that provide access to messaging applications will be embedded in operating systems. Rather than have to leave an application to send or receive mail, users will access messaging functions from any program running on the network. Instead of exiting applications to go to the electronic mail program, users would be notified when messages have arrived by simple prompts or open windows on the screen.

Messaging, directory, and database functions will also become more integrated. Despite the wider acceptance of "open systems," many programs, protocols, and computers used on networks weren't originally designed to work together. As a result, there are often duplicate or incompatible directory, naming, messaging, administration, or management systems. By integrating many of the functions of a messaging server into a database server that also performs key organizational database functions, messaging can be more easily extended across the enterprise to large numbers of users.

Putting in place a network that provides a distributed computing infrastructure through common or standard software services, such as messaging, allows organizations to run "mail-enabled" applications that utilize electronic mail to make key functions or data accessible to hundreds or thousands of network or remote users. In this way, messaging becomes a standard transport mechanism for delivering requests or performing tasks on large networks. Combining voice and electronic mail with other collaborative technologies holds the potential for automating even more business operations through the use of information retrieval and delivery or workflow applications.

As business moves from an industrial base to an information-driven economy, there are new pressures to look for greater cost savings and efficiencies from the use of technology. Over the past few decades, business made gains by automating key manufacturing-floor processes that involved labor-intensive tasks. Now, businesses are looking to realize some of these same benefits through information-intensive operations such as customer service. At the same time, greater access to information is redefining efficiency in the manufacturing process itself, creating a state of continual change and improvement in many manufacturing-floor processes. For instance, new software is being introduced that can process voice, fax, or electronic-mail inquiries for the status of an account or an order by checking various databases for the appropriate information. Once the software has compiled the data, it replies automatically through various delivery methods, such as fax or electronic mail.

With wider adoption of these applications, users look toward ways of combining multimedia data to provide a greater degree of functionality and integration in processing, managing, and delivering information. This means integrating voice and electronic mail, providing broadcast or store-and-forward fax capabilities, support for data integrated with video, and access to information from personal communication devices. The support of integrated voice, data, video, text, and images in applications requires the creation of a new class of multimedia data that will be accessible through information services that are as widely available and easy to use as today's telephone system.

As a step in this direction, major computer companies such as Hewlett-Packard, Digital Equipment, and IBM have begun to move away from proprietary, monolithic systems and toward open, standards-based systems that support a certain degree of functionality based on different types of computers and software working together through common interfaces and portability. This "plug and play" approach became necessary as organizations increasingly turned to the distributed network as the platform for applications. As a result, business systems and procedures are being fundamentally reworked as many companies reengineer these operations according to new hardware and software technologies. Very often, at the center of these changes is a company's database environment.

In developing or maintaining these databases, companies increasingly need to locate and gather vast amounts of information—whether from databases or from real-time news feeds—by the fastest possible means. Then, once the information has been accessed, sorted, and stored, it has to be disseminated to the relevant employees or customers who can act on it.

What was a centralized, rather rigid "body" of data becomes even more purely a data flow that is made available through CSC applications to the workers actually designing the products, setting up the marketing programs, conducting the sales, and providing the support services.

In the Virtual Office, the Next Meeting Is Scheduled for Your Personal Computer

For years the personal computer has been one of the most commonly used tools to prepare information, slide presentations, and reports used in meetings. But now, as it evolves from a desk-top productivity device to a business communications tool, the personal computer is becoming not just the source of materials for meetings but also the site of the meetings.

The communications and computing developments of the last few years will bring personal-computer-based video conferencing one step closer to simulating face-to-face interaction and will help establish the concept of the virtual corporation. With virtual corporations defining themselves through the sharing of information among business partners, new efficiencies in communications and meetings will be possible. Corporations will be able to create electronic links between partners, seamlessly binding appropriate resources to build a product, solve a problem, or perform research.

Although large-scale video conferencing equipment is already available, it is expensive and it may require participants to go to a special facility. Despite the fact that these systems enable people to exchange information in a manner much more nearly like person-to-person communication, they fail to provide low-cost, personal-computer based access to the documents and tools needed for many different types of meetings and conferences.

Users of personal-computer-based video and communications applications at different sites will share a common electronic desktop and will be able to update electronic documents. Multiple users will be able to share single-user applications by taking turns interacting. In addition, some applications will be specially designed for real-time shared use. Video conferencing capabilities will enable participants to see one another's physical gestures and reactions.

But new conferencing capabilities will not be limited to the desktop. Innovations in networking technologies, such as the growth of high-bandwidth and wireless networks, have been accompanied by a corresponding increase in the use of multimedia-based presentations and communications by companies seeking greater impact and differentiation in the market.

Simultaneously, computer companies are adding increased communications capabilities, in many cases now wireless, to a range of new portable devices. Software companies such as Microsoft and Lotus are expanding mail systems to support electronic messages that can now consist of data, graphics, images, voice, and video.

Taken together, the advances in networking that provide more access to information and the increased reliance on multimedia information are creating the need for an information-management system that is scalable to process large amounts of data very quickly, is open to support industry standards, works with the leading client environments, and is capable of storing and manipulating complex objects consisting of multimedia data. This information-management system will provide the underlying network, messaging, database, security, communications, and administration services to support the development and deployment of enterprise-wide CSC applications.

The emergence of the capacities and the components that will create the virtual office has just begun. It began by removing barriers of time and location by linking offices and adding mobility through portable and wireless computing. It will continue as the software used to allow workers to collaborate evolves into applications that seamlessly tie together messaging, databases, and other project-specific data.

Over the next ten years, as new technologies are developed and lower costs are achieved, many powerful new ways to integrate video, voice, and data will arrive. Some of these services will provide access to huge databases on public information networks that store both relational data and the new multimedia information. These public on-line databases will act almost as libraries providing access to data that could not have been available so easily before. Business, education, and entertainment will be able to employ the public digital communication infrastructures to provide new services based on increased access to information. From a computer, a television, or a personal digital assistant, people will be able to conduct business, take educational courses, be entertained, or communication with friends or associates.

As publishers, media, and entertainment companies convert to digital format all types of reference information, news, and historical data, new multimedia servers will emerge as the platform by which those information services and public databases can be made accessible over the digital communications infrastructure to a wide range of CSC applications. Yet CSC is more than just the networks and new applications.

Since the main computing platform of the 1990s is not the mainframe but the distributed network of computers from many vendors, the sharing of information has become an absolute necessity.

CSC is actually the discipline of using computers and software to achieve new levels of interpersonal communication and information sharing. For example, effective collaboration requires mechanisms and controls that allow unattended communication, unstructured or discussion-like databases that facilitate group interaction, or the ability to use multimedia in representing ideas more vividly and visually.

Since it is the goal of CSC to improve group productivity quantitatively and group awareness and intensity qualitatively, teams of individuals require basic networking and messaging services in order to collaborate effectively. For example, one of the earliest CSC applications to be widely used was Lotus's Notes product. Since Lotus developed Notes at a time where there were no standard network services such as messaging, directory, or security, it built those functions directly into Notes, thus launching it as a self-contained environment on the underlying network for these services. But as standard network services emerge, Lotus is opening up Notes to allow users to take advantage of them.

With standard interfaces for exchanging messages between clients and servers on a network, team members can send and receive messages, automate common office procedures, and conduct real-time conferences. As the corporate world adopts standards in messaging and implements these standards as part of the operating environment of the network, much greater levels of intra-office and inter-office communication and information access will be possible.

CSC will also bring new benefits in the areas of education and training. As a new order of accessible information pours into easily updated network databases, new ways of learning will be possible through on-line systems.

To stimulate interest in history, the Port Hueneme School District in Oregon developed an interactive CD-ROM based on the travels and diaries of Lewis and Clark. Allowing the students to work in either English or Spanish, the program allows students to follow the great expedition on a map that uses images, voice, animation, and video to unfold the story.

This project works upon the assumption of "cognitive latency," which asserts that as information density is increased the learning time for users will be reduced. Highly visual applications employing graphical interfaces, pictures, video, and voice will enhance the learning process beyond what old text-based systems could do.

Computer users retain more information when more than one mode of communication is employed. For example, when sound is added to visual images there is greater impact. When the visual images are enhanced by video or graphics there is even more impact.

As interactive multimedia learning programs are being developed that use video, sound, graphics, and text, students are allowed to explore more personal progressions of logic and inquiry. Students can learn more by going at their own pace in the manner that allows the most understanding.

Most CSC applications use several of these classes of service. For example, a claims-processing application uses the information-sharing capabilities of a database to store account information, interpersonal communications to route claim forms among multiple reviewers, real-time conferencing if two or more reviewers wish to jointly discuss some aspect of a claim form, and interoffice automation to analyze financial aspects of the claim.

Ultimately, CSC helps people communicate and collaborate by providing an infrastructure that enables any member of a group to communicate with any other at any time or from any place. With any-to-any communication, a user has the ability to communicate with one or more users, choosing the level of interaction most suited for the purpose. "Anytime/anyplace communication" refers to the idea that users must be able to send information in either broadcast or interactive mode and must also be able to retrieve information at any time, regardless of the location of other people or the information.

The "mail" by which team members collaborate now commonly embraces fax, voice, and electronic mail. Efforts are underway to build electronic-mail systems that will allow group members to send and receive messages using a variety of data types—text, graphics, images, audio, video—over various electronic communication channels. Although it is as easy to send and receive messages from within applications as it is to print the information, the real breakthrough for mail and CSC applications has come from the transparent access to other users over interconnected corporate and public networks.

Early local-area-network-based e-mail systems were designed for the workgroup and did not provide security, communications, and processing capabilities that could be used effectively across the enterprise. Now, as mail systems are being segmented into "open" clients that can be used from a wide variety of personal computers and other devices, there are also messaging servers that can scale to the needs of the enterprise. As CSC applications are fitted into distributed databases and other applications, an enterprise messaging system is vital as the transport link connecting individuals or teams of workers.

CSC makes possible computer-mediated conversations that use electronic mail, database, or group-discussion technologies to allow two or more people to interact in real time or in a time-deferred mode. As information becomes a much richer resource, technology companies will need to find ways to remove traditional barriers of time and location in offering simple and transparent access to the new messaging services.

In the future, as messaging systems are implemented to take advantage of the digital communications architecture, personal computers will be better integrated with two of the most important information and message-delivery systems: the telephone system and cable. Automatic acknowledgments will inform users when messages have been delivered. Filtering mechanisms will receive, categorize, and prioritize messages on behalf of users. Users will receive and act upon their messages at any time from any place, using computers or other devices.

The personal computer will, in fact, replace current message systems, since it will gather electronic mail, voice messages, faxes, phone slips, and other forms of communication into one integrated messaging system. A single "in box" on the graphical user interface screen will list all types of messages, and there will be an interface to support voice commands that, in turn, can control the system and speech synthesis for information delivery. This system will also be customizable so that users can select different formats or media for sending or receiving messages, even offering filtering or prioritization.

Software systems on networks will be so sophisticated that ever more routine tasks will be performed automatically, providing monthly summaries of various messaging and task transactions, much like a bank statement today. Personal digital assistants will be able to integrate messages with information from a variety of sources.

Since businesses and individuals will all have on-line in boxes, many coordinating, scheduling, and confirmation arrangements will be made automatically. A mailbox for messages won't be a physical place; it will be a defined set of parameters that can proactively coordinate functions and, at the same time, be open to anyone anywhere with proper security privileges.

The expectations of information accessibility will change. Eventually, people using digital or wireless networks will want their data in a multimedia format, as well as wanting more general services, news, entertainment, and reference information to be readily available. To make many of these messaging capabilities available to a broader range of users, telecommunications companies will provide electronic mailboxes, voice mail, video mail, classifieds, directories, and information-search services. But, as customers entrust their personal data to communications companies, they will expect the freedom to access it anywhere at any time with a variety of new devices.

In essence, CSC uses computers to supplement the way we communicate with one another in a workgroup, an organization, or an enterprise. Although the first attempts at personal-computer productivity software were heavily dependent on text or numbers as the primary mode of expression, CSC relies on rich and natural data—images, voice, and video—to create a more sensory approach to learning and communication.

Putting Intelligent Agents to Work in Workflow Processes

Interoffice automation allows computers to closely simulate the way people work in organizations; for example, to facilitate the automation of related tasks in a company's operations. This automation of interrelated tasks—usually called *workflow*—is accomplished by the "intelligent" or specifically defined routing of electronic forms, essentially moving a piece of work from one person to another on the network. Through electronic mail, these forms and any relevant data are circulated to designated individuals on the network, who must process, approve, or in some way be notified of the task or the end results.

In addition to helping users communicate and collaborate, with CSC the computer expands its traditional role of automating tasks that users find tedious, boring, and repetitive. Many business procedures lend themselves to computer automation, including expense reports, claims processing, travel approvals, and status reports.

Most likely, many of these workflow functions either will be incorporated into or will work in conjunction with other applications, such as workgroup spreadsheets or databases, that will automatically tabulate the results, summarize the findings, and process the results.

As these CSC applications become more sophisticated, it will be possible to establish certain preset thresholds for approvals, ordering, requests, or other common office jobs. When the aspects of these functions that most require judgment are performed by office workers, highly intelligent systems will operate as file clerks and move the order or request through the appropriate electronic offices or checkpoints required to process the item. These systems will include built-in logs that provide managers with daily summaries of automated tasks that have been performed.

An early example of such an application is a networked multimedia training program at a telecommunications company. Since the company requires its employees to review monthly developments in new regulations and policies, a whole layer of management was needed just to handle the paper flow for the 50,000 or so employees who needed to see that information. By implementing an automated, interactive multimedia system that can present the information, quiz the employee, and bring about a review of the mistaken entries, it was possible make the material more interesting and shorten the time it takes an employee to review it. To help with auditing, the system also creates a list of employees who have reviewed the data for managers, and alerts those individuals who have not signed onto the training system that month.

In an automated, decentralized work environment, team members constantly create information that they want to share—documents, reports, memos, papers, spreadsheets, photos, audio tapes, and video tapes. To accommodate this need, these files are stored electronically and in hard copy.

In the future, information will be shared by capturing, storing, searching for, retrieving, displaying, editing, and printing electronic documents stored in an electronic file cabinet. Powerful query utilities will help users locate desired information. When a team member checks out a document from the electronic file cabinet, a copy will always remain there for other team members to access.

This component of CSC applications provides users with access to both highly structured information (e.g. from databases) and highly unstructured information (e.g. from human interaction, news feeds, information bases), helping them to make more informed decisions. In addition, by combining data or information from both types of sources, CSC opens up new ways of doing business or communicating that simply weren't possible without electronic document storage and retrieval.

For instance, the daily output of government information—rulings, press releases, studies, records, and requests—can be made available on line at a fraction of the cost of producing and disseminating it on the paper. With this type of information available to be downloaded to corporate electronic file cabinets for a fee, this information could be used to make more accurate decisions, speed the process of communication, and make information that is now difficult to obtain more readily accessible.

In addition to text and numerical data, the electronic file cabinet will be able to store sound, video, images, and graphics, thus extending the notion of a corporate database in a dramatic way. Multimedia files could make it possible for companies to develop new applications. Real estate companies could show pictures of properties. Multimedia databases could reinforce their files with the pictures or video segments needed for an insurance file or a legal briefing. And multimedia data could be stored in an object-oriented environment to be reused as components of other programs, thus saving time and resources on programming. In addition,

PC users will be able to access these compound documents from one common, intuitive human interface that incorporates voice and handwritten text annotation.

Like workflow, automation is also being used for tasks or processes in information access, retrieval, and delivery. These automated information-processing systems will evolve to address major corporate applications. In the same way that manufacturing systems were automated over the previous decades, many customer-service applications will be automated to be made more efficient, cost-effective, and flexible to various modes of inquiry.

For example, an investment banking firm seeking to establish the status of a trading order for a customer could request the information by voice, electronic mail, or fax; all would be recognized instantly by the CSC application. The system could access the customer's file in the order-processing database and deliver the information in whatever format the customer requested. Some of these new CSC applications will even employ "agents" (intelligent modules of software and data) to process information that would otherwise require human intervention.

In this way, the use of intelligent agents is much like that of server-to-server procedures in distributed database environments. In a database, when a set threshold is violated, an alert is triggered that activates a database process. Intelligent agents also perform tasks and activate application processes. They will eventually do more.

One day intelligent agents will operate as personal assistants on the digital communications infrastructure, running errands, tracking down details, checking on facts, returning simple messages, and searching databases. Potentially, an intelligent agent could search databases listing available products, find a product, and alert someone to approve its procurement. Agents will grow in sophistication as there are CSC applications and network services to support their interaction on either a network or the digital communications infrastructure.

How will intelligent agents work in the year 2000 and beyond? In the virtual office, many common tasks and jobs will be done by agents. Since all forms of electronic equipment will be connected either by wires or by wireless communications, many operations will be automatically "monitored" to ensure that consistent or expected operations are maintained. For instance, users will choose the news sources that affect their business and social interests. Agents will be able to check news, entertainment listings, and even classifieds to locate appropriate events or items. Then the agent could compile and sort the list before presenting it in fully integrated multimedia format. If a user wanted to buy a car, the agent could show available cars on the market that meet the user's specifications. If a plastics business wanted to move into a new international market, the agent could gather information from international news sources.

Agents will operate as personal assistants. They will be as flexible and powerful as the communications networks supporting their interaction will allow, redefining in some ways the nature of purely human work. Agents will play a pivotal role in an information-driven culture that needs faster and more efficient ways to gather and store information.

A Virtual Community: The Telluride InfoZone

Located in the picturesque mountain town of Telluride, Colorado, the Telluride InfoZone is a pilot project designed to explore community development and education in rural areas through the use of information and telecommunications technologies.

In the first phase of the project, completed in 1993, a dedicated phone-circuit connection was established to Colorado Supernet/Internet providing local access and a gateway connection to commercial networks for any personal computer users in the town or the surrounding area. The InfoZone is also initiating the beginnings of a Community-Wide Information System (CWIS) that utilizes added channels on the existing cable TV system and public-access computing stations.

"The InfoZone intends to be a site-specifically pragmatic response to our community's needs and desires and an intelligently creative model that can be used by other communities," explains Richard Lowenberg, program director of the Telluride Institute, a nonprofit organization that is developing the InfoZone. "By considering the social and economic impact of these new technologies on previously isolated rural communities, the InfoZone hopes to be a long-term research and test-bed project that, by example, hopes to promote an ecology of the information society."

Along with the Telluride Institute, the public library, the school system, the medical center, and local governments are participating in the creation of a virtual community database connected to a growing web of global databases. The InfoZone aspires to be an electronic library for its community.

The InfoZone is developing a research alliance with universities and corporations to closely examine the social, political, and cultural implications of creating a "telecommunity" of rural computer-literate citizens who gain high-speed telecommunications access to anywhere in the world. When it is not necessary to be near commercial or transportation centers to accomplish the required tasks, the work force can live and work where it is most affordable, desirable, or practical.

Lowenberg believes Telluride will be a place of new and fresh ideas. "Communities like Telluride will become vital economic engines in the information society and highly attractive nodes in a global telecommunications web," he says.

Implementing CSC Enterprise-Wide

In the first CSC applications, which arrived in the early 1990s, it was common to find various messaging, database, directory, security, and communications services built into the application (as in Lotus' Notes). Since standard distributed services or interfaces are emerging for these areas, CSC applications can now be built on top of the operating system and the network services.

For example, the use of intelligent agents will require standard messaging interfaces and fast, transparent network access to allow the transmission of multimedia data. In most cases, objects or self-contained software modules containing both data and the instructions on how to use the data will be used for those purposes. Since objects encapsulate the data and instructions inside their structure, they can contain different types and amounts of data: video, millions of records, or a simple command. Since common interfaces are being defined for how objects interact over a network, it is likely that the agents of the future will be objects on the move.

But enterprise-wide CSC applications will not be implemented on a large scale until corporations define the underlying architecture that can facilitate this level of transparent data access on the network. For many corporations this will take time but still will most likely be implemented as a distributed object computing model by the late 1990s.

However, in highly regimented organizations where control of computing resources is centralized, information systems managers may be responsible for the development and deployment of CSC applications, with workgroups and end users playing the role of consumers.

In addition, for organizations with independent remote offices or task-specific groups that do not need to be part of the enterprise network, a strategy that allows these users freedom to develop custom CSC applications should be encouraged and documented. The strategy should include recommendations on the look and feel of the user interface, the security considerations, the documentation requirements, and the eventual distribution and deployment of the applications on the corporate network. Examples of such applications could include a department-wide workflow forms-routing application, a task-specific mail-enabled application using attachments, or an application designed for a proven workgroup collaboration environment (like Lotus' Notes) with easily modifiable templates. In some cases, linking messaging and database functions on the corporate or campus network will be a good start.

Whichever strategy is followed, there are basic requirements for supporting CSC applications in a network environment. First-time adopters of CSC applications should start with a test application in a workgroup environment. This will help the organization understand and learn the capabilities of CSC incrementally without incurring major risks. In addition, a specific training and support plan for the CSC application will help ease the transition from personal applications to collaborative applications.

The Infrastructure of the Networks and the Operating System

As the acceptance of CSC applications grows within an organization, it is critical to adopt standard network and application services. The ability to quickly replicate databases and update information on users' systems requires highly efficient and powerful networks and servers. In addition, a high level of fault tolerance is required. For example, certain messaging and database applications, such as banking operations, require successful updates for a transaction to be completed. The failure to register a deposit accurately could disrupt critical payouts, credit ratings, and asset-aggregation data.

CSC applications mandate a consistent way to locate and access users, resources, and devices on the network, usually accomplished through a network naming service. The capacity for communication should be facilitated via a powerful and intuitive naming convention.

A consistent naming services architecture—to be provided, ideally, through the network—needs to be developed and should follow the formats most consistent with the organization. Searches through wild cards, aliasing, and yellow pages within the naming system must be supported. For example, a naming convention that uses several different layers of parameters would be very beneficial in performing searches on a large enterprise network. A multiple capacity to search on name, department, organization, or location would prevent users and devices from getting lost on the network.

Information systems managers also need to guarantee consistency across desktop and portable platforms in the organization. Minimum requirements must be set and standardized for all hardware and software components. For example, CSC-enabled systems should have adequate processing power, graphics, adequate disk storage, a fast network connection, natural data support (audio, video, etc.), and support for the leading graphical user interfaces. Whenever possible, companies should also try to select standard applications for word processing, spreadsheets, electronic mail, drawing, and so on. This level of standardization helps in ensuring consistent capabilities and minimizing support problems.

Supporting anytime/anyplace communication also requires a robust, high-speed (14,400 BPS) remote access or dial-in support for the network. The objective of providing this kind of a capability is to ensure consistency of access regardless of location. For example, a person using a CSC application from a laptop computer on a business trip should be presented with the same environment and usage model as an in-house user.

Finally, the security and integrity of data are major concerns in the enterprise-wide deployment of CSC applications over a corporate network. A clear strategy and guidelines must be established to ensure that information is accessible only to authorized users, that information remains intact, and that changes can be tracked and traced.

Messaging and Database Standardization and Integration

Messaging and database access are crucial to the deployment of CSC applications. Although different messaging and database systems will continue to be used, standardized access and greater integration of these programs will be required for future CSC applications.

Electronic mail is the simplest form of a CSC application. For CSC to gain acceptance and for users to understand the benefits from CSC, information systems managers should provide e-mail and messaging capabilities at every desktop and portable device. Providing e-mail on every system also provides a consistent and standard base for future e-mail-enabled CSC applications.

Standardization on e-mail application programming interfaces (API) at the client personal computer is the first step in the process. This guarantees that all applications deployed in the enterprise are communicating to a single, standard API, regardless of which messaging server is being accessed. Another standardization requirement is to establish the type and richness of data that can be sent through gateways to other e-mail systems. Since messaging systems differ, it is not always possible to know what types or formats of data are supported for communication to another system.

For example, a Windows user sending mail to a user on the UNIX-based Simple Mail Transfer Protocol (SMTP) may have difficulty with embedded objects that may be used to store video segments. This problem will be solved through standards for the various aspects of messaging, including the format, the communication, and the storage of mail files.

Databases are also crucial to the deployment of CSC applications. While there are databases that work only as proprietary solutions, there are a number of client/server databases that support broader access through standard client interfaces. The tight coupling of messaging server functions with databases affords a highly effective transport mechanism for inter-platform communication.

A client/server approach in both messaging and database gives companies greater flexibility in mixing and matching client applications with different servers. Cooperative and distributed applications can be designed to provide CSC capabilities.

Application integration is very important to any CSC applications strategy. In order for a CSC application to be fully utilized, other applications must be able to run in conjunction with it in standard graphical operating environments, such as Windows.

Vendors of CSC applications need to provide consistent and easy-to-use development tools. These tools should help managers develop ways to oversee the deployment and the tracking of the application across the enterprise. Such tools should provide support for managing application distribution, information dissemination, security, and monitoring performance.

CSC applications for use throughout the company should also be scalable from a workgroup to a department to an enterprise. This is a very important aspect of CSC because in most cases CSC applications will be used in small groups before being distributed across the enterprise. An enterprise CSC application should be designed to scale to larger platforms encompassing more users, more locations, or more servers.

Support of Natural Data Types

CSC must also communicate in the user's language. The networked computer world uses graphics, audio, and video as well as keyboards. Determining the type of data required will help managers of information systems understand and prepare for capabilities that are required of personal computers. For example, companies requiring voice annotation and audio conferencing need to invest in audio boards and dedicated phone lines.

The level of information flow required by audio and video is difficult to incorporate into computing, because audio and video require enormous bit storage and network capacity. Advances in semiconductors have enabled silicon technology and software to squeeze down these images to a much smaller number of bits. In addition, new hardware and software offerings keep improving the quality of video playback on personal computers.

Intel, with its Indeo technology, offers a standardized software video playback mechanism for personal computers that use Intel processors, going back to the Intel386 chip. Because Indeo technology is scalable, the size, resolution, and smoothness of the video improves as the chip is run on more powerful central processing units. The use of dedicated video hardware also improves the quality of the video. Future versions of Indeo technology will compress video to even smaller file sizes, making it less onerous to send video files over phone lines.

The Power Spiral

CSC requires high-performance processors. There is always a need for more performance, because next-generation software is developed to run on the current high-volume CPU. The software runs slowly, however, because developers put on "bells and whistles" and load down the CPU, requiring another generation of CPU to run the software well. At Intel, this phenomenon is called "the power spiral."

To illustrate this spiral: the 8086 and the 286 volume were driven by the success of the IBM PC. They used 16-bit software based on DOS. Then came the Intel386 microprocessor, which ran 16-bit software better and faster. Gradually 32-bit software was developed for the Intel386 CPU, but it really took the power of the Intel486 chip to run the software well. The power spiral motivates us to bring higher-performance CPUs to the personal computer.

If we break the personal-computer microprocessor market into three segments, we see at the high end the computers used for critical business tasks and organizational group work. Typically, these computers cost over $5000. In the middle range ($1000-$5000) we see broad business and home use. At the low end we have computer users who are very price-conscious. Their home computers often supplement work that they do at the office, so software compatibility is important. These computers are sold by mass merchandisers and typically cost below $1000. Let's use this model to review how the insatiable appetite created by the power spiral is being fed.

Every three years or so, a new processor family comes out to occupy the high end of the market. In 1985 it was the Intel386 processor, in 1989 it was the Intel486 CPU, and the cycle continued. The Pentium chip has taken the high-end position. The Intel486 processor dominates the mid-range market, and the Intel386 CPU is obsolescent. Such developments keep the power spiral rising.

The Pentium processor is more than twice as fast as the highest-performance Intel486 processor, and it brings new capabilities previously found only in mainframe-type applications. This processor is 100 percent compatible with all the previous software written for the Intel X86 architecture. When the Pentium first arrived, the business world had made the Intel486 architecture the processor of choice for personal computers, partly due to the appearance of large numbers of Intel486 CPU-based computers at prices below $2000.

At the same time, the Intel486 DX2 microprocessor became popular because it permitted the processor to run internally at twice its normal speed without requiring the rest of the computer to speed up. It is easy for Intel's original-equipment-manufacturer customers to adopt this technology and bring this higher performance to the marketplace, because they can reuse their existing designs. In the lower end of this three-tier market model, the Intel386 CPU had become the standard architecture for personal computers in the sub-$1,000 market, meaning that many first-time users started out on 32-bit Intel-based machines.

The Future of CSC Applications

It is essential that information systems managers clearly identify business requirements, such as the linking of geographically dispersed groups for tasks that warrant CSC. In many cases, the deployment of CSC applications will save enough to make a real, positive difference to the plans for a program or a product. These benefits should be documented and researched to provide a clear understanding of the quantitative and productivity gains associated with the use of CSC applications. Identifying the savings associated with CSC can also help justify the purchase of equipment required for deployment. For example, insurance companies spend millions of dollars on forms and on their processing. A demonstration of CSC's capacity to save money and raise productivity in processing claims should really get management's attention.

Most large organizations have no idea of how work really flows through the system or of how the company gets things done overall. Workgroups that have processes and methodologies quite distinct from the company's standard ones are often unaware of or indifferent to the differences. It is very important for enterprise-wide deployment of CSC that those in charge of information services understand the range of processes and methodologies within the enterprise's various workgroups. Understanding these needs will clarify the mixture of choices.

Just-in-time business requires CSC applications. To support CSC, personal computers will need to continue to have increased processing power, be more portable, be better connected to other computers, and support a wider range of data types.

CSC applications provide a new approach to computing that allows intellectual property to be harnessed and disseminated across the organization.

One of the biggest benefits of CSC will be its ability to provide users with transparent and quick access to all the relevant information necessary to fulfill a task, no matter what type of data is used and no matter how or where it is stored. For example, CSC applications will be used to gather data from multiple types of computers and networks and provide the user with access to that data from a single graphical user interface on a personal computer or a mobile device.

Treating the network as a single computer, CSC masks the network's underlying complexity from the user and combines database, communications, and messaging technologies to increase collaboration and access to information. CSC will also provide highly flexible and efficient dissemination of information to individuals, functional groups, organizations, or diverse combinations of groups through selective broadcast facilities. With electronic mail, the originator of the information must target recipients for specific messages; with CSC, database applications can propagate the information among all authorized users, thus reaching a far wider audience.

An equally important aspect of the technology is the automation of expensive and time-consuming tasks.

CSC enlarges the range of the people involved in completing the tasks. By their very nature, CSC systems provides their users with access to qualified and skilled individuals within and outside the functional group without those users' needing either to have heard of them or to know where they are to be found. In this way, these CSC systems will serve as the basis for a powerful and distributed bulletin-board-like system. Using a computer for discussion, brainstorming, and problem solving also reduces the level of inhibition many people may have in expressing their opinions in a public forum.

The intelligent use of electronic mail and databases in a CSC system will provide a repository for the collective intellectual property of the organization—an asset greatly underutilized today. Today much of the work in an organization never goes beyond oral discussion and handwritten notes. Since people are a vital asset in an information-driven culture, it is vital to find a way to capture electronically as many ideas and discussions as possible. CSC applications will serve as a repository for the collective intelligence of a group of users who contributed to any discussion held or any work done on a particular subject.

Although the benefits of CSC are numerous, its acceptance in the office still faces many challenges. The annual market for CSC applications is now more than $1 billion, but there are many factors holding back the growth of this new area. Although ultimately the payoff from CSC comes from the ability of different people and systems to work together, it is often difficult to overcome the communications and interoperability hurdles involved in linking people and technology in enterprise-wide operations.

The lack of training and support is certainly slowing the acceptance of CSC. Successful CSC implementations require grassroots buyer programs and a high level of integration and support. Few vendors can afford the investment, and few integrators are able to handle the long sales cycles required by interdepartmental decision processes. For years, Lotus shouldered the responsibility of selling Notes through a direct sales force in order to absorb and control the risk of "missionary sales" in a new market. As the market matures, Lotus and other vendors are turning to companies that want to leverage the profit potential of CSC applications on what would otherwise be commodity-priced network installations.

Moreover, successful implementation of CSC requires that individuals adapt the technology to a fundamental reshaping of more efficient work processes and procedures. This can be difficult when key individuals involved in the task or project have difficulty changing from ingrained work habits or procedures. Some people prefer to work alone and may not want to participate in electronic group discussion. The fact that users can now easily be mobile or remote presents new management challenges, as well.

There will also be technical problems, including the lack of client versions of CSC applications to support all platforms within the workgroup or organization, incompatibilities among complementary workgroups, limited platform performance, and network operational problems due to increased traffic and bandwidth constraints. There are many horror stories about companies' spending months or years trying to fit together all the pieces of the hardware-and-software puzzle. Nothing works perfectly "out of the box" when network complexities and multiple operating systems are involved.

Organizational issues also play a role in the acceptance of CSC. Some people resist out of the fear of being deprived of privacy or autonomy. One of the primary reasons management in major corporations has slowed the movement of mission-critical applications from mainframes to networking has been the lack of distributed management tools and the possibility that access to vital corporate data will be harder to control. Certainly new CSC applications that make information available to users anytime or anyplace require dependable security at the network and application level.

It is very rarely possible to implement a strategic corporate application without the endorsement of senior management. That is why it is advisable to include senior managers in the planning and review cycles of the CSC application. Once they become aware of its potential as a flexible tool for collaboration and for the automation of workflow processes, these managers can become internal evangelists for the CSC application.

However, despite any of these obstacles, the market forces driving just-in-time business will force both vendors and corporations to find cost-effective and timely means of persuading their people to welcome CSC and its possibilities. In fact, CSC applications will prove to be essential for businesses that are dependent on rapid access to and dissemination of information within and outside the organization. As the use of computers at home and at work increases, existing boundaries, expectations, and definitions must give way to the unlimited possibilities awakened by the emergence of CSC.

Since much of the new development of CSC applications will be done by means of object-oriented technologies, it will be possible to create interdependent, reusable software modules that can serve as building blocks for various aspects of CSC applications. In this way, messages composed of sound or of full-motion video can be integrated with other objects storing relational data from a corporate database. This approach to software development will benefit all businesses, but it will be especially beneficial in those industries that require companies to respond rapidly to competitive pressures—for example, financial and banking services.

In 1977, Citicorp was able to differentiate its service through the introduction of automated teller machines. Only a few years after their introduction, ATMs were commodities. Although the bank wanted to move quickly to introduce new services, it was hampered by the complex and lengthy process of software development. Citicorp turned to object-oriented programming for its development environment. This approach, which allowed the bank to rapidly develop the internal CSC applications that management needed to collect and analyze market information, also enabled the bank to quickly design and implement new banking services. Object-oriented design allows technologists and end users to work together to have the application closely simulate actual work processes. Since common portions of applications exist as objects that can be quickly and easily reused for other CSC applications, Citicorp now has more flexibility in identifying and responding to its market.

In a similar way, telecommunications firms have used object technologies for years to create and manage new phone services. Since many of the elements of any phone service (such as billing or customer information) are repetitive, the phone company can reuse those modules in order to design and develop services more quickly. CSC applications automate many of the tasks of monitoring and managing the operation of these services.

In 1990, executives in the oil and gas industry recognized the need to share data in order to minimize the risks and costs associated with the exploration and development of new oil reserves. To formalize the agreement to work together, they formed the Petrotechnical Open Software Corp. (POSC), a consortium of over 50 organizations, including the leading petroleum companies, service companies, and research organizations of eight countries. POSC is defining the specifications for a software integration platform in which software and hardware vendors can supply applications to the oil and gas industry. One of the key objectives of the effort is to manage huge amounts of data from various databases and business applications. CSC applications that facilitate the gathering of data from various industry sources are expected to help the oil and gas companies get better technical results and better analyses.

In another example, a major computer company is testing the use of computer screens, built into the backs of airplane seats and linked through a local area network, for collaboration and discussion among passengers. It is expected that, if the pilot program is successful, this airplane network, supporting full multimedia, will be used in the next few years for collaborative work and entertainment throughout the airline industry. Eventually, the network is expected to be connected to other public and private networks, allowing passengers to send and receive messages via satellite.

Along the same lines, remote access will also be facilitated by personal digital assistants (PDAs). Although some PDAs are being designed to be as thin and small as a wallet, some of these devices are expected to include a built-in cellular phone. With cellular phone network coverage all over the globe by way of satellites projected to be in orbit by the late 1990s, these PDAs will allow CSC applications that can truly break through previous limitations of time and place. Integrating telephone service and messaging into a single device for scheduling, data access, and mail will make it possible to introduce a new generation of CSC applications.

In publishing, there will also be dramatic changes. In terms of on-line information services, the amount of electronic information available is small compared to the amount that is produced in print and other traditional formats. Multiple forms of publishing, including print, images, music, and video, will be combined into multimedia databases, with users employing CSC applications to search, collect, and combine data from various sources to create presentations, messages, reports, news, entertainment, and other types of products.

For much of this digital information, there will be virtual libraries that will automatically manage the access and the fees associated with intellectual property rights and then be able to ship the information over the appropriate data highways to the requester. As information is gathered from electronic public discussion forums conducted on interactive discussion-like databases, the reports on what has been gathered could be periodically broadcast over the communications network to subscribers.

At this stage, the uses for CSC applications appear limitless. As more and more information services and databases support greater interactivity, users will take advantage of messaging to query, to respond, and to share information that otherwise would be communicated in more static environments. Taking advantage of networks and the emerging digital communications infrastructure, CSC will help bring order and structure to the largely undefined realm of interactive multimedia and information processes.

The Fall of Software's Aristocracy: Realizing the Potential of Development

Scott Brown

The history of all hitherto existing society is the history of class struggles.
—Karl Marx and Friedrich Engels

The world watched in awe and anticipation as the Berlin Wall came down, heralding the fall of the Soviet empire. "The masses" would no longer be controlled by self-serving bureaucrats preaching liberation but practicing a hideous form of aristocracy. Social and economic freedom came into the hands of individuals. The opportunities are theirs to capitalize on or to squander.

We are poised on the brink of a revolution with the potential for greater economic impact worldwide than the fall of communism. It will be a revolution in computer software, currently the domain of computer scientists and highly trained professionals. Over the next decade the development of application software will shift from the technological elite to the software proletariat. Emphasis will shift from large, horizontal, shrink-wrapped offerings for the masses to individually developed custom creations based on widely distributed software components called *objects*.

The tools now being created will allow computer users without programming skills to design software for their individual needs. Nearly everyone who uses a computer, from elementary school students to baseball coaches to accountants to scientists, will have this freedom. After all, these are the most qualified people to develop such software, because they have the best understanding of what is needed. We envision a world where every application program is custom developed by and for the end user. Simplifying the development of computer software will give individuals easy access to the tremendous power of computer technology in a way that will complement personal needs and habits. The long-promised potential will finally be realized. The impact of this change will be astounding.

Imagine that you are sitting at a workstation. In front of you is a marketing study saying that more widgets could be sold over the phone if the caller's name and number were to be delivered to the sales operator's screen while his line was ringing. In one part of the workstation's screen is a browser for scanning and selecting icons. Each icon represents a block of functions that perform specific tasks. There are icons for building customer data records, for answering the phone, for constructing billing screen outputs, for collecting digits from a touch-tone phone, etc. Using the mouse to identify your choices, you select icons by dragging them from icon browser and dropping them onto the palette (a blank area in another part of the screen).

After identifying which icons are needed and placing them on the palette, you begin to construct the logical flow of the application by identifying which icons are successors to other icons in the flow. The logical flow represents which events are performed in what sequence. For instance, you select an icon labeled *CallersName*. An information window and help screen tell you that *CallersName* captures the name delivered by the phone company when a call is connected to your factory. You connect *CallersName* to an icon labeled *FindCustomerDataBase*. Such connections are accomplished by first pointing with the mouse to *CallersName* and dragging a line to *FindCustomerDataBase*. The information window informs you that *FindCustomerDataBase* can accept a customer name and will search the purchase-order history for past sales to this customer. You then connect *FindCustomerDataBase* to *DisplayOnOperatorConsole*.

The tool you are using is a visual programming environment. It allows you to develop an application program by selecting icons, connecting arcs, pruning a graphical tree, condensing limbs, and zooming on icons instead of by the traditional method of using a language such as COBOL or C. Dynamically, the visual editor prevents the joining of icons that cannot be logically connected. You would hear a beep if you attempted to connect *CallersPhoneNumber* to *DisplayCallerName*. As successor paths are identified and validated, arcs appear on the screen and connect the icons. The icons with their connecting arcs form a flow chart that graphically represents your program.

At any time during this process you can simulate your program. Simulation allows you to try your program in a safe, controlled environment and get immediate feedback about how well it works. You decide to proceed by clicking the mouse on the Simulate button. The simulator displays the graphical representation of your program with the icons and their connecting arcs colored blue. As the simulation continues, the icons change to green when they are running and to gray as they are completed. An error is indicated by a red or yellow icon along with an explanation of the error and suggestions for correcting it.

By alternately creating or modifying portions of your program and immediately simulating its execution, you are able quickly to complete and refine the software you have created. Once you are satisfied that your program works as intended, it is subjected to a battery of tests. After these tests are completed, you are given a report that describes any defects and an estimate of the computer resources required to run your program. The whole process is completed and the new application is deployed in less than a day.

Computer hardware technology has advanced rapidly during the past two decades. At the same time, the demand for new software applications has outpaced our capacity to create them. Corporations, faced with stiff international competition, are turning to information technology as a means of improving productivity, which further increases the demand for software. Yet computer users struggle to remain current with an industry in which product life cycles resemble those of first-run movies. Technology now allows many things that were impossible only a few years ago: speaker-independent voice recognition, dazzling multimedia presentations, data communications at speeds exceeding 100 million bits per second. Such capabilities are now economically viable for many uses. But they are not in widespread use, because the software required to apply them is missing. The inability to realize the full potential of these technological advances causes immense frustration.

Trained programmers have traditionally been required to develop application software. They are skilled in using computer languages and algorithms, but they often know little or nothing about the actual problems they are asked to solve. Developing a software application requires those who understand the problem to communicate their knowledge to the programmer(s) involved. Because this is a complex, error-prone process, critical information is often not conveyed. The results can be programs that don't perform as intended and further frustration among those who expect computer technology to boost productivity.

Developing software with traditional programming languages (such as C, COBOL, Pascal, or C++) is difficult and time consuming. Long development cycles can result in obsolescent applications. Many corporate information-technology professionals are mired down just keeping their company's systems operational and have little time to develop new applications. Moreover, less technologically sophisticated users often do not understand the possibilities offered by computer technology and therefore make little use of them.

Personal-computer-based spreadsheet programs, such as Lotus 1-2-3, were the first software tools to offer nonprogrammers a limited ability to customize the software for specific applications. Users found that capability so attractive that they could justify the purchase of a personal computer on the basis of a spreadsheet program. What is needed is a software-development environment that extends the full capability of computer technology to nonprogrammers by allowing them to develop their own programs.

Emerging software-development tools will resolve many of these issues and unleash a new era in application software development. These tools include a visual programming environment, commercially available libraries of software objects, the ability to simulate the execution of a program, and facilities for version control and application deployment.

Visual Programming

Visual programming will dramatically simplify the building and maintaining of software. By expressing programs in visual rather than textual form, we can achieve the same productivity gains now associated with the graphical user interface (GUI) of operating systems such as Macintosh and Microsoft Windows.

Figure 1 shows the visual representation of a program segment that replaces hundreds of lines of C or C++ code in a windowing application.

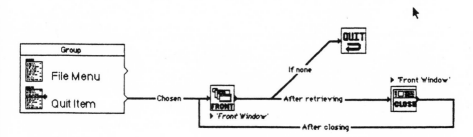

Figure 1

In a typical windowing application, it is necessary to make sure that all windows have been closed before the program terminates. In order to translate this requirement into an application using a visual programming tool, the logic is interpreted as follows:

• When *Quit Item* in the *File Menu* is chosen, the *Front Window* is retrieved and is passed to *Close Window*.

• After closing the *Front Window*, the program loops back to retrieve the next *Front Window* until there is no front window, at which time *Quit* is executed.

This program segment can be briefly described as follows: When the Quit menu item is chosen, the program closes all windows that have been created and quits.

Visual programming tools associate graphical icons with objects. Software objects are computer programs created in a very disciplined way such that data and methods for accessing and manipulating data are encapsulated in a single unit. Encapsulation is the property of objects that requires that data be accessible only through well-defined methods. Each instance of an object may have different data values, but the methods are the same. For example, the object *Bank_Account* might include data elements such as *Name, Address, Account_Number,* and *Balance* and methods such as *Deposit, Withdrawal,* and *Change Address.* Each instance of *Bank_Account* will have different values for *Name, Address,* etc., but the methods will be the same. New objects can be constructed from combinations of existing objects, and they inherit the properties of the objects used in their construction. A new object called *Checking Account* could be based on the *Bank Account* object. Figure 2 is shows the *Amortization* method from a *Loan* object written in C++. (The entire

```
void FAR PASCAL _export AmortizationFunc(pAEvtInfo, pAObjMessage theSystem)
    {
    OBJECTID oiLoan ; // the ID of the Loan Object
    OBJECTID oiPayment ; // the ID of the temp object holding the payment
    LoanData far* pLoanData ; // pointer to a structure with default values
    long double loanValue ;
    int periods ;
    long double interest ;
    double payment ;

    oiLoan = AFuncGetTypedParameter(1, OTYPE_LOAN) ;
    pLoanData = (LoanData far*)AObjLockData(oiLoan, 0) ;
    if (pLoanData == NULL)
        {
        theSystem->message1 = 2 ; // follow flow #2 (ERROR) and return
        return ;
        }

    ONmbrGetReal(pLoanData->oiLoanValue, &loanValue); // Get value of object
    periods = (int)ONmbrGetInteger(pLoanData->oiPeriods) ;
    ONmbrGetReal(pLoanData->oiInterestRate, &interest) ;

    if(loanValue < 0 || periods < 1 || interest < 0)
        {
        AObjUnlockData(oiLoan, 0) ;
        theSystem->message1 = 2 ; // follow flow #2 (ERROR) and return
        return ;
        }

    payment = CalcPayment((double)loanValue, periods, (double)interest) ;

    oiPayment = AObjCreate(OTYPE_NUMBER) ; // Create a temp Number Object
    ONmbrSetReal(oiPayment, payment, TRUE) ; // Set the value of the object
    AFuncSetParameter(1, oiPayment) ; // Output this number object

    if (pLoanData->oiPayment)
        ONmbrSetReal(pLoanData->oiPayment, payment, FALSE) ;

    AObjUnlockData(oiLoan, 0) ;
    theSystem->message1 = 1 ; // follow flow #1 (SUCCESS)
```

Figure 2
AppWare Loan object's amortization method (copyright 1993 Novell Inc.).

object is several hundred lines of code.) Figure 3 shows an icon that could be used to represent the *Loan* object.

In order for a visual programming environment to be effective, the objects being manipulated must have the proper granularity. Granularity refers to the level of functionality encapsulated in a single object. Whereas constructing a program using fine-grained (low-functionality) objects will typically require many objects to complete the task, a program constructed using coarse-grained (high-functionality) objects requires only a few objects.

Objects can be differentiated by their granularity. At one end of the granularity spectrum are massive horizontal applications such as Lotus

Loan

Figure 3

1-2-3 and WordPerfect. Such applications are software components at an ultrahigh level of functionality. At the other end of the spectrum are C++ classes (i.e., language objects), each of which provides narrow functionality. In any given application, hundreds or even thousands of classes might need to be combined.

There is a threshold of object granularity above which visual programming fails. If one simply replaces a line of C or C++ code with a picture or an icon, tens of thousands of icons are needed to represent a complete program; the area of screen or paper required to express software logic increases to the point of unmanageability. The usefulness of icons in GUIs comes from their ability to hide underlying detail. Doing the opposite—displaying the full detail of code-level logic in a visual metaphor—is not particularly helpful. At the level of C or C++, textual representation of code is preferable.

As the software objects becomes coarser-grained (in other words, as the software components become more functional and intelligent), visual programming technology becomes more appropriate. If one can represent 1000 or 10,000 lines of traditional code with a single icon, then the visual metaphor is efficient and powerful. By combining two dozen icons, a user can develop a sophisticated application equivalent to tens of thousands of lines of code.

With tight encapsulation of coarse-grained objects, the quality, consistency, and reliability of derived applications can be extremely high. All program "bugs" arise when a programmer manipulates data in an unintended way. As the number of access points to data increases, the likelihood of introducing a bug increases. By restricting access to data to a limited set of methods, the use of objects in the construction of programs tends to reduce variability and improve quality. Applications constructed from high-quality objects are likely to be high-quality applications and can be developed without detailed knowledge of the objects being used.

Despite the benefits of larger software objects, a contrary force also emerges as software components become coarser. The flexibility to build a custom application diminishes as the software objects grow in size and functionality. To illustrate this point, consider the construction of a house. If the house is built of fine-grained objects (boards, nails, wire, bricks), there is a great deal of flexibility in customizing the arrangement of these objects. It is possible, however, to speed construction by using prefabricated, coarse-grained objects (walls, rafters, even rooms). As the coarseness of these objects increases, the ability to customize the house decreases. Just as these coarse-grained construction objects are made up of fine-grained objects, coarse-grained software objects are often constructed by combining fine-grained objects.

When software is developed using fine-grained objects, nearly complete control can be maintained over every aspect of the program. Any function can be developed, and underlying system software routines can even be overridden if necessary. When applications are constructed using very coarse-grained objects, much flexibility is lost. The resulting program may be large and cumbersome and may lack desired custom features.

The use of prefabricated components in constructing a house improves productivity and reduces the skill level required to assemble the components by reducing the complexity of the task. Likewise, as the coarseness of objects increases, visual programming tools will improve productivity and decrease the required skill level. Visual programming environments are most effective when it is possible to combine a few objects to do a big job.

Clearly, the need for flexibility must be balanced with the need for efficiency. As software components become coarser, the usefulness of visual programming increases. At the same time, the flexibility of development decreases. At some point, the lines representing these two tendencies cross. That intersection represents the critical combination of flexibility, granularity, and usefulness that marks the ideal visual programming environment.

It is important to note that both fine-grained and coarse-grained objects are important and useful. Just as it is not possible to build a house using only prefabricated components, it is not possible to develop software using only coarse-grained objects. A combination of objects of varying granularity will be required to complete the job.

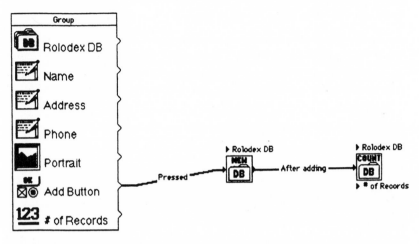

Figure 4

Novell's Visual AppBuilder attempts to draw the ideal compromise between the effectiveness of visual programming and the flexibility of development. AppWare's software components—called AppWare Loadable Modules (ALMs)—are much larger and more functional than C++ classes, but are much smaller than large commercial applications such as Lotus 1-2-3 and WordPerfect.

The snapshot from Novell's Visual AppBuilder shown in figure 4 is a segment of an electronic rolodex application. A database object called *Rolodex* contains the data elements *Name, Address, Phone,* and *Portrait.* The Rolodex object also contains a Button object, which is used to create a new rolodex "card" and which then return a count of the total number of "cards" in the database.

Visual programming will create two classes of programmers:

• Professional programmers, who will develop systems software and object libraries using a combination of traditional languages such as C++ and visual programming tools. They will handle the details of interfacing with operating systems, networks, storage devices, etc.

• Users of visual programming environments (visual programmers) are usually consumers of object libraries and other "shrink-wrapped" software. These programmers will deal at a higher level of abstraction and won't need to be concerned with the details of how the underlying system works.

These two groups will work at different levels and have different needs. The visual programming environment will have to accommodate both groups. AppWare, for example, provides two levels of object control and communication: one is for object creators (the professional programmer) and is invisible to object consumers (the visual programmer); the other is for object consumers and is invisible to object creators.

Commercially Available Objects

Since objects are the raw material used by the visual programmer to create and modify applications, the usefulness of visual programming will depend on the commercial availability of objects. The emergence of visual programming will create a segment of the software industry in which the focus will be on developing and marketing software objects. These two forces will build on each other—the widespread usage of visual programming will motivate professional programmers to create more objects, and the commercial availability of high-quality objects will make visual programming more attractive. Market forces will ensure the proper granularity of objects, as visual programmers will purchase those objects that provide the right combination of functionality and flexibility. By making technology accessible to most people, visual programming is likely to expand the market for computer products, making it very lucrative for the software companies that create the best-selling objects.

It is important to remember that software objects are constructed using other software objects. This provides a convenient mechanism for one person to build on the work of another. Over time, commercially available objects will become richer and functionality will increase.

The leading software companies of tomorrow are likely to sell both objects for use by visual programmers and complete application programs such as word processors or spreadsheets. There is a high degree of synergy between these activities. Software companies will use the objects they create to develop applications in a visual programming environment. For example, suppose NuSopht is a leading supplier of software objects for the visual programming market. Since NuSopht is a major source of the raw materials required to develop software applications, it is well positioned to develop and market its own applications. Using visual programming, NuSopht develops an electronic mail program, MediaMail, that allows text, graphics, audio, and video to be sent in mail messages. The MediaMail product includes not only the application program but also the visual programming environment used to create it. By selling the product in this form, NuSopht will encourage customers to customize the application, using visual programming. It will also increase the market potential of future add-on objects. The creative efforts of millions of people are likely to be focused on developing extensions to popular products.

Simulation

An essential element of a visual programming environment is simulation. Simulation allows the visual programmer to visually trace the logic of the program that has been created. Simulators display the tree of icons and arcs that represent the program and visually follow the step-by-step execution of the program. The icons are often color coded: gray for completed, blue for pending, green for executing, yellow for exceptions, and red for fatal errors. The display shows icons changing color and data values changing as the execution proceeds from icon to icon.

Simulation gives the visual programmer the immediate feedback necessary for rapid iterative development cycles. It encourages experimentation, and it will bring out the best in application developers as ideas will be refined to levels not previously practical. It is also an aid to quality. The powerful visual metaphor will exaggerate logic errors that may have otherwise been difficult to detect.

Version Control and Application Deployment

Visual programming will give application developers the ability to create new versions of programs at an astonishing rate—perhaps several per day. At this rate it will be difficult to keep track of which version is current or which version should be used at different locations in a network. The tools required to solve this problem include version control mechanisms and application deployment mechanisms.

As new versions of applications are completed and become ready for deployment, responsibility shifts from the application developer to the operations management group. The operations management group must have mechanisms to clearly identify each version of an application for several reasons, including these:

• There may be times when it is necessary or desirable to switch back to a prior version of an application.
• Some applications may be custom developed for each user.
• Applications distributed internationally may have different versions to support different languages.

Whatever the reason, the operations management group will need the ability to monitor and control which version of an application is running at each location. This must include the ability to change or upgrade the version of an application running on a single workstation or on every workstation in the network.

The tools and mechanisms for software management and control exist today. However, they must be integrated into the visual programming environment. This will occur as part of the natural evolution of visual programming.

Economic Benefits

The traditional approach to software development usually involves a group of several individuals, some programmers and some nonprogrammers. This approach is inherently inefficient for several reasons:

• The communication problems extend beyond the nonprogrammer/programmer issues. As their number increases, communication between programmers and other programmers becomes more important and difficult as well. The difficulty of coordinating the efforts of a large group of programmers cannot be overstated.
• It is very common to discover that the problem being addressed by a software development effort is not very well understood. Often even the most outspoken proponents have only a general understanding of what they are trying to accomplish, and this often results in software that must be discarded once the problem is really understood.
• Nearly everyone underestimates the difficulty of the job being done. Software development is difficult to estimate because projects frequently have enough unique aspects to make it difficult to base estimates on past performance. Programmers usually underestimate because they don't understand the problem, nonprogrammers because they don't understand the complexity of developing a solution.

• Whenever more than one person is involved there are usually disagreements about priorities and about approaches to solving the problem. This is another cause of software that must be discarded or significantly reworked.

As a result of these factors, software projects are notorious for taking longer than expected and costing more than anyone estimated at the outset. Visual programming will improve the efficiency of software development in the following ways:

• The use of visual programming will dramatically reduce the size of development teams (possibly to one), and the communication required will be reduced correspondingly.
• When the process of application development is faster, a lack of understanding will be discovered sooner and therefore cost less.
• Since visual programming dramatically reduces the time required to develop software, the impact of underestimation will be diminished to a tolerable level.
• Smaller teams usually means fewer disagreements.

As a result of these changes, the productivity of application software developers will improve at least an order of magnitude. Application development will become an infinite and thus inexpensive resource.

Marketing as the Bottleneck

The process of creating software has traditionally been the bottleneck in the development of new applications. However, once it is possible to develop and distribute applications in a single day, the time *for* marketing rather than the time *to* market becomes the constraint. This will significantly change the software sales cycle. Features currently available only through lengthy custom development will be easily provided.

Here is how the sales and development cycles may become intertwined:

"Thank you for meeting with me," says Jane, the sales representative for the local phone exchange.

"No problem. I was interested in your ad and called your sales center to download your demonstration program. We are interested in your ability to customize your services to our specific needs," replies Tom, local owner of a small chain of pizza stores. "And we already have a service developed with help from your support staff."

Jane sets her laptop computer on the conference table. "After the demo program ran, it asked you some questions and faxed your answers back to us. On the basis of those responses, I believe we can provide just the solution for your needs," she says, turning on the laptop. "As I understand it, you currently maintain a central phone number where your customers can place orders. The current application then routes the call to the store that is nearest the caller."

"Yes. This was an improvement over having the customer look up the nearest number to dial. But what the fax from the demo doesn't mention is that we want to field mobile vans with ovens. These mobile ovens will receive calls via cellular phones and bake the pizzas while en route to the delivery point. But how do we route to the nearest van? How do we even know where the vans are?"

By now the color screen on the computer shows the logo of Jane's company. "Let's see," Jane murmurs as she examines a row of graphical buttons and clicks on the one labeled Edit Service. A box with a question mark appears and asks: 'Enter current service name.' Jane enters 'Tom's Terrific Pizza'. "The cellular modem is calling the billing center to retrieve your records," Jane states. After a moment the screen clears and is replaced with a diagram of Tom's current service.

Jane begins by pointing at the first icon after the one labeled *Start*. "Your subscription is for basic number delivery with geographic routing. The first icon is labeled *Call Delivery*." After she selects 'Examine Icon' from the menu, a window opens, listing the features of call delivery that Tom has selected. "You have chosen to receive the customer's name, address and phone number. This is received by your answering computer before the caller hears the first ring. From there this information is passed to a database that we maintain for you." Next she examines the Search icon. "This object uses the caller's number and searches the database for the nearest store." She pauses to scroll the screen, as the service cannot all be seen at once. "We then place a call to the store and connect the caller, who now hears the phone ringing. Approximate elapsed time for the caller is 2 seconds."

Tom continues: "Ultimately, on our display phone at the local store, you show the caller's purchase history and last purchase made. We still choose to have a person answer the phone, I still don't like voice response units."

Jane makes a mental note to later demonstrate parallel voice processors. "Do you want to modify your current service or create a new one?"

"I want a new service. The stores will be converted to walk in traffic only. All deliveries will be made via the vans."

"OK. Let's edit this to what you want."

Another set of icons appears. "These are our features available to mobile customers. As I propose it, instead of placing a call to your store, you will now want to place the call to the van nearest the caller. I know we have an icon that determines the location of the mobile phone that is nearest to a specific address, but not to a list of phone numbers. I'll need to call back to the office for programming help."

With that, she hits some keys on her laptop and a telephone pad pops up. She types in a number, and the laptop makes a wireless telephone call. Over the speaker from the laptop, a voice says "Hello, Jane. This is Tina."

"Hi, Tina. I'm here with a customer and I've got a question. We want to select the closest location to an address, but we want to select the closest from a list of mobile numbers. The palate I've got will only return the location from one mobile phone, not a list. Got any tricks you're holding back?"

"No, no tricks. I've retrieved your screen and I see the problem. Wait a sec, I'll send you another choice." After a pause, the voice speaks again as a new window opens on the laptop's screen. "I'm sending you a module we developed for another customer that does the same thing. Watch, I'll insert the logic just after you receive the customer's call." The windows change sizes, and the original screen returns. The *Call Delivery* icon changes colors, and the new icon, *Select Nearest Mobile Phone,* appears beside it. A line appears, connecting the two. The distant voice continues its narration.

"You still get customer information delivered by our telephone switch. The caller's phone number is now passed to the *Select* icon. I've retrieved your mobile numbers and initialized the list of numbers for the *Select* module. If they ever change, just use the modify window to adjust the list. The *Select* module will locate the mobile phones within the network and return the number of the phone nearest the caller. The rest of the service will remain the same, except the call will be routed to a van instead of one of your stores. Just to show you how it works, we'll let the laptop simulate the new service using your phone number." The laptop's speaker makes the sound of a telephone ringing. The *Start* icon changes from green to gray. Tom decides that green must mean active and gray must mean completed. Finally, Tom hears one of his van installers answer with a crisp pizza-van greeting. Jane points to the speaker on the laptop, and Tom takes the hint. "Hi, Bill. Just me. How's the installation coming?"

Bill finishes the status report and hangs up. Tom then tells Tina that the service was satisfactory. But then he asks: "You said this was done for another customer. Can you tell me who?"

"Let me check," Tina continues. "We develop logic modules either for general release or for exclusive rights. Exclusive is more expensive because we can't reuse it. This module was paid for as a 'general release' module by Gina's Gourmet Delivery. Looks like Gina should have paid to keep the module exclusive. You're going to build on her efforts. Jane, talk to you later. Bye."

The laptop's speaker falls silent. Jane produces a disk from her pocket and copies the service from the laptop. "Here's the copy for your use. When you are ready to turn the service on, select the Initiate option from the menu. We will receive a work request in operations and your billing will begin."

Tom thanks Jane as she packs up her laptop. She is already planning her next visit, which will be to a local medical specialists' practice. She is going to sell them the same geographic routing service, but first she must change the pizza box icon to a stethoscope, the pizza company's logo to a hospital cross, and the icon of the van into a convertible.

Beyond Visual Programming

Most of the basic technology described thus far is available today. However, it needs further development and assimilation to meet the objectives that have been outlined. Visual programming tools need further development to make them easier to use and more intuitive. There also must be a critical mass of commercial-grade objects available in order to make visual programming an attractive option. I am confident that this development will take place as companies invest in products for the visual programming market. The assimilation process, however, is much less predictable. Even though personal computers have been available for more than 10 years, there are still many people who are not comfortable using them. Symbolic of this apprehension is the number of video cassette recorders that still flash 12:00 because the owner is reluctant to learn how to set the clock. Overcoming these phobias will be a major challenge in the decade ahead. Of course, public education is vital to this effort, as is training for those in the workforce. But the assimilation will truly happen when we are immersed in the technology. Just as color television was viewed as a novelty in the early 1960s, a significant portion of the population today views the computer as a novelty. We need to stop viewing the computer as a novelty and start viewing it as a significant multipurpose tool.

Concerning visual programming, we are definitely in the early adopter stage of the product life cycle. The tools are still immature and require a significant amount of technical sophistication, but significant productivity gains can be achieved by those who are ready to use them now.

This process of refining and assimilating visual programming will take several years, and even though it is a tremendous step forward it will fall short of the goal of true computing freedom without the addition of some key technologies. These key technologies include fuzzy logic, speech recognition, and artificial intelligence.

The visual programming environment will be refined and simplified to the point that most people will be able to easily learn to program their computers. The problem that still remains is that for most people the logic of programming is an unnatural process. It contradicts the way we think. For example, the natural way to program a traffic-activated traffic signal might be 'When traffic is *heavy*, keep the green light on *longer*.' This program is easy for most people to understand, but is difficult to translate into a computer program because the terms *heavy* and *longer* are not specific. But the use of such ambiguous terms may be required to make programming understandable by untrained computer users. Fuzzy logic is a software technology that provides techniques for dealing with the ambiguity of human thought processes. It will provide a means of expressing terms such as *heavy* and *longer*.

Fuzzy logic, as a technology, will be invisible to the visual programmer. It will be incorporated into the objects created by professional programmers. We will likely see fuzzy objects (encapsulating fuzzy logic) as important additions to visual programming environments. Fuzzy objects may have the same names as other objects. The *ProcessLoanApplication* method within the *Loan* object, for example, may approve loans when the applicant is *close* to the payment-to-income ratio as long as the applicant's credit rating is *good*.

By merging speech recognition and artificial intelligence into the visual programming environment, the computer will become an intelligent assistant to help us with the programming task. Through these technologies, we will be able to develop programs by talking with our computers. Rather than create applications object by object, the intelligent assistant will create sections of logic based on verbal descriptions and previous conversations concerning the application. The visual programming metaphor will still apply—object icons and their logical connections will still appear on a screen. The intelligent assistant will become a personal programming coach, providing suggestions, interacting with the visual display, and providing information on the pros and cons of various approaches to solving a problem. It may also be possible to delegate such tasks as documentation, collection of measurements, and software management to the intelligent assistant. This conjures up images of HAL in *2001: A Space Odyssey.*

A conversation with a digital assistant might go as follows:

"Good morning," said Dan to MIDGE, the computer mounted on the kitchen wall. "We need to review the thermostat object—the heat ran all night, and I woke up several times with a dry throat and nose."

The dim screen brightened and displayed a visual program. "Dan, I think the problem was the humidity. It was 20° below zero last night, so the heat had to stay on to maintain the temperature. The thermostat object does not adjust the humidity as the outside temperature drops."

Dan looked at the program on the screen and said "I thought I bought a new thermostat object that adjusts humidity."

"The thermostat object in use is the one you wrote last summer, but there is a new one in the object library," replied MIDGE.

"Replace the thermostat object with the new one and display it on the screen," said Dan, irritated that he had forgotten to do this earlier. Satisfied after examining the visual display of the new object, he turned to fix breakfast. "One last thing, MIDGE. If Compcor stock is still trading below its historical average PE ratio, place an order for 500 shares."

We are entering a new world where software development is no longer limited by resources. Just as microprocessors have made processor power virtually limitless, the ability to rapidly develop or modify applications will be viewed as infinite. The only limits will be our creativity. Infinite processor capacity and infinite applications-development capacity will make computer technology applicable to almost any problem. Programming a computer will become as commonplace as programming a microwave oven. It will become a part of everyday living. Computers themselves will be less prominent as components of the infrastructure of homes and offices. Computers will be viewed as appliances that can be easily programmed to handle foreign currency trading or monitor the activities of household appliances.

Tightly encapsulated software objects are the software equivalent of hardware integrated circuits. Just as integrated circuits revolutionized hardware development, software objects will revolutionize software development. The visual programming environment can be thought of as a computer-aided design tool for software. It can be used to arrange objects to create programs, to control development such that only valid operations are included, and to provide rapid prototyping capability. Visual programming will enforce standard ways of connecting and interacting with objects. Some may view this as restricting creativity. To the contrary, it will focus creative effort where it will be most productive: on creating new objects and on combining objects to create new applications.

The software aristocracy has long held control over all software development, including applications. This has been mostly out of necessity rather than choice. Those who benefit the most from new or modified applications will have the ability and the motivation to take control of application development. Just as the fall of the Berlin Wall is bringing sweeping changes in Europe and Asia, these changes will dramatically change the business landscape. Though it is difficult to comprehend the impact of this change fully, it is clear that—like the recently liberated residents of Eastern Europe—we have before us an opportunity that we can either capitalize on or squander.

Acknowledgments

I would like to acknowledge the assistance of Joe Firmage and James White.

Naturalware: Natural-Language and Human-Intelligence Capabilities

Gustave Essig

"The time has come," the walrus said, "to speak of many things,
Of shoes and ships and sealing wax, of cabbages and kings,
Of why the sea is boiling hot, and whether pigs have wings"
—Lewis Carroll, "The Walrus and the Carpenter"

Why are computers still so difficult to program, so time-consuming to learn, and so hard to use? The answer is simple and obvious: computers cannot communicate with human beings in the same way that we communicate with one another. We humans use *natural language.* Computers, lacking this capability, have not been able to exhibit the levels of intelligence that we normally assume in human interaction. The difficulties of using computers remain so extensive that most people choose not to use them at all (except maybe for games and entertainment with little functionality and simple interfaces) unless they are forced to in their job or profession. In fact much of the potential power of these new computer systems is unused—and wasted.

The lack of natural-language capability (the way humans *communicate*) and human-intelligence capability (the way we *think*) remain major barriers to usefulness and to future computer capability, both in terms of programming and in terms of human-computer interaction. It is also the reason software development remains an enormous and expensive undertaking and the reason it is so costly for organizations to implement advances in computer capabilities.

Computer scientists have created a great many different programming languages. They have similarly created different kinds of knowledge-representation structures to store and access data for these languages to manipulate. One result of these efforts has been an explosion in "off-the-shelf" programs. Sadly, despite tremendous effort and investment, these programs remain very "user unfriendly".

Software systems engineers face many of the same challenges as their earliest predecessors in computer software design, including how to make computers easier for people to communicate with and how to make computers more intelligent. An understanding of how natural language works has proven elusive; indeed, after nearly half a century of intense effort, determining what the "rules" of natural language are has been much more difficult than anyone had imagined.

In spite of dramatic increases in computer speed and memory capacity and even specific functionality, not only has the dream of human-like machine intelligence not yet been realized, but it seems with each passing year to be further from becoming a reality. We have yet to build a computer that has any reasonable degree of human-like intelligence, except in very limited knowledge domains. The term "artificial intelligence," originally introduced in the 1950s, has proven an appropriate description for computer capabilities that emulate only a small subset of human reasoning. Computer intelligence today is indeed very limited. It is not natural— it is "artificial."

Software engineers continue to try (so far, unsuccessfully) to move from data bases to knowledge bases, from word processing to knowledge processing. Yet whenever software development has run into human language and human reasoning it has ground to a halt. Voice recognition alone could offer vast productivity increases. The mechanics have been perfected, but problems with semantics (meanings in language) remain.

Where computer science is now most challenged is not in developing better-performing hardware, although that race is certainly continuing, but in improving software design so as to make the computer a still more functional tool while at the same time minimizing the difficulties of using it. Essentially, this is a challenge to develop better *human* communication and intelligence capabilities.

Computers continue to lack important practical capabilities that, if achieved, could make all the past achievements in computer science pale in comparison. Natural-language and human-intelligence capabilities will have tremendous benefits for human-computer interaction and for communication. If present communication and intelligence limitations could be removed, or even significantly reduced, not only would productivity greatly increase, but in a practical sense the current very high human cost of computer use would dramatically decline.

The Human Cost of Current Software Limitations

The human (i.e., personnel) cost of computer use has long since far exceeded the costs of hardware and software, and with new programs and functionality making computers harder to learn and to use the human cost is steadily increasing. At the outset of the computer industry, and for many years, the high hardware and software systems costs far outweighed the human costs of computer use. Human-computer productivity did, however, significantly improve with the explosion in the use of low-cost microprocessors and mass-marketed software produced for them. With advances in hardware capabilities came increased software functionality, accompanied by increased complexity. Until recently, however, program developers managed (more or less) to shield users from this increased complexity. (Programs that did more were not necessarily harder to learn and to use.)

However, we are now facing much longer learning curves, more difficult use, and, as a result, increasingly lower real computer productivity. This has several direct causes. Computer systems continue to migrate from expensive mainframes to moderately priced minicomputers to low-cost microcomputers. From a few well-trained computer operators, the class of users has expanded to include millions of novices. Faster and more powerful hardware is preparing the way for new software capabilities (e.g. audio, video, groupware). The integration of existing applications and capabilities with new ones has made programs appear even more complex to the users. The result of these increases in program complexity is that the major cost of implementing and maintaining computer capability has shifted from the cost of the machines and the software systems that run them to the cost of the people who use them.

A computer is a complex tool that can be made to be almost chameleon-like simply by changing its software. But no longer is a computer user expected to know just one program. The constantly changing (and improving) software that massive commercial software-development efforts have produced (corresponding largely to increases in hardware power) has yielded many different kinds of software *systems,* including these:

- operating systems
- network systems
- interface systems
- application systems (word processing, spreadsheets, graphics, database management systems, communications, multimedia, etc.)

Not only is each of these "systems" composed of different kinds of software that each do a specific job, but within each system are many different programs offered by various software vendors. Each program, even if developed by the same vendor as another system, has a unique "interface language." Those "interface languages" consist of what is called the "user interface," which amounts to all the specific actions that the user can take to command the software to execute its functions. The actions most often consist of typing command words, pressing keys, and/ or using a mouse to point a cursor at a word or an image on the monitor screen. Other communication methods are occasionally used, including limited voice recognition and touch and pen-based input screens, but text, key, and mouse input are now by far the most common.

The many different "languages" all these programs use to communicate with us are not at all like the natural language that we use to communicate with one other. Try as they might, software developers have yet to crack the mysteries of natural language—at least not sufficiently to mimic on a computer system the far greater capabilities of natural language. As a result, almost every computer user must learn not one but many different computer interface "languages." Although they are not at all similar to our natural language(s), they are "languages" nonetheless, because they are the systems we use to communicate with computers. In fact, every programmer and every computer user must constantly reduce the complex requirements of what he or she wants the computer to do into a number of much simpler actions. In other words, users must *translate* their needs, whether consciously verbalized or not, into the available functions of the interface language that the computer currently is using to communicate with them.

In an attempt to make this translation easier, in the last few years the use of simple pictures (called "icons") in these user interface "languages" has largely replaced word and key input, resulting in what is called a "graphical user interface" (GUI). This attempt to solve the problem of human-computer communication has had some success, and nearly all new programs that are designed to be used by nonprogrammers now use this approach. However, simple pictures convey little of the enormous information-content capability of natural languages and do not represent a significant interface advance. (I am reminded of primitive men who drew pictures on cave walls before the advent of language!)

Now different programs may use similar or different command words, keys, and/or icons to represent many different kinds of actions: some simple, some complex, some with "hidden" and far-reaching consequences. To learn to use a program, one now must learn what each command word, what each keyboard key or key combination, and what each icon means—all, of course, in terms of human (i.e. natural) language. For example, a user can point to a small picture of a printer and click a mouse button, which might be equivalent to the command "PRINT SCREEN" or saying to the computer "Convert the numerical equivalent of the images on the screen into a specific sequence of numbers that will cause the output of the printer to duplicate the appearance of the screen on paper, and then send those numbers to the printer." Many programs give you several ways to accomplish the same thing. For example, if you want to print out a quarterly accounting report, you can type "PRINT RPT(QTR)", or push the Alt-F6 key combination on the keyboard, or use the mouse to point at and click on an icon that looks like a miniature report with a Q on it.

Today the commands in many programs are grouped in hierarchical menus of keywords or icons, with each keyword or icon signifying a particular action. (Seldom-used commands are rarely represented by icons; already there are so many icons that often the user must know what icon menu a particular icon is on in order use it.) Let's say you need to change the resolution of the computer screen in the middle of using a program. That doesn't happen very often, so you are not aware that there is any icon for the resolution-change command(s) (or you don't remember what the icon looks like or where it is). First you must remember what the specific keyword is to change screen resolution in this particular program. Then, if you remember that, you must guess which major category the keyword is in (out of eight), then which subcategory (out of sixteen), then which sub-subcategory (out of six). If you guessed wrong at any point and it's not there, or you were trying to find the wrong keyword all along, you're lost.

A single program might use many hundreds of textual commands, key combinations, and icons. A single user commonly uses many different application programs, different interface programs, and maybe even different operating and networking systems. And, to make matters worse, user interfaces keep changing as new programs (and new versions of the same program) are offered. Recent attempts to standardize the various application interfaces by using an additional layer of programming to create an "interface system" (such as Windows) have done little more than encourage the addition (but not yet the replacement) of text or key commands with developer-specific icons.

In addition, the ongoing integration of programs and program capabilities, as well as computer network communication, adds still further to the complexities faced by computer users. For example, spreadsheets and graphics are integrated into "presentation software packages," word processing and graphics are combined to offer "desktop publishing," and database and communications and word processing are united into "personal information managers." The impending integration of the computer, the telephone, and the television is a staple of feature stories in magazines and newspapers. We read that word processing, spreadsheets, graphics, database, electronic mail, facsimile transmission, audio, and video are together evolving into comprehensive "desktop communications" software.

Intercomputer communication adds still more complexity. Computers now often communicate with other computers over local-area networks, which are becoming wide-area networks and international wide-area networks (such as the Internet). This progress in developing, updating, and integrating software is both remarkable and expected. The need for such functionality is unquestionable. However, all this functionality increases difficulties for the user and greatly reduces productivity. The result is often fatal to widespread use.

The interface and intelligence limitations of current software, coupled with the increasing number of available programs and the constant changes to these programs, have added tremendously to the time requirements and the difficulties of computer use. This is especially true when there is a need to use many different programs (e.g. in a business or a profession), each of which gets updated or replaced almost annually.

Remembering how to use what amounts to thousands of specific functional text commands, keys, and icons, each of which mean different things in different programs, is an enormous educational challenge. The task is now so daunting and time consuming that it is rare that an individual can adequately learn one program before it is time to learn new ones. Formal user training is an expensive investment, especially in view of the nearly constant retraining that is necessary. For practical reasons, learning how to use a program now is often on a "need to know" basis. User manuals (both in print and on line), how-to books, software support personnel, and computer gurus are all taking bigger and bigger chunks out of otherwise productive time.

All the improvements in hardware and software capability have greatly expanded what an individual person is potentially capable of accomplishing with a computer. But the cost is very high: *greatly reduced use* and *significant reductions in real productivity*. Learning how to use a single computer program with hundreds of commands is an expensive investment in time and effort. That investment is multiplied by the number of different programs each person uses (or should use) and by the number of people in the company or organization that must productively use all those programs. And all this is due to the continuing lack of adequate human (i.e. natural) communication capabilities.

Another critical consequence of this lack of natural-language capability is that computers cannot exhibit broad intelligence capabilities that are associated with normal human interaction. The reasoning power of computers today is so minimal that programmers and users must not only decide what specifically it is that they wish the computer to accomplish, they must often supply the intelligence (i.e. the knowledge and reasoning power) that the computer needs to execute their commands and accomplish the desired tasks.

What is preventing the development of human natural-language and human-intelligence capabilities in computer systems? Has computer hardware performance not yet reached high enough levels? Do we not have a sufficient understanding of how the human brain produces natural language and natural intelligence? Or is there something so fundamentally wrong with the way software is designed that without a major change it will not be able to break through the barriers that, thus far, have prevented human language and intelligence from being incorporated into computer system software?

The answer might be surprising. Brilliant work over the last 10 years or so in many areas outside of computer science, including neuroscience, linguistics, cognitive science, and philosophy, has led to fundamental insights into the structure and function of language and intelligence, including how they are functionally produced by the human brain. This research now offers a much clearer understanding of the human brain's cognitive and linguistic functionality. However, those developments also reveal that software design as it has been done since the computer was invented has basic functional and knowledge-representation deficiencies. It is primarily these deficiencies, and not the lack of computer processing power, that have prevented software developers from bringing natural-language and human-intelligence capabilities into the world of computers. These functional deficiencies can be traced to the origin of software itself.

The Software Model for the Digital Computer

In the beginning, there was the theory of the Universal Turing Machine, based on the principles of mathematical logic. Then there was the hardware of the very first electronic computers (ENIAC in the United States and Colossus in England), which were built from thousands of electronic switches that could be automatically turned on and off very rapidly, controlled by hundreds of other switches. Then came the idea of the stored computer program (first formally described by John von Neumann and first embodied at the British Radar Research Headquarters), with once-manual "program" switches now controlled by hundreds and then thousands of instructions (or "rules") stored in various memory mediums. And with the "soft" ware came the data—the quantification of the variables that the software instructions used to turn those many switches on and off. Switches, instructions with variables, and numbers. Hardware, software, and data. The computer was born.

In 1935 Alan Turing was not interested in automatic computing machines. Conceptualized visually, Turing's calculating machine was an endless strip of paper tape with squares on it in which data (symbols) could be encoded. A read/write device could read the symbol(s) or write new symbol(s) on any one square on the paper tape at a time, moving it back and forth as necessary. The "program" that controlled the read/write device consisted of a series of instructions ("functions") to be executed, and that program and the data upon which it acted were all pre-encoded on the paper tape. The simple functions envisioned by Turing included "Read the symbols in one of the squares on the tape," "Write a symbol in a square on the tape," "Move the tape one square to the right," and "Move the tape one square to the left."

Turing's concept arose from a direct effort to reduce complex computation procedures into a small set of elementary operations (functions). Turing reasoned that, since humans methodically follow simple rules to change one set of numbers into another set of numbers, a mechanical device could do the same thing. Replace the input set of numbers and/or the rules and the machine would produce an entirely different output set. Turing found that sequential repetitions of these elementary functions could replace virtually any mathematical operation, no matter how long or complex. The computing machine Turing envisioned was thus a "universal" machine that could perform any kind of computation.

With Turing's calculating machine used as a guide, the first electronic computing machines were built. Programmed to accelerate the human performance of arithmetic calculations, they were first used to replace human "computers" in breaking codes and calculating ballistics during World War II. (The machine was called a "computer" not because of what it could do but because the people who had done this job were called "computers.") The early nonmilitary applications included calculating census statistics and (in the television introduction of the computer to the public) predicting the results of elections.

But Turing saw that there was more to this new machine than met the eye, so to speak. He realized that it used symbol manipulation to emulate the results of the brain functionality which we call "calculation," and he realized that symbol manipulation could be used to simulate other mental functions. In fact, he proved that his new machine was a universal machine that could simulate any other process or machine that could be described by mathematical logic.

Because of important parallels between the new machine and the human brain which were then clearly evident, the invention of the electronic computer in the 1940s spawned widespread speculation by many eminent people that the functions of natural language would soon be simulated on a computer and that "disembodied intelligence" was inevitable. This created the specter of powerful man-made nonbiological brains that would one day compete with (and, many thought, ultimately exceed) human intellectual capability.

Like the hardware of electronic computers, the human brain also basically consists of many switches. With enough switches, and the right rules to control those switches, and the appropriate data, it seemed quite plausible that an electronic brain could do anything that a human brain could do: calculate, talk, even think. Much as we had built and then (in just a few decades) substantially improved mechanical horses and birds that could go much faster and further than their biological counterparts, it was often asserted, it would not be long before this new "brain" machine would be faster and smarter than any human biological brain.

At first, programming a computer to have natural-language and human-intelligence capabilities seemed to be fairly straightforward. Just as the rules of mathematics were replicated in a computer, so (it was thought) the rules of natural language and human intelligence could be identified and replicated. Human language and reasoning had been targets of philosophers, logicians, and mathematicians since Socrates and Aristotle. The way our brain works, the "laws of thought" (coined by Boole in 1854), had been described variously by rules in the form of logical statements, axioms, theorems, and predicate calculus. With all this tremendous intellectual effort already completed, surely it could not be too difficult to use these logical rules (and new ones if necessary) to develop a system that could emulate the human language and reasoning processes.

Some of the earliest computer pioneers were very excited about this possible result of their work. Turing himself suggested in an early paper ("Computing Machinery and Intelligence," *Mind*, 1950) a simple but seemingly objective test (now known as the Turing Test) for those who might claim such a result. He suggested that we answer the question "Can a machine think?" by comparing computer intelligence with human intelligence. The test consists of a human and a computer system answering questions asked by a human "judge." Intelligence is ascribed to the computer to the extent that the human judge cannot distinguish the responses as being provided by the machine or by the other human. There has even been a suggestion of a "reverse Turing Test" in which a computer and a human ask questions of a third human who must judge the origins of the questions.

Thus far, however, all attempts to develop software to achieve natural-language and/or human-intelligence capability in a computer system have failed. Computer scientists have yet to imbue the computer with any significant natural-language capability, or even one that can carry on a simple human-like conversation. Needless to say, no computer system has come close to passing the "simple" Turing Test, and the human-computer communication blockage remains. We seem to have reached a barrier in the effort to design software that can exhibit significantly greater human-like functionality, specifically natural language and human intelligence. The barrier seems to be not physical (hardware) but intellectual (software).

It is becoming more and more apparent that the problems involved with simulating human language and intelligence have now left the hardware (physical) arena. Even in the infancy of the computer industry, computers were amazing machines, solving mathematical problems at speeds no human could match. And they were much better at storing and retrieving data than a human brain. Today, with microprocessor chips containing millions of transistors and operating at speeds that exceed 250 million cycles per second (compared to billions of neurons that fire only 1000 times per second), computer systems are (grossly speaking) approaching the theoretical performance capabilities of the human brain.

The barrier that has prevented the development of natural language and intelligence is not one of operation; it is one of *function*. In spite of some very general surface similarities, the human brain's operation is significantly different from that of today's single-processor digital electronic computer. More important, however, so is its functionality. Both the bird and the airplane exhibit the function of flying, but their operation in doing so is very different. Function is the result of operation, but substantially the same functionality can be produced by different operations. Think of the car and the horse, the camera and the eye, and now the computer and the brain.

Computers, with software based on the mathematical logic of the Universal Turing Machine, were not meant to be "brain machines" in the sense of producing the same functionality (in other words, the same results) as the human brain. *Computers were designed to be, and with the ways software continues to be developed still are, only "logic" machines.* They exhibit the functionality of mathematical logic, nothing more.

However, compelling new research now strongly indicates that the human brain, functionally, is not simply a "logic" machine; its "reasoning" capabilities go far beyond the functions of mathematical logic.

While computer scientists have struggled for decades without significant success to build a computer system that has substantially the capabilities associated with human language and intelligence, significant progress has been made in other seemingly unrelated areas in understanding the *functional* operation of the human brain, including new understanding of the mechanisms of natural language and the basis for real or "natural" (as opposed to "artificial") intelligence.

There is increasing evidence from areas far outside of computer science—neuroscience, linguistics, cognitive science, and philosophy—that the processes by which human intelligence capabilities are produced by the brain incorporate functionality that extends beyond existing mathematical logic, knowledge representation, and sequential program execution paradigms, and that this functionality is embodied in the production of natural language and "human" intelligence.

The intellectual barrier faced by software designers appears now to be that there is much more to natural language and human intelligence than is currently within the realms of logic or mathematics, and consequently beyond computer science in its current state.

Beyond Logic and Data

We have always used physical or conceptual models to create machines that improved upon the functionality of the products of natural evolution. One could suppose, for example, that a rock and a stick became a hammer and then an ax. A round rock with a hole in it and a stick may well have been the inspiration for the wheel. The horse-drawn carriage with a gas engine (less the horse) became a car. The way birds flew were the inspiration to construct mechanical gliding and then flying machines. The human arm was transformed into the crane, the ear became a microphone and a speaker, the eye became a camera, and so on.

But the model used to create the electronic computer (and the software to control it) wasn't the human brain: computers were not designed to broadly emulate brain functionality. The model wasn't intelligence; it wasn't natural language; it wasn't even a brain function, neuroscientifically speaking. The model Turing used to conceive a computer was basic, simple, mathematical calculation, and underlying the processes of calculation were the functions of mathematical logic.

The multifunctionality of a Universal Turing Machine is obviously very important to its acceptance and increased usage. The computer is not a single machine; today it can be programmed to function as one or more of a wide range of machines: word processor, database management system, graphic arts studio, financial modeling and analysis system, expert system, etc. Uniting all these different functional machines is mathematical logic. Regardless of its transformation, regardless of its program, the software computers use today is conceptually designed like Turing's first computer; it remains a machine based on the principles (and hence the functions) of mathematical logic.

Unlike such breakthrough hardware developments as the integrated circuit and the microprocessor, software design has *not* fundamentally changed since the first computer was programmed nearly half a century ago. Virtually all software today still retains its heritage of *mathematical logic*. Current computer software design still uses, almost exclusively, functions grounded in mathematical logic. Although it is not widely appreciated yet, the functions of mathematical logic are indeed very limited relative to the functional robustness of natural language. The tools that software developers have in their programming arsenal have remained small and inadequate to the task of mirroring natural language and human intelligence. Those attempts that have tried to expand the available functions (as in the relatively new "object-oriented" and "functional" programming languages) have done so in very limited ways (again, relative to the much more numerous functions of natural language).

Outside of the brain, most knowledge is stored in the knowledge-representation structure of natural language, such as in books, newspapers, and magazines. Many computer systems use this representation structure (*free-text* databases). More and more, however, knowledge is being transformed at great expense from the flexible and robust linguistic knowledge-representation structure of natural language into rigid computer database structures. The simplified database structures offer faster retrieval and greater storage and data-modification efficiencies than have been possible with knowledge represented in natural language. But in the course of that translation, from the complex structure of natural language to the simplified structure of relational databases, something very important is lost: knowledge.

Scientists and mathematicians historically have endeavored to *remove* complexity (i.e. knowledge) from their theories and representations of the world. Einstein recognized this impact of the "scientific method" years ago:

Science [and mathematics] is the attempt to make the chaotic diversity of our sense-experience correspond to a logically uniform system of thought. . . . The scientific way of forming concepts differs from that which we use in our daily life, not basically, but merely in the more precise definition of concepts and conclusions; more painstaking and systematic choice of experimental material; and greater logical economy. By this last we mean the effort to reduce all concepts and correlations to as few as possible logically independent basic concepts and axioms. (Albert Einstein, *Ideas and Opinions*, pp. 315–316)

Maximizing "logical economy" through the reduction of "all concepts and correlations to as few as possible" produces not a gain but a reduction of information, a *loss* of knowledge. Thus, Einstein concurs that human knowledge and intelligence expressed in mathematical/logical terms necessarily implies a *reduction* in knowledge and intelligence. The information content in natural language is similarly reduced when "translated" into an artificial language based on mathematical logic (or some other rationale utilizing the "scientific method"). The reductions are accomplished not by magic but simply by replacing existing cognitive functions ("all concepts and correlations") by fewer "artificial" functions—or, as Einstein put it, "as few as possible logically independent basic concepts and axioms." Note his use of "logically independent," which means, simply, that independent variables are used in place of dependent variables. The result is a "sanitized" independence from the real world.

Yet that is exactly the opposite of a major current goal in software development. The world is a complex place. Sparse programming functions and simple knowledge-representation structures are fine for limited applications in controlled knowledge domains; however, enabling computer systems to more completely mirror that world entails more complexity, not less. Human cognition and natural language reflect that "natural" complexity. Natural language is by necessity very complex. It is also by far the most capable knowledge-representation system known.

True to the "scientific method," computer scientists have done away with considerable complexity in their development of artificial languages and knowledge-representation systems. Programming languages still are all based on the limited functions of mathematical logic. Database structures (other than "free text") are likewise very limited in the variety of information they can store. It is not surprising, therefore, that the artificially intelligent and expert systems that have been developed with these programming and database tools to date have not approached the complexity that is reflected in human intelligence or natural language.

There is a fundamental deficiency in software design. Its cause is the limited functionality of programming languages (stemming from the "logical independence" of the functions of mathematical logic). This limited functionality is evidenced by the difficult interface languages that computer users must learn and use, which severely limit the way computers can communicate today (compared to the way humans communicate). It is further evidenced by knowledge-representation structures that are applicable to only very specific and narrow domains (hence, computers *are* like idiot savants).

Software developers must recognize that the fact that computers may not *operate* like the human brain today doesn't mean that in the future they cannot be made to *function* as the brain does. Humans are still the only machines that can produce two of the most important and needed human functions: intelligence, and communication capabilities using natural language. Humans are managed by an internal machine (the human brain). It is not how this machine operates but the *functionality* of this machine that produces its power. If important natural-language communication and human-intelligence capabilities are to be achieved, computer software must *function* as the human brain functions. It is the *functionality* of the brain that gives it its *capability.* Only through different and new approaches in the way software is designed that more closely emulate the functionality of the brain (but not necessarily the operation) will the computer of the future be made capable of true human intelligent interaction in natural language.

Applying new understanding of the brain's functionality to the development of computer software will result in new approaches to the way software is designed and implemented. Here will be found many of the answers that software developers have been seeking for many years. The answers will not consist of how to simulate the brain's operation; that was attempted in neural network programming systems. Instead, we will discover how to go beyond current programming and knowledge-representation paradigms to duplicate more and more aspects of the brain's functionality, which will lead to natural-language interfaces and human-cognitive-intelligence capabilities.

But (and this is especially important) new approaches in software design must not only incorporate functions beyond those of traditional mathematical logic into programming languages; they must integrate these functions into a new functional knowledge-representation paradigm. In order for the human brain's functionality to be emulated in a computer, a way to store knowledge must be developed that is functionality similar to the way the brain stores it. Knowledge-representation structures must be flexible and robust enough to be able to capture the real-world complexities of brain (cognitive) functionality *as expressed in natural language.*

Knowledge Representation: The Missing Link

What is "knowledge"?

With the advent and the continuing development of computer science, the answer to that once purely philosophical question has taken on a practical demeanor with important scientific and economic implications. The lack of an adequate theory of knowledge has now become a major obstacle in advanced computing projects around the world, including Japan's Fifth Generation computer project, Europe's ESPRIT, MCC in the United States, and thousands of other privately funded efforts. The fundamental goal of all these efforts is to discover better ways to store and manipulate knowledge, and yet undeniably all have proceeded without any true understanding of what "knowledge" is. Yet how knowledge is stored, not only neurologically but also cognitively and linguistically, will be one of the keys to the long-sought natural-language and human-intelligence capabilities of computers.

The current study and multi-level understanding of the brain's functionality and of natural and artificial languages can be summarized as in figure 1.

Mathematics, Computer Science:	Logic
Linguistics:	*Natural Language*
Cognitive Science:	Intelligence
Neuroscience:	Neurologic Functions

Figure 1

The operational and functional organization of the brain is hierarchical. In the brain, the operations of individual neurons form groups that operate in small networks (neurologic functions). These networks communicate with many other networks to form larger networks, which continually communicate with and modify one another in a process broadly referred to as "reason" (intelligence). Still other networks transform intelligence (cognitive functions) into language (linguistic functions) and then organize them syntactically (according to the rules of grammar) prior to communication. It is the task of still other networks to reverse this process.

How knowledge is stored in the "cognitive" brain is fundamentally critical to how we can construct a machine that can not only find it quickly but also compare it, manipulate it, apply it, communicate it, and ultimately create it. A new knowledge-representation structure that is consistent with the way the brain functionally stores (and manipulates, applies, communicates, creates, etc.) knowledge is the key not only to achieving natural language capabilities in computers also to achieving human natural-intelligence (vs. "artificial intelligence") capabilities.

What is needed is a philosophical unification of these now-separate descriptions of the same thing: the functionality of the human brain. That unification will be in the form of a common set of functions integrated with a common knowledge-representation structure.

Today we can "see" the workings of the brain in only very limited ways. Neuroscientists have determined that it is primarily the area of the brain called the "cerebral cortex" that produces our thought and our language. The cerebral cortex is only about 15 percent of the brain's mass, but it contains around 10 billion intricately connected neurons in neural networks. The vast majority of these connections are internal only; relatively few of the higher brain's neurons are interconnected to the body's sensory systems. While we do have a fairly good idea of the inner workings of individual neurons, we don't yet know exactly how networks made up of billions of neurons produce language and intelligence. However, through "reverse engineering," a good idea of how the brain functions on the levels of cognition and communication is rapidly emerging. We can see some of the results of all that neuronal activity—what we do and how we react to the world around us. Human activity consists of interactions between an "inner world" that for now is hidden from our understanding and an "outer world" that we all have nearly common access to. We do not yet comprehend the operational changes that take place inside our brains, but we can closely examine those interactions to see how we respond to external events functionally, and from that we can determine the functionality of the "hidden" inner operations that produce those external responses.

This approach has enabled neuroscientists to establish what the major functional systems of the higher brain are. And several of those functional systems give us the capability for one of the most important things we do: *communicate* with the outside world. We share knowledge about our perceptions of both our inner and outer worlds using language. In other words, we transform the products of our internal operation—what I will call "cognitive knowledge"—into signs that are available to others (and their "inner worlds"). One of the ways we represent our knowledge of the world is in the spoken and written signs of natural language.

In their essence, we can describe all languages as functional sign systems. The human species is not the only living entity on this planet that communicates with the outside world using functional sign systems. Bees do it. Cats do it. Porpoises and whales do it. In a sense, even bacteria do it. They all exhibit observable responses to corresponding external stimuli. They function (in part) in reaction to their perceptions of the outside world, and in some cases they create signs that cause reactions in other entities. Humans, however, as a result of the processes of evolution, had physical and neural systems that were able to create many more and different kinds of signs (such as the phonemes of speech and the characters of written language). Those signs, in order to be signs, must be accompanied by functional responses. Many of those responses are internal neuronal-network responses, each a function of a particular sign or combination of signs. Spoken and written language evolved from those responses.

A key word here is "evolved." Evolution is a process by which an entity is transformed into another entity. Before language, humans transformed internal responses to the outside world into external ones in order to survive. Before language, humans had knowledge of the world around them, in terms of how objects spatio-temporally related to one another and how those objects that could do so ("living" objects) functioned in response to outside-world stimuli. But they had no way of representing in external signs their internal representations of that outside world, no way of sharing their knowledge of it. They had no language.

Somewhere during the course of *Homo sapiens'* existence, the capability to share that knowledge came about. Maybe it was in particular movements or grunts and groans, or pictures on cave walls. However it happened, those external responses became signs to other humans. The grunts and groans became speech, and relatively recently (perhaps only about 7000 years ago) the phonemes of speech were translated into written signs. But *the basic underlying cognitive processes didn't change*!

Before language, our perceptions of the world around us, our knowledge of that external world, were (as they obviously still are) *functional relationships between objects*. Spatio-temporal relationships are but one kind of functional relationship. With the advent of language, we represented those relationships in verbal signs—in other words, cognitive knowledge was represented as linguistic knowledge in language. Then verbal signs were transformed into written signs, still representing objects in the world in functional relationships. For our purposes here, let us call knowledge as represented in natural language "linguistic knowledge" (as opposed to knowledge functionally represented in our brain, which we will call "cognitive knowledge"). Knowledge represented in a structured database or as programming rules in a computer, for lack of a better descriptive term, we will call "artificial knowledge."

By definition, cognitive knowledge dwarfs linguistic knowledge. Cognitive knowledge includes sights, sounds, smells, tastes, and the products of the imagination, much of which have not yet been translated into linguistic knowledge. We create words to use as we need them; in the last several centuries thousands of new words and thousands of new meanings for existing words have been added to our lexicon. Nevertheless, we have large amounts of cognitive knowledge without the need to transform it into linguistic knowledge, into natural language, into words. Art and music are two kinds of cognitive knowledge that we have not yet adequately transformed into natural language.

The capabilities of all of the knowledge-representation structures and systems that have been created by software developers and programmers over the years (artificial knowledge) are likewise dwarfed by those of natural language (linguistic knowledge). That is why computers, even those blessed with artificial intelligence, are so "dumb."

Obviously, without an understanding of how the transformations occur, and of what is lost (and/or gained) in the process, these are very general (and, practically speaking, unhelpful) observations. But what if we did understand how these transformations occur, and could objectively and quantifiably specify exactly the knowledge that is lost when cognitive knowledge is transformed (represented, converted, translated) into linguistic knowledge, and/or when linguistic knowledge is transformed into artificial knowledge?

We could do several things. We could expand artificial knowledge to be as capable as linguistic knowledge, which means as capable as a significant component of cognitive knowledge. We could fully represent the linguistic knowledge of natural language in artificial (i.e. programming) terms and much better emulate what we are calling "human intelligence." But to do that we have to know what are the structures of cognitive and linguistic and artificial knowledge and what are the processes by which the knowledge content in each kind of knowledge gets transformed from one knowledge-representation structure to another.

A New Beginning

It is true that we don't yet completely understand how the enormously complex machine called the human brain works—how billions of independent cells working together give us capabilities no other known entity has (great power to communicate, and intelligence far beyond that of any known machine). And we clearly have not been able to describe natural language using just the "sanitized" functions of mathematical logic.

Using primarily sequential programs operating on static data, we have yet to invent a system of knowledge representation that remotely compares to natural language in scope and capability. And, although some aspects of natural intelligence have been described extensively in formal mathematical terms, no logical system has yet been presented that accounts for the variability, flexibility, and robustness of human intelligence. To the contrary, the combination of limited functions, static data, and sequential program execution that is still incorporated into software-design paradigms has created what amounts to an intellectual barrier to the attainment of these capabilities.

It is becoming increasingly apparent that to halt the decline in computer productivity, and indeed to enhance productivity, we need far greater natural-language and human-intelligence capabilities in computer systems. The old software-design paradigms do not correspond to the new understandings of brain functionality, cognition, and natural language. But, thanks to the dedicated research efforts of leading neuroscientists, linguists, cognitive scientists, and philosophers, cognitive and linguistic knowledge representation can now be applied to software development to yield these capabilities. It is time to focus software development on the achievement of these goals through the application of the results of these efforts.

What are these insights? What has been learned about the functionality of the human brain that could bring about a new beginning in software development—enabling a more accurate duplication of its function in a different and more productive way than has been attempted before in a computer system?

Breakthroughs in neuroscience have been expanded upon and corroborated by independent research in cognitive science and are further supported by new developments in linguistics. An analysis of these efforts leads to the conclusion that human reasoning, memory, and (to a great extent) natural language all operate using a principal functional operation—a complex process that (in simplified forms) we commonly call *categorization*.

Neuroscience continues to establish the functionality of ever larger groups of neuronal networks, and is now describing functional systems at or certainly near the level of language production. The widely distributed memory structures of the brain are becoming far better understood. Each functional system is now understood to have its own memory. One of the most surprising things about how each functional system works is the importance of categorization in all the major functional systems of the brain so far identified.

Generally speaking, the new understanding of fundamental brain functions includes (but is certainly not limited to) the following major processes: categorization, concept formation, linguistic knowledge representation, and semantic/syntax interaction. These processes correspond to human reason, memory, and natural language production. In the brain, functional relationships of many kinds are ascribed to objects both real and abstract (categorization). New categorical representations are created in many ways from instances of old categories (concept formation through recategorization). Categorical representations are transformed into appropriate natural-language symbols (linguistic knowledge representation). Complex signs (formal language) are produced from natural-language symbols using the rules (grammar) of language formation (semantic-syntax interaction).

Table 1 (from *Bright Air, Brilliant Fire,* by Gerald Edelman) summarizes the major brain functions and the areas in the brain in which neuroscientists believe these functions primarily occur. Notice that the functions of categorization are involved in every one of these major brain functions. Note also that a part of the brain (Broca's and Wernicke's Area) has the function of language production, involving communication and mediation with other functional areas. Many scholars over the centuries have suggested that humans think using natural language. The Sapir-Whorf Hypothesis, for example, proposes that our reasoning capabilities are limited by our language. Neuroscience now tells us that the Sapir-Whorf Hypothesis as it applies to human intelligence is fundamentally incorrect—we do not reason using language. In other words, the brain first decides what it wants to say and then passes that knowledge on to the language-production area of the brain, which then attempts to determine (using the rules of grammar) how to say it. This conclusion is also supported by Einstein: "The words or the language, as they are written or spoken, do not seem to play any role in my mechanism of thought . . . Has not every one of us struggled for words although the connection between the "things" was already clear?" (*Ideas and Opinions*)

Table 1

Brain area	Major function
Primary and secondary cortex	Perceptual categorization
Broca's and Wernicke's Area	Language production; language categorization
Brain stem, hypothalamus, and anotonomic centers	Internal homeostatic systems— memory (categorization) of states and values
Hippocampus, amygdala, septum	Correlation (categorization) between internal systems and memory; current perceptual categorization
Frontal, temporal, and parietal cortex	Conceptual categorization

Human *communication*, however, is limited by language. And since human intelligence is externally embodied only in the media of communication, natural language as a primary medium of communication limits the *expression* of thought, not the underlying cognitive processes. (The Sapir-Whorf Hypothesis does accurately characterize computer intelligence, which, as we know, is dependent on the available functions of the programming languages that control its operation.)

Neuroscience is now ready to give computer science some very important lessons having to do with the emulation of the brain's functionality. Consider the following:

• The functionality of the brain shows far greater diversity than can be exhibited by the characteristics of limited human mental constructions, such as mathematics and logic. The brain uses many more and many different types of functions than the few defined by mathematics and logic (which are still the backbone of computer software development).

• Biological memory is not static; it is dynamic. It cannot be described as data using symbolic codes; nor can it be emulated using rules. Knowledge representation in the brain is not like "data" now represented in a computer, and rule-based knowledge-representation systems do not function like biological memory. Memory is *functional categorization*: the process of ascribing relationships between objects, where those relationships and objects may be (and often are) in themselves categories.

On another level of human brain functionality, researchers working in the field of *cognitive science* have established the importance of categorization to intelligence. They have developed theories of what the functions of categorization are on the basis of many years of research and testing. The following list (from *Women, Fire, and Dangerous Things*, by George Lakoff) outlines some of the new tenants of cognitive brain functionality:

• Thought is not a result but a process. More accurate, it is the interaction of many processes, principal among them the process of functional categorization.

• Human reason is centrally based on the functions of categorization that create relationships among objects (our perception of things in the real world, abstract entities, and categories of things and abstract entities).

• Human reason cannot be described by classical categorization, which assumes that the world comes in fixed categories and that there are categorization criteria that are singly necessary and jointly sufficient.

• No *fixed* formal semantic system can account for novelty. New categorical functions are created as needed through interaction with the outside world.

• Human reasoning is often nonlogical. The functions used in categorization are often chosen without logical basis; it is not so much that they are illogical as that they are "extralogical."

• Some aspects of thought are embedded in the brain at birth through evolutionary processes (including the capability and methodology of categorization—for example, the way certain perceptions such as colors are categorized). These initial processes are often modified through external experience and communication.

What cognitive scientists are saying is that we reason using categories, and that those categories are not fixed (they cannot be fixed, or we couldn't recognize or respond to anything new that didn't fit in an existing category) but are created as we need them and in any way we need them. Those cognitive functions not limited to the functions of mathematical logic or any other discipline. They are "extralogical" and, as Einstein noted, extraphysical: ". . . the concepts which arise in our thought and in our linguistic expressions are all . . . the free creations of thought which cannot be inductively gained from sense experiences" (*Ideas and Opinions*, p. 33).

Thus, we have learned from neuroscience that all major brain functions involve categorization. Cognitive science has discovered that categories are functional and that they are interrelated, without boundaries. Neuroscience and cognitive science agree that there is a transformation from functional categorical representation in the brain to symbolic representation in natural language.

On still another level, studies in linguistics have suggested that the knowledge-representation structure of natural languages can be adequately represented as "semantic networks" using cognitive categories of relationships between cognitive categories of objects. The idea of semantic networks as a representation of human associative memory was first proposed by M. Ross Quillian in 1968 and was later expanded upon by many artificial intelligence researchers including Marvin Minsky (1975) and Roger Schank (1975). In general, these efforts used limited numbers of linguistic relationships without reference to "cognitive" relationship functions, and their use was appropriate to only limited knowledge domains.

More recently there has been a realization by linguists that there is a "psychological complexity of lexical knowledge" reflecting different ways of categorizing experience that should be included in semantic network knowledge representation systems. (George Miller et al., "Five Papers on WordNet," p. 3). The result of this application of "functional categorization" has been the incorporation of "cognitive" relationship functions underlying an expanded number of linguistic relationships in a semantic network (such as the one being developed at Princeton University called "WordNet"). A "cognitive" semantic network is actually a linguistic categorization system using a variety of linguistic representations of cognitive categorization functions and objects that parallel cognitive categorization processes.

An additional process occurs when the rules of natural-language syntax (see e.g. Chomsky) are applied to linguistic knowledge to produce sentences containing complex constructions of corresponding linguistic signs. This, of course, concurs with neuroscience's identification of a separate functional area of the brain dealing with "language production," and is a potentially significant confirmation of our understanding of how cognitive categorical functionality can result in natural language.

The complexity of natural language is, on the surface, overwhelming. But the world it represents is also overwhelmingly complex. And, clearly, the artificial functional relationships in current programming languages and knowledge-representation structures reflect only a small subset of the underlying linguistic relationships, which reflect only a subset of the underlying cognitive relationships, which further reflect but again may be only a subset of the underlying neural network functional relationships.

I have noted that human beings reason using the processes of functional categorization. It is one thing to represent knowledge; it is quite another to use it as a component process of intelligence.

To clarify the processes of cognitive functional categorization, we should examine in more detail what may turn out to be the fundamental processes underlying both human language and human reason.

Functional Categorization

What was it about shoes, ships, sealing wax, cabbages, and kings that induced Lewis Carroll to include them in the category of things it is time to speak of? What is it to *categorize* an object?

The traditional ("classical") view is that it is to group objects by the things they have in common. New views on the subject from cognitive science now expand upon that limited definition, suggesting that, as with "new" views of logic, there is a "fuzziness" (i.e. complexity) to categorization that has not been seen before—a complexity that was omitted on the basis of *a priori* assumptions made by philosophers nearly 2000 years ago and subsequently included as an essential component of the "scientific method."

This "fuzziness" has surprising significance. Knowledge is functionally represented in the brain ("cognitive knowledge representation") as relationships between objects, where all relationships are represented by functions marking categories of functions and where all objects are also markers of categories. The kinds of relationships between objects can be described as "functions," but they are not exactly like the functions of mathematical logic. In contrast with mathematical logic, where the operation of a function is "logically independent" of the content of the variable to which it is applied, cognitive categories are defined by both the function and the object to which it is applied. *The function of a unit of knowledge is to represent an object's "membership" in a category, as defined by a function and an object.* The inclusion of the applied object into the "meaning" of the function is the source of the "fuzziness."

Because mathematical logic (and computer program statements) and natural language are languages, their underlying structures are the same: functions applied to objects. The difference lies in the purpose of the representations. Mathematical logic abstracts from the objects acted upon, enabling the same function to be applied to many different objects with consistent results. Different objects can be substituted for one another without affecting the "meaning" of the function. That is why variables can be used in mathematics (and traditional programming languages). And that is why they cannot be used in natural language: the object acted upon by the cognitive function is intrinsic to its "meaning"—which is to say intrinsic to the category definition.

For example, consider our knowledge about trees. Not only can the word "tree" refer to a physical object; it can also represent categories of objects. We know that certain things are "attached to" trees. "Attached to" is an abstract cognitive function that defines categories of things that are physically connected to other things. "Attached to (tree)" is not abstract; it defines the category of things that are connected to trees. Its members might include branches, leaves, and bark.

If we abstract from "attached to (tree)," following the lead of science and mathematical logic, we are left with "attached to (x)," where "x" can be any object. This makes sense because, as we all know, many different objects can be "attached to" other objects. As long as you already know what "attached to" *means,* this abstraction accomplishes its purpose. However, without that underlying meaning (read: without any related categories, which we removed by replacing an object "tree" with the variable "x"), the abstraction removes any knowledge represented by "attached to." "Attached to (x)" in this instance has no meaning (in the natural-language sense) whatsoever if what 'x' is has not been specified.

Although this overview of categorical abstraction highlights just a few of the major issues of functional categorization, it is important to an understanding of functional knowledge representation. Functional knowledge representation facilitates processes of human reason more sophisticated than the processes that can be facilitated by existing AI and expert systems, which are based almost exclusively on the limited functions of mathematical logic. The original Universal Turing Machine replaced "calculation" with elementary mathematical processes. The intelligent computer of the future will simulate "intelligence" and "language" using the processes of functional categorization, which, as was mentioned above, could be the fundamental processes of reason and natural language. In a computer those processes will be embodied in a system of functional knowledge representation.

Functional Knowledge Representation

The discoveries of neuroscientists, cognitive scientists, linguists, and phi-losophers aside, the ever pragmatic (and necessarily so) software develop-ers will ask: How can a logical machine simulate extralogical functions? How are these extralogical functions so different from logical functions that they can produce natural-language and human intelligence capabili-ties? How is knowledge to be represented and manipulated using these extralogical functions?

What kind of knowledge-representation structure should be used? How will that knowledge be input, retrieved, manipulated, and even cre-ated? And can that knowledge-representation structure and manipulation system be efficiently implemented in a digital computer?

Here, once again, I am talking about knowledge representation not at the operational level but rather at the functional level. For example, oper-ationally a computer stores data as strings of binary code; functionally it might store data as rows and columns in a spreadsheet or a database.

Put another way, these questions ask: Is the cognitive brain in fact a machine that a Universal Turing Machine, a digital computer, can simu-late? Can the cognitive functionality (as opposed to the operational func-tionality) of the human brain be described in terms consistent with the limited functionality of mathematical logic?

For future software-development strategies, these are the important questions. If a computer with appropriate software can sufficiently simu-late cognitive functions of the brain, this should lead to a machine that exhibits natural-language and human-intelligence capabilities, thus solv-ing many of the problems of communication, productivity, and human cost that the widespread use of computers now engenders.

Functional knowledge representation is the key to these capabilities. It might even be called the "fundamental" structure of knowledge, whether neuronal, cognitive, linguistic, or (now) artificial. We now have a quanti-fiable definition of "knowledge": *Knowledge is a representation of cate-gories of functional relationships between objects.*

Each object-relationship-object representation is a basic *unit* of knowl-edge. Units of knowledge with the same function-object components make up functional *categories* of knowledge.

To see this another way, consider a universe with just two objects (and with us as external observers). What is all the possible knowledge in that universe? The answer, by definition, is "all possible relationships that those objects could have"—for example, spatio-temporal or logical. A *different* question is: What is all the possible knowledge that could be expressed (represented) about that universe? Expressing (externally representing) knowledge requires language.

Spatio-temporal and logical relationships are just some of the possible relationships that can be represented in language. In fact, since every verb or verb phrase in natural language represents a possible relationship, all possible representable knowledge about that universe could be expressed in thousands of statements about the possible relationships between those two objects, each using a different verb and/or verb phrase.

How many linguistic functions (verbs) representing discrete cognitive relationships are there in common English? At last count, over 4500! How many linguistic objects (nouns and pronouns)? Easily over 26,000. That's over 100 million potential categories. Modifiers and specialized lexicons skyrocket the number of potential categories into the trillions. The knowledge-representation capability of natural language is extensive, to say the least. But underlying it all is *knowledge*—our perceptions of the world—whether represented in neural networks, in cognitive categories, in linguistic semantic networks, in artificial programming languages, or in computer databases.

The realization that verbs and verb phrases in natural language function just as operators do in mathematical statements is essential to understanding natural language as a functional system.

Functional categorization is a primary process used in human knowledge representation. One result of that process has been mathematics. In fact, as we saw before, functions in mathematics are abstractions of categorization. Mathematical functions and cognitive functions and linguistic representations of cognitive functions all have the same functional structure:

$y = f(x)$　[mathematical]

branches = attached to (tree)　[cognitive]

Branches are attached to trees.　[linguistic]

Because of the similarities in structure, the cognitive relationships we use in categorizing objects—in all languages, natural and artificial and the hybrids in between—can be treated like functions in mathematics, giving us the real possibility of a mathematically tractable model of natural language that can be operated automatically using a Universal Turing Machine (a computer).

That possibility notwithstanding, knowledge-representation structures using functional categorization with linguistic representations add considerable functionality (and the capability to represent much more complexity) to existing programming languages and current knowledge-representation methodologies. Just expanding the list of functions available to programmers and to users will go far to add new levels of natural-language and human-intelligence capabilities to computer systems.

For example, consider the use of the function of "entailment" in software-development efforts. Entailment is commonly represented by the "if . . . then . . ." structure of rules used in almost every programming language. The entailment (if . . . then . . .) relation holds regardless of time or the content of the variables used.

Linguists have found that the function of entailment in natural language comprises at least three relationships, based on both temporal implications and semantic contents. For example, two pairs of entailed variables may occur at the same time without being semantically (categorically) equivalent. *Limp→walk* and *snore→sleep* both are temporally simultaneously entailed, but *snore* and *sleep* are obviously different activities. A limp is a kind of walk, but snore is not a kind of sleep. The *limp-walk* entailment relation is called "troponomy with co-extensiveness"; the *snore-sleep* relation is called "troponomy with proper inclusion." A third non-temporally simultaneous entailment relation has also been identified. For example, *succeed* entails *try,* but *succeed* presupposes *try.* This entailment relationship between *succeed* and *try* is called "temporal inclusion with backward presupposition." Likewise with *die* and *live.*

Adding new cognitive aspects of linguistic functionality to the basic logical entailment relation is but one example how new functions can be added to programming logic through the use of linguistic representations. It illustrates how linguistic (natural-language) representations can break the communications barrier that computer users now face, leading to easier and far more productive (and less expensive) computer use.

This functional knowledge representation solution dramatically extends the number of functions used in structured programming and even in object-oriented programming by using cognitive functions as represented in natural language. It also integrates those functions into a database structure that mirrors the knowledge structure of natural language— i.e., relationships (functions) between objects. (See table 2.)

Though there is much left to do before functional knowledge representation is a viable software paradigm (such as determining how the formation of new categories is controlled), it seems to me that it will be achieved relatively easily by effectively combining the present object-oriented and functional programming styles with a tremendously enhanced set of functional relationships to create a functional, dynamic knowledge-representation system that conceivably could be easily integrated into existing relational database management systems.

This functional method of categorical knowledge representation has many important advantages, including these:

- fact extraction and storage from free text without loss of knowledge
- manipulation of individual units of knowledge
- integrated use of logical processes such as deduction and inference
- relating facts in many new ways beyond what has been input
- increases in the productivity of programmers and users
- natural-language and human-intelligence capabilities in computer systems.

In knowledge-representation theory, evidence of a viable storage structure that parallels the structure of natural language but that also reflects underlying cognitive processes would be very exciting. It would allow knowledge to be stored in a computer in exactly the form in which we use it: natural language. It would also, for the first time, give the computer

Table 2

Natural language			Database fields		
subject	verb	object	function	object	value
Trees	*have*	*leaves.*			
			are attached to	trees	leaves
Leaves	*are on*	*trees.*			

system a way to relate objects in new ways, thus creating new knowledge, and perhaps to reason with that knowledge in the ways that humans reason. Furthermore, through the use of well-established syntactical structures, stored knowledge could be expressed in grammatically correct sentences, giving a computer system full natural-language-production capability. These are capabilities that only a naturally intelligent machine capable of communicating by means of natural language could possess.

What will emerge when we finally fully integrate programs with data using the knowledge-representation structures and functionality of human cognition as represented in natural language will simultaneously be a new style of programming and a new knowledge-representation structure. It will be "naturalware."

Conclusion

Software development is at a critical point. Today's computers (maybe even desktop microcomputers) may well have the operational performance necessary for substantially greater human communication and intellectual capabilities. Certainly computers early in the next millennium will. It is now up to software developers to begin to supply this needed and very important functionality. Until they do, pressures to develop these capabilities will increase, accompanied by sharp increases in the gap between potential and actual computer productivity. To turn the productivity decline around through improved human-computer interfaces as well as increased computer intelligence, the development of natural-language and human-intelligence software systems will emerge as one of the most critical challenges facing computer science.

There can be no doubt that software systems will be more and more like the cognitive functional systems that enable and control us. The application of a new understanding of how the brain produces language and intelligence to software development will result in new generations of computer software that will emulate large functional systems of the brain. But we will develop software systems that will enable computers to exhibit human intelligence only if we incorporate central aspects of neurological, cognitive, and linguistic *functionality* into the design and the development of computer software—not the brain's operation (neuronal networks, the "hardware"), but its functions (cognitive knowledge, the "software").

To some, this was clear even 40 years ago. Stored-program pioneer John von Neumann saw that computer systems using the Turing paradigm operated very differently from the human brain (even as the brain was then understood). He said one should not expect the intellectual capabilities of computers to match those of the biological brain in certain critical respects until those functional differences are incorporated into computer functionality. "When we talk mathematics, we may be discussing a secondary language, built on the primary language truly used by the central nervous system." ("The Computer and the Brain," p. 82)

I have presented only an overview of new aspects of the functionality of the brain, human cognition, and natural and artificial languages that are emerging from research outside of computer science. One of these important insights is *functional categorization*. In the future these revelations and other that are being developed will, more and more, open new doors to software development.

Specifically, the importance of functional categorization to all aspects of brain functionality will become increasingly evident. Using the cognitive processes of functional categorization, software design and development efforts will see beyond the limitations of the few present-day mathematical and logical functions. An explosion in the number and kinds of new functions will form the basis of a new functional knowledge-representation structure, revolutionizing software development. Blessed with the additional power of thousands of diverse, "fuzzy" categorization functions, these efforts can then enter the world of natural language, the most efficient and flexible knowledge-representation structure nature has been able to develop after many millennia of evolutionary work.

What these new "software" functions are and how they work can only be derived from a new understanding of how the human brain functions and represents knowledge. In fact, identification and use of the cognitive functions of categorization and their corresponding linguistic representations could be critically important to future software (and eventually hardware) development.

If Turing and von Neumann were alive today, I believe they would both acknowledge that the computer programming and knowledge-representation methods developed thus far are so lacking as to require a major software redesign move into the functional capabilities of human intelligence and natural language. This requires recognition of the contributions of many scientists outside of computer science to an understanding of the processes by which the human brain produces these capabilities. That redesign involves extending now-limited basic object-oriented/functional relationships into other much larger cognitive and linguistic knowledge domains through incorporation in a dynamic functional knowledge representation structure. It is, I believe, an advance in software design that both Turing and von Neumann would appreciate.

Although the computer, with its superior calculating and memory capabilities (but limited communications and intelligence) has had a profound effect on society in a very short time, when computer natural-language and human-intelligence capability are achieved the impact will be unimaginably greater. No longer will programmers and users have to translate their needs into another "artificial" language. Difficulties with "user interfaces" will be greatly reduced, and software capabilities will not have to be sacrificed to "user friendliness." Voice and optical character recognition systems will be able to incorporate context and semantics into recognition algorithms. Stimulating conversations with electronic machines will, at long last, become a reality.

It is too early to predict the ultimate result, but it certainly is possible that history will show that these new capabilities will not only usher in a new era in the computer age but also signal a major evolutionary advance.

In the future, as brain functionality is increasingly implemented in new kinds of software (e.g. "naturalware"), we should look for a totally new generation of software capabilities, including advanced intelligence approaching that which is inconceivable to us now. When natural language and human intelligence are attained through new "naturalware" design approaches, such as functional knowledge representation, the digital computer may achieve its destiny as the successor to the human brain in both complexity and capability.

The digital computer is an "evolutionary tool." Unlike any of the other tools (and machines) created by mankind, the computer theoretically can recreate any other tool (or machine), including the machine that created it (the human brain). In spite of the wonderful achievements computers have made possible, the computer commands a unique distinction in history not because of these effects on humanity to date, significant though they are, but rather as a result of its theoretical potential to match and maybe exceed the functionality of the most powerful and complex machine now known in the universe: the human brain.

The digital computer is thus not only the invention of the human species, but an evolutionary product of it. Beyond that, look to Arthur C. Clarke.

Bibliography

Gerald M. Edelman, *Bright Air, Brilliant Fire (On the Matter of the Mind)*. Basic Books, 1992.

Albert Einstein, *Ideas and Opinions*. Dell, 1954.

Donald G. Fink, *Computers and the Human Mind*. Doubleday, 1966.

George Lakoff, *Women, Fire, and Dangerous Things (What Categories Reveal about the Mind)*. University of Chicago Press, 1987.

George Miller et al., Five Papers on WordNet. Princeton University Cognitive Science Laboratory, 1993.

Sebastian Shaumyan, *A Semiotic Theory of Language*. Indiana University Press, 1987.

John von Neumann, *The Computer and the Brain*. Yale University Press, 1958.

III

On the Knowledge Frontier

Where's the "Walkman" in Japan's Software Future?

Edward A. Feigenbaum

On shining altars of Japan they raise
The silver lamp; the fiery spirits blaze.
—Alexander Pope

The software sector of the computer industry is, paradoxically, booming
yet troubled. Nowhere is this more true than in Japan, in many other
areas a fine model when it comes to things technological.

Measured by annual revenue, how does Nintendo compare to the U.S.
software giant Microsoft? (Microsoft, of course, is an everything-you-
need software supplier; and Nintendo makes only games.) The surprising
answer is that Nintendo is 25 percent bigger than Microsoft, with approximately $5 billion a year in revenues versus Microsoft's $4 billion.
Of the four largest packaged-software companies in the world, if you
include the games companies, the United States has only two. Nintendo
is number one. The list of the top five also includes Sega, another
games software company. That is one side of the Japanese software
industry.

What is the best-selling Japanese (non-game) software package in the
American market? If that question is too hard, try this variation: What is
your favorite Japanese software package? Nobody has an answer to this
question, because there is no Japanese presence in the huge American
software market. Now consider some analogous questions about consumer electronics: What is your favorite Walkman-type device? What's
your favorite CD player? What's your favorite television set? What's your
favorite laptop computer? In light of Japan's success in those markets, it
is all the more interesting that Japan has no presence in the American

software market. This chapter tries to explain why. It also addresses a broader range of issues concerning the Japanese software industry in an attempt to understand its future.

The total size of Japan's business is about $100 billion annually for all kinds of software—including packaged programs, programs custom prepared by a contractor, and software made within a company that has its own programs. Of that $100 billion, half is spent on in-house programming. Approximately $35 billion is spent on packaged software or custom programming services. Computer makers spend about $15 billion on system software for their equipment. In the Japanese way of doing things, customers prefer to have software customized for their own interfaces and their own ways of doing business, and they are willing to pay for it. Approximately 90 percent of sales are custom software, whereas only 10 percent are packaged software—although for software use, rather than revenues, the ratio may be less because so much use of packaged software is from illegal unpaid-for copies.

As already mentioned, Nintendo is the world's largest packaged-software company, at $5 billion in annual revenues. In custom software, Japan's largest company is NTT Data, a subsidiary of NTT with annual revenues between $3.5 billion and $4 billion. Two Hitachi subsidiaries each have annual sales over $1 billion. A financial-software subsidiary of Nomura Securities has about $1.5 billion a year in sales. Japan's largest independent software house, CSK, is the parent of Sega. Not counting Sega's revenues, CSK itself has annual revenues (from software plus services) of about $1 billion.

In numbers of people employed, the Japanese software industry firms range from the huge NTT Data down to what we would call "garage shops" with only a few employees.

The Industry's Problems

In January 1993, Tokyo officially declared software a "distressed" industry. That status allows the industry to get certain kinds of government subsidies and special considerations. But these businesses still lack the proper interplay of market forces. The result is a narrow, focused, uncompetitive Japanese industry where there is no honing of software products in world markets and no opportunity for the high-volume sales needed to make packaged software profitable.

Moreover, the future of Japan's software development is plagued by the structure of the industry itself, by the way Japan's culture treats software, and by problems in the educational system which ultimately supplies the creativity and management for this industry's future.

Officials at the Ministry of International Trade and Industry referred to the software industry's troubles as an "urgent" problem in the title of a draft white paper. Why is the problem so urgent? What is making MITI nervous? The source of MITI's anxiety is a perception that is quite correct: hardware is becoming a commodity produce with eroding profit margins; meanwhile, the high profit margins are moving to the high-value-added software part of the computer industry. This is true not only of the sale of packaged software but also of the sale of software embedded in other products. It is often said, dismissively, that "hardware is the box that software comes in," because software is where the major value is added. So the Japanese look nervously past the year 2001, when software will decisively be the locus of commercial competition in the computer field.

With students from the Stanford Japan center, I recently interviewed employees of the large computer makers Fujitsu, Hitachi, NEC, and Toshiba. We also interviewed employees of packaged-software companies. One of the latter was JUST Systems—the largest packaged-software company in Japan, with revenues of $100 billion per year. Another was Japan Lotus, a subsidiary of Lotus Development Corporation. We wanted to see how an American company operating in Japan's packaged-software industry saw the situation. We also interviewed employees of IBM's new subsidiary Encyclosoft, a combined software publisher and distributor that is trying to enter Japan's market for packaged software. And we interviewed two system integrators, because that task is clearly playing an ever greater role in the software industry. As the industry moves away from mainframes and toward the client-server architectures, the situation is much more "plug and play" and the users are often not knowledgeable enough to do the "plug and play" totally on their own. One of the system integrators was Argotechnos 21, which has 800 employees and is a spin-off of Nippon Univac; the other was the Japanese branch of the U.S. firm

Andersen Consulting. Also interviewed were representatives of several small, independent software houses.

For an academic view, we interviewed the dean and some members of the faculty of a new engineering school of Keio University. Furthermore, we interviewed the director of MITI's Electronic Policy Division and the president and top officers of the Japan Information Processing Development Corporation, a quasi-governmental promotion organization for the computer industry. In all, 20 different interviews were conducted. How did I know that was enough? I had a strong feeling as we came to the end of these interviews that we were hearing the same story over and over again, and it appeared that we had reached the point of diminishing returns and that we had essentially surrounded the issue.

In contrast with the American approach, the large Japanese computer makers have established many software subsidiaries. For example, Fujitsu has about 100 wholly owned subsidiary companies. The number of employees in a software subsidiary ranges from about 80 to about 500, with 200 considered optimal. Independent software houses serve these computer-maker subsidiaries. The independent house is the last firm to get work, and usually gets the low-value-added tasks. The high-value-added work is done in the parent company. The Japanese have mated their liking for hierarchies with the hierarchies of structured programming, saying (in effect) "Some people will do design, some people will do top-level coding, and some people will do lower-level coding." This is dysfunctional in the sense that the people doing the lower-level work don't learn how to do tasks at the higher level because they are never given those tasks. And the feedback channels are very noisy. It can take a long time for information (for instance, that some piece of the design won't work, or that some logical alternative wasn't explored) to be passed up from the coders.

Much of Japan's "custom" software may in fact be built out of hidden packages. The big system integrators, including ones the size of Fujitsu, may have libraries of large packages that they use when producing custom software systems. Large custom software jobs may have many "packages" inside. In the United States we might sell them separately, but in Japan they are sold as integrated custom systems.

Japan's software-distribution networks are not mature by American standards. There are three distributors for all shrink-wrapped personal computer software. If you are not covered or handled by one of those distributors, you simply have no way of selling your software. I failed to find a similar network for workstation software.

I went looking for Japanese database software. IBM sells a lot of DB2 worldwide. Oracle sells about $1.8 billion worth a year. Among the other large American vendors are Informix and Sybase. What are their Japanese equivalents? There are none. A buyer can get database systems built by the system integrators or the large computer makers, but there is no separate market for Japanese database software. How about CAD software? With minor exceptions, the answer is the same. The best-selling CAD program in Japan is an American package, AutoCAD, and other U.S. packages do nearly as well.

Knowledgeable Japanese who have studied the software industry explain that it will be unable to progress until it begins to compete worldwide. The firms producing software will have to hone their products. Unless some force were to emerge that would cause the introduction of new products, the domestic industry would not be competitive even in Japan. The companies would not have a big enough market in which to compete. In fact, the market's size is a major problem for the Japanese in the area of personal computers. In the United States there are many tens of millions of personal computers, which are potential recipients for any particular piece of software. In Japan that number is many times smaller. Competition took a different form in the Japanese personal computer industry than in the American one, and this compounds the problem of the small market. The Japanese industry took the form of incompatible proprietary operating systems, further fragmenting the market and requiring software companies to produce seven different versions of their programs.

The latter problem is going away because Microsoft jumped in and said: "We'll guarantee that Windows 3.1 in its Japanese version will be a common platform. That is, if you, the developer, will write for Windows 3.1, we will guarantee that it will operate on all those seven otherwise incompatible systems." Microsoft has created something of a common standard among the Japanese and is therefore selling very well in Japan.

Another major problem of Japan's software industry is "bundling." In 1968 the U.S. Justice Department forced IBM to sign a consent decree saying that the company would not include software in its hardware prices—that software would be priced separately. The reason was obvious: there couldn't be a software industry when IBM was producing all the software and giving it away. A competitive software industry would not come into existence. The United States has had more than a quarter century to build up a highly competitive software industry, one in which it is difficult even to survive. Microsoft and a few other flourishing large companies are anomalies.

The Japanese have no such dynamism. Until a few years ago bundling was the norm. The large companies would bundle their software with their computers, and it was difficult for anyone else to compete. Then the government issued an "advisory," which normally is the equivalent of the government's telling firms what to do. In this case, however, it didn't work. The advisory was: "Don't bundle your software. Japan is supposed to go to unbundling [i.e., selling separately]." In 1993 Japan's government issued another directive putting teeth into that first one: "If you don't unbundle, we're going to take you before the Fair Trade Commission." Until the Japanese unbundle software, there will not be room for the competition that would invigorate the domestic industry.

The Demands

The independent software "body shops" supply workers for large projects. Yet the need for large numbers of programmers has decreased significantly because of Japan's recession (a firm is going to save money by not redoing a system that it might otherwise have redone) and because firms don't want to add new applications to mainframe systems. But companies are not yet secure enough with the client-server idea to commit money to reprogramming their systems along those lines. So they wait. These factors have made redundant at least 250,000 Japanese programmers from those "body shops," many of whom seem to have ended up driving taxis and doing menial work.

Two or three years later than their U.S. counterparts, the Japanese are beginning to discover distributed computing, client-server networks, open systems, and the overall move away from mainframes. Customers are beginning to insist on this type of computing, yet the industry is nervous about supplying it. Businesses are unsure of their own skills and knowledge, and of the software needed for open systems.

At JUST Systems, the largest Japanese packaged-software house, the CEO mentioned the main factor inhibiting the growth of his company. It was not the deep recession, nor was it heavy-handed government intervention. It was the extent of illegal copying of JUST's software. He said that JUST has determined that a piece of software sold to a business is, on average, copied four or five times. Sold to the government, on average it's copied ten times. In spite of what MITI says about bundling and unbundling, the Ministry of Finance does not budget for government agencies to buy software. It only budgets for computer hardware. This forces government agencies to pressure manufacturers to bundle their software. Otherwise, they scrape together miscellaneous funds to buy a single piece of software and then make a large number of copies.

One government official called Japan "a copier's paradise." A contrary view came from a Japan Lotus executive: "We just lowered the price of Lotus 1-2-3. We had a price which was about $1000 taking into account the fact that so many illegal copies were made. We just decided to cut the price in half. We figured that at a lower price the Japanese will want the manual and they'll want our service, so they'll stop copying our software."

The president of a small software boutique tells a poignant story. He was the first person in Japan to produce good word-processing software; then he expanded into desktop publishing. He soon learned that a retailer in the electronics district of Akihabara in Tokyo was giving away his company's software as a gift if a customer bought an NEC computer. He went to court to halt this practice. As soon as he sued, the word got out and his sales dried up. Potential customers knew that they too were making illegal copies, and they feared that action might also be taken against them. After he withdrew his suit, sales picked up again. The man told me that Microsoft had sent out letters to the 5000 largest purchasers of Microsoft software in Japan, informing them bluntly that Microsoft will prosecute to the fullest extent of the law anyone caught copying. "That's great," says the original word processing entrepreneur. "Only the Americans can tell them that, and we're very happy that Microsoft has done so."

Japan's laws regulating copying are satisfactory, but their enforcement is essentially nil. Anyway, the Japanese prefer not to enforce the law, because of their profound cultural dislike of going through the legal system. The social ethos apparently contains no "don't copy" restriction.

Few if any authoritative Japanese are satisfied with the quality of the computer science and information science departments at Japan's universities. In the United States, I have never heard a single software industry executive claim to be unhappy with the output of the computer science departments of U.S. universities. Furthermore, in Japan the Ministry of Education limits the number of students in each department. A typical computer science department has about 40 undergraduates, a few Master's students, and maybe one or two Ph.D. candidates. Some departments have had dispensation to graduate 80, but that is rare.

The Japanese are trying to fix the problem of inadequate numbers. For example, they created two big computer science departments at new institutions, one near Kyoto and one at Kanazawa. In each place they are trying to hire 64 professors, and each department will have hundreds of students graduating every year. Until Japan can train more Ph.D.s to become professors in those departments, it will have great difficulty solving its "urgent" software problems. And any solution may take 10 years.

The Japanese system does graduate many people called "programmers" from trade schools and high schools. However, these are the people who are becoming increasingly redundant. The real need, now and into the future, is for highly trained university graduates.

Underlying all the malaise in Japan's software industry is this question: Does the culture respect software? Is software "real"? Years ago, software writers were called "programmers" and were paid less than electrical, hardware, and other engineers. As software writers came to be in great demand, Japanese firms changed the name "programmer" to "software engineer" and raised salaries. But, alas, the status did not change.

In the Japanese mind, software is not real. It is considered something like a service—something that comes along with the hardware. You expect it; it's supposed to be there; it makes the hardware run; but it's not distinct. It is not a product in its own right. It is a kind of vapor. You can't feel it. You can't lift it. Can you really sell it? Is one comfortable selling something that is not tangible, is not hard? Is software worthy of respect as a field? If it's vapor, it's nothing. Would you invest your money in nothing? Would you invest your career in nothing? It is hard to motivate young people to go into this business. The Japanese do not have a folk hero who made $8 billion in the industry. The cultural attitude toward software will have to change if Japan is to resolve what it calls an "urgent" problem in the decade ahead.

What is Tokyo doing about all this? It has issued that directive on unbundling. It has paid subsidies to the packaged-software industry. (Although good ideas for packaged software can win large government grants, this is not venture capital: the government doesn't take equity.) MITI is pushing the Ministry of Finance to introduce software line-items budgets into the agencies in order to reduce the amount of copying. The government is taking a strong stand against copying. It is instructing its agencies not to copy illegally, and is jawboning businesses about this illegal practice. And the Ministry of Education is starting more computer science departments and is trying to introduce more personal computers into the schools.

Japanese Views of Software's Future

The Japanese realize that value is moving from hardware to software, but they still feel more comfortable selling software in a substantial package. They have invented a term that describes their new attitude toward software. It is pure, wonderful Japlish: the "new hard." The "new hard" is the new way to contend with the idea that "hardware is the box that software comes in." Think of a function; imagine the software capability that is going to realize that function; then invent a box that actually does the job. You embed software in the box; then you sell the box, not the software. This is becoming an increasingly common practice in the United States. At a recent meeting at Stanford, Joel Birnbaum, Hewlett-Packard's vice-president for research, told about a new HP stethoscope which will contain a microcomputer that will do signal processing of the sounds the doctor is hearing and will be able to give intelligent readouts. That is an example of the way that an intellectually and economically valuable product gets embodied in something that is actually hardware. What the customer buys is an intelligent stethoscope, not a piece of software that is read into a stethoscope. The Japanese plan to make a major business out of this paradigm.

The Japanese also see multimedia as a large part of their business future. There is great uncertainty about "when" and "how much" but not about "if." "Given that IBM's mainframe business is declining and Fujitsu's business is modeled after IBM's, what is Fujitsu's future?" I asked one of Fujitsu's executive vice-presidents. His answer was "Multimedia."

The traditional large Japanese computer manufacturers are worried about the upcoming confluence of consumer electronics, communications, and computing. They worry that the firms that will master this new world will be the same ones that mastered the consumer electronics industry in the past—Sony and Matsushita, specifically. Sony, indeed, is a company considerably skilled in computer science and technology. Nintendo is also a potential winner. Nintendo game computers are present in more Japanese and American homes than any other computer. If Nintendo's alliances with Silicon Graphics and other firms bear fruit, Nintendo may become a major player in this new era of computing.

Several faculty members of the Stanford Computer Industry Project and I have a hypothesis about how the Japanese software industry is going to evolve. On one hand, the large computer manufacturers in Japan (such as Fujitsu) will "circle the wagons" around their customer bases. These companies and their customers are not going to move away from mainframes rapidly. At great cost the companies will protect their cherished customer relationships. Hence, they will vigorously oppose trends that allow customers to mix and match, buying hardware and software from many different vendors (i.e., "open systems").

Here is a good example of protecting the customer base: Japanese customers seem to want to buy Sun workstations. Fujitsu offers its version of the Sun workstation, licensed through Sun. But the workstation says Fujitsu and not Sun. If you are a Fujitsu customer, you buy the Fujitsu box, not the Sun box, because Fujitsu doesn't want Sun relating to its customers. It will be very difficult for American firms to break into several Japanese markets because of the long-standing relationships which Japanese vendors have with their customers. To say the least, these relationships are difficult to disrupt.

The second part of our hypothesis is that there will be smaller startup firms, ones which believe they can prosper outside Japan, and that these firms will energetically pursue overseas markets, following a Nintendo-like model. Somehow Nintendo introduced a proprietary standard, set up a distributor network, made foreign alliances, and so on. There probably will be some niche products (as defined by Japanese companies) that make dents in the American market. These companies may do very well, as did Nintendo. Except for Nintendo, there is absolutely no current evidence for this portion of the hypothesis. The future will tell.

American firms will do very well competing with the Japanese in the packaged-software industry, where the United States' 75 percent market share currently dominates the world. But Americans should not set their expectations too high for penetrating the Japanese market for big-business software. The alliances and relationships which the Japanese have developed over a long period of time are famously durable, and Americans will very much remain "outsiders."

Acknowledgments

Stanford University has an ideal base for studying Japanese societal phenomena, the Stanford Japan Center. It was my good fortune to have a faculty assignment there that allowed me to conduct a study of the paradoxical Japanese software industry. I was doubly fortunate to have as research assistants fourteen very smart students from Stanford and Dartmouth who were "students abroad" in the spring of 1993. Their contribution was stimulating and substantial. The students were S. Chang, M. Chen, A. Cho, N. Eustance, R. Gaines, E. Iwami, A. Goore, L. Jen, H. T. Liao, C. Meindl, M. Moore, N. Morgan, K. Pascual, and R. Sandoval.

Property of the Mind: Software and the Law

Jeffrey P. Cunard

STOP

BEFORE OPENING THIS PACKAGE CONTAINING THE SOFTWARE, CAREFULLY READ THE LICENSE AGREEMENT INCLUDED WITH THIS PACKAGE. DO NOT OPEN THIS PACKAGE AND USE THE SOFTWARE UNTIL YOU HAVE CAREFULLY READ AND AGREED WITH THE TERMS AND CONDITIONS. IF YOU DO NOT AGREE WITH THE TERMS OF THIS LICENSE AGREEMENT, PROMPTLY RETURN THE SOFTWARE AND ANY ACCOMPANYING ITEMS. IF YOU OPEN THIS PACKAGE YOU WILL BE BOUND BY THE TERMS OF THIS LICENSE AGREEMENT.[1]

Which of us has ever returned the software we purchased after reading such a warning? If none of us ever has, why does a software vendor even bother? The answers to these questions are deeply embedded in a worldwide debate over the type and the scope of legal protections that should be available to prevent unauthorized uses of software. This fight, which has lasted for more than 30 years, has spilled out of academic journals and trade publications into the world of business. It is the subject of increasingly contentious litigation in the courts and of study in the halls of governments in the United States and abroad. The battle is not just about who should profit from the tens of billions of dollars generated annually by the computer software industry, nor is it simply about competition and competitiveness—which companies or, indeed, which countries will be globally preeminent in the computer sector. No, it is a fundamental dispute over economic philosophy: What is the optimal path toward a productive post-industrial, high-technology civilization?

This debate has largely been veiled from those of us who use software in our businesses or at home. We who buy software generally believe that the nature of legal barriers to unauthorized use of software is entirely settled. The ordinary consumer may pay just as much heed to the "shrink wrap" license reproduced above as he does to the FBI warning at the beginning of the videocassette he rents from his local video store. In truth, the question of how the law protects such novel forms of creative output as computer software is one of infinite complexity.

Safeguarding Creativity: The Framework for Legal Protection

The laws of intellectual property (including copyright and patent laws and the legal regime for the protection of trade secrets) are intended to protect intangible works—the products of artistic, scientific, or other creative activity. We are all familiar with the laws prohibiting the theft or unauthorized use of such physical objects as books, machines, and floppy disks. The intellectual-property laws, in comparison, protect the poet, the engineer, and the software developers—the individuals or enterprises whose brainpower produced the works embedded in those objects—against unauthorized copying and use.

In the last few years some economists have begun to scrutinize the traditionally unquestioned assumptions that underlie intellectual-property laws. People, they point out, create a great amount of intellectual property—Great American Novels and poems, garage-band songs, water-cooler jokes—that is never published. In fact, in these and a myriad of other situations there may be no expectation of publication or of any economic reward. In other words, the urge to create, at least for individuals, may not depend on the incentives that assertedly justify copyright, patent, and other legal schemes. These heresies, however, have less relevance for copyright industries, which depend on legal protection for their products. Accordingly, this revisionist view has not yet penetrated public-policy discussions on the nature of future protection for computer software deeply, nor can we expect it to do so anytime soon.

Virtually everyone recognizes that pirating intellectual property is both wrong and illegal. By "piracy" we mean unauthorized large-scale reproduction of creative works for resale. Unquestionably, commercial piracy of all intellectual property, including software, poses a continuing and significant threat to the software industry and is morally repugnant. There should be no debate on this point.

What is less well understood is that there are many uses of intellectual property that fall shy of piracy. Rather than being considered illegal, some might well be encouraged. The legitimacy of these uses is grounded in what is described as the "intellectual-property bargain" of U.S. law. Here is the bargain: The law safeguards economic incentives for the production of intellectual property by granting individuals the monopoly right to exploit their works for a limited time. In exchange, society benefits from the flow of artistic and innovative works into the market and from technological development. Ultimately, the works so created will become available after the term of exclusive use expires. In a nutshell, individual property rights are in a delicate balance with the goal of ensuring that the public benefits.

The debate over the extent to which the intellectual-property laws should protect such relatively new products of intellectual genius as computer software is joined just here: What are the terms of the intellectual-property bargain that would generate optimal benefits for society? The crux of the controversy is whether society benefits more from affording creators broad, enduring, and exclusive rights to foster creativity than from limiting their rights in order to encourage adaptation and innovation by others.

As a preamble to all that follows, it is worth emphasizing the understanding inherent in the bargain by quoting from the 1909 House of Representatives report that accompanied the Copyright Act:

The enactment of copyright legislation by Congress under the terms of the Constitution is not based upon any natural right that the author has in his writings, for the Supreme Court has held that such rights as he has are purely statutory rights, but upon the ground that the welfare of the public will be served and progress of science and useful arts will be promoted. . . . Not primarily for the benefit of the author, but primarily for the benefit of the public, such rights are given. Not that any particular class of citizens, however, worthy, may benefit, but because the policy is believed to be for the benefit of the great body of people, in that it will stimulate writing and invention, to give some bonus to authors and inventors.

The fine points of this contract lie in the metes and bounds of the protection that the law accords creators. Essentially, protection against unauthorized use, reproduction, or distribution is not available for creative works that are already in the public domain. Similarly, no monopoly will be granted for principles that exist in nature or for broad ideas or concepts. Conversely, the law does protect inventions that are new, works that are original, and specific expressions of ideas.

To be more concrete: under patent law, inventors are only entitled to claim ownership of features that are "novel"—that is, different from all previous inventions. Patent law has not protected scientific principles and mathematical algorithms. In return for the statutory monopoly, however, and in furtherance of the underlying bargain of intellectual-property law, the owner of a patent on an invention must disclose the details of the invention so that the public can come to understand it.

Under copyright law, to be protected a work must be original in the author (it need not be novel). Copyright accords no monopolies to creators for abstract ideas, procedures, principles, concepts, systems, or themes—for what the Supreme Court long ago described as "the common property of the whole world." [2] Granting creators a monopoly on mere ideas would thwart the fundamental goals of the law, which are embedded in the intellectual-property bargain. Consequently, copyright only protects the "expression" by authors of ideas.

Much of the current debate is over the meaning of such recondite notions as the nature of a mathematical algorithm and the difference between an idea and the expression of that idea in the context of computer programs. More recently, very substantial industrial, judicial, and academic resources have been expended in trying to apply to software the all-important dichotomy between an idea and the expression of that idea—the distinction that, at least in the copyright domain, separates what cannot be protected from what can.

Generally speaking, applying this idea/expression dialectic to the more familiar literary works that are protected by copyright law is not impossibly difficult. No one would think, for example, that an author should have monopoly rights for each and every play about a man and a woman who come from feuding factions and promptly proceed to fall in love; we would not question, however, Stephen Sondheim's right to protect the libretto for *West Side Story* or (if he were alive today) Shakespeare's being able to protect *Romeo and Juliet*. In the world of computer software this distinction between an idea and its expression is far from clear, however.

Copyright and Patent Protection for Computer Software

Software is most commonly protected, in the United States and elsewhere, under copyright laws and as a copyrighted "literary work." Indeed, the text of the Uruguay Round agreement concluded at the end of 1993 states expressly that the Berne Convention (which provides international protection for copyrighted works) should protect computer software as a "literary work." In addition to copyright law, resort is increasingly had to patent protection. That the copyright law should be the most available form of protection is the direct result of congressional enactment and judicial decisions. Yet we do not need to be highly skilled Silicon Valley programmers to know that software is different in many respects from plays or poems, and other kinds of works (movies, paintings, sculptures) that are also protected by copyright. Indeed, the more we rely on our everyday common sense, the more apparent it is that software is not like other "literary works," which convey meaning to human beings.

Computer software is functional: it makes machines work. To be sure, software is not unique in its functionality. Some conventional copyrighted works have utilitarian purposes. A navigator's map and a cookbook recipe come to mind; so, too, do accountant's blank ledger sheets and automatic player-piano rolls, both the subjects of early Supreme Court cases.[3] Architectural works, which integrate function and aesthetics, are now expressly protected under a 1990 amendment to the copyright law.[4] Nor is software alone in being copyrightable yet essentially unintelligible to people; think of the digital bits of a sound recording embedded on a compact disc or the image fixed in a videotape. Each of the latter, however, is intended to convey information to—to produce music or movies for— and to be appreciated or even inhabited by real, live people.

Even if software is not unique in either its utilitarian nature or its lack of immediate human intelligibility, for many (though far from most) observers the chasm between software's fundamental characteristics and the underlying objectives of the copyright regime—to impart information to the public—is deeply disturbing. Another aspect of software raises more difficult issues for the industry and for the law: because computer software actually implements or is part of an electrical or mechanical process or operation, how can we separate its unprotectible elements—procedures, processes, or operations—from that protectible quantum of expression created by the programmer?

What about patent law, which protects novel processes but not what the law deems "mathematical algorithms"? Thirty years ago the U.S. Patent and Trademark Office refused to issue patents for programs because they were thought to be creations in the area of thought or "mental steps." Soon patent protection was made available for a process that did not require human intervention. The courts played an active role in determining whether certain programs were unpatentable, because they were mere mathematical formulae, or whether they could be patented when incorporated in an overall process. Over time, a series of closely argued and somewhat abstruse decisions have separated the chaff of a "mathematical" algorithm, which is not protectible under the law, from a "nonmathematical" algorithm, which may be embodied in a patentable claim. Today the Patent and Trademark Office is issuing patents in significant numbers for computer software.

American and International Debates

The unsettled state of legal protection for software in the mid 1970s caused the U.S. Congress to throw up its hands and create a special commission to tackle the legal issues raised by the intersection of copyright law and new computer technology. In 1974 the U.S. Congress, confronting the anachronistic 1909 Copyright Act, the special characteristics of software, and the substantial uncertainty as to whether copyright and patent law would be available for software, established the National Commission on New Technological Uses of Copyrighted Works ("CONTU"). CONTU, which represented authors, other copyright owners, users, and the public, held three years of hearings. Its report concluded that computer programs are expression, should be treated as literary works, and are protectible under copyright law, that proprietors of software should have the same rights as owners of other kinds of copyrighted works, and that it is not an infringement of copyright to use a program as it is intended to be used in conjunction with a computer.[5] CONTU commissioner John Hersey, the noted author, dissented vigorously, pointing out that the essentially utilitarian qualities of programs distinguished them from other kinds of copyrighted works. A relieved Congress adopted the recommendations of CONTU's Final Report, expressly adding a definition of "computer program" to the 1976 Copyright Act.[6]

The CONTU Final Report expressly recognized that many of the most critical and sensitive issues would be left to the courts for ultimate resolution. At least the commissioners were right on that score. The courts have been intensely and increasingly active in determining how the copyright laws might apply to computer software.

Today the entire computer industry champions strong intellectual-property protections for software. However, a vocal and active subsector of the industry—including such eminent American companies as Sun Microsystems, Storage Technology, and Amdahl and also some European and Japanese software houses—wants to tailor the exclusive rights available under the copyright law to allow the production of "interoperable" computer devices and programs that can interconnect with existing systems without the risk of a suit for copyright infringement.

IBM, Digital, Apple, Microsoft, Intel, and other large and established developers are fighting back. These are the companies that have the most at stake (their software assets), and the most to lose from the weakening of the copyright law. They have joined the debate with a vengeance, arguing that those who want to narrow or refine the scope of copyright protection for computer software are not innovators but merely beneficiaries of technology developed by others. The establishment's rapid retort to the smaller software houses has been that there is no need for the law to afford developers special access to interfaces for the development of compatible programs.

Lest the patent side of the controversy be forgotten, there continues to be litigation over software-related patents. Debates over whether computer processes and algorithms should be patentable have swept the software industry. A U.S. Commerce Department report in the early 1990s, however, concluded that computer programs are quite properly subjects of patent protection, that the existing U.S. laws for protection of software were adequate, and that no specialized statutory framework would be necessary or even helpful.[7] The debate over software patents promises to continue; the Patent and Trademark Office held two hearings on software patents in early 1994 in which large corporations supported continued issuance of software patents while smaller houses and individual programmers were more skeptical of the benefits of patentability, if not downright opposed to patenting software.

Before examining the future, it will be helpful to summarize the current state of the law in the United States. In particular, the law evolved slowly to protect different aspects of computer software under the copyright law.

In the first generation of litigation, the courts protected, as literary works, the "literal" elements of a computer program. These literal elements include the actual lines of code, whether object code or source code. Courts have protected both operating and applications programs, as well as microcode and programs embedded in ROM chips.

In the second generation of litigation, the courts protected structure, sequence, and organization (SSO) or selection, coordination, or arrangement (SCA)—the so-called nonliteral components of a program. The literal lines of code, even if not intelligible by humans, might be said to be like other literary works. It may not be intuitively obvious, however, why we should protect elements of expression in a program that are at a more abstract level than those literal elements, though traditional copyright law does not limit protection to the text alone.

In a third generation, the courts protected under copyright law the "look and feel" of a program. "Look" refers to a program's expressive elements: menus, command language, tile displays or "windows," icons, scrolling features, and other elements of the graphical user interface (GUI). "Feel" refers to the use of keystrokes and commands, and other aspects of the program's interaction with the user.

Aside from the user interface, other aspects of a program's external design that might be protected under copyright law include its interface with other programs. (Applications programs need to have access to functions provided by the operating systems software of the computer.) It is in trying to fit all these nonliteral elements of a program to the Procrustean bed of the idea/expression dichotomy that courts, developers, and users are increasingly finding that the copyright law is not quite as helpful as it might be.

Protecting a Program's "Look and Feel"

We can assume, at least for now, that there is a consensus that copying lines of code constitutes copyright infringement. Far more problematic for the courts is trying to determine to what extent the SSO or the "look and feel" of one program might infringe another. The critical issues here will center around determining on which side of the idea/expression line of demarcation the nonliteral elements of a program for which protection is asserted might fall. The American judiciary and the courts of other nations have struggled valiantly but without complete success to develop a test for infringement based on determining at what level of abstraction two programs should be compared, what elements of a program are not protectible, and whether two programs being compared are indeed substantially similar.

The seminal decision in *Whelan Associates, Inc. v. Jaslow Laboratories, Inc.*[8] (which decided that program copyrights can be infringed even absent direct copying of source code) recognized the importance of the programmer's decision in arranging the program's SSO and subroutines. The appeals court rewarded the programmer's efficient arrangement of modules and subroutines and the programmer's organization of the way the software obtains and makes use of data. In doing so, the court applied some more traditional notions of copyright law to software, to ensure that some of the most commercially important elements of the program would be protected. The crucial first step of the court's analysis is a comparison of the functions or purposes of the programs at a relatively high level of abstraction: management of a dental lab. The consequence of determining the program's function, or idea, at that level is to draw the idea/expression line so far to the idea side of the spectrum that virtually every other aspect of the program would be considered protectible expression.

Many courts have embraced the *Whelan* decision and have concluded that a program's SSO can be protected. However, determining what constitutes the function of a program continues to be difficult for the courts. One vexing issue for the courts is whether they should simply look at the overall function of the program or whether they should examine more carefully the functions of the various discrete processes or applications that are embedded in it. The court that decided the *Whelan* case failed to provide much guidance for its successors in this respect.

The idea of a program is far from self-evident. As the ongoing litigation involving Lotus 1-2-3 demonstrates,[9] the search for a program's idea can be perplexing, both for courts and for software houses wishing to avoid litigation. Is the idea underlying Lotus 1-2-3, at its most abstract, "a menu-driven electronic spreadsheet?" At the other end of the spectrum of particularity, is it a spreadsheet that uses the exact menu commands of Lotus 1-2-3? The trial court's ruling on whether Borland's Quattro and Quattro Pro infringed on the Lotus 1-2-3 user interface settled on a level of abstraction that was above the most specific; it defined the idea of

Lotus 1-2-3 as a spreadsheet with hierarchical menus linked by command operations but not necessarily using the same command names and organization as the Lotus product. In applying this test, the court in a decision of monumental significance to the software industry, decided that the user interface of Borland's programs infringed the expression of Lotus 1-2-3.[10]

Several courts also have struggled with the problems inherent in applying the suggestion of the court in *Whelan*, which it borrowed from more traditional copyright principles, that if there is more than one way to express an idea then the copyright holder's expression of that idea must be protected. Conversely, where there is only one way of expressing a particular idea it is said that the idea and the expression merge. When that occurs, the expression, which otherwise might be protectible, is not within the scope of copyright. This doctrine of "merger" (or *scenes a faire* in the literary world) developed out of the proposition that certain common themes, such as the shoot-'em-up Western and the cops-and-robbers film, may not be copyrighted.

But the general theme of a play or a novel, which may not be protected by copyright, differs considerably from a standard or a requirement for a computer program! Courts are looking at the programs of third parties to determine whether there are alternative ways of expressing an idea or a function differently than the expression of the plaintiff (though, as we have seen, this review requires that a court first determine the program's function).

Infringement litigation increasingly is examining the role of "externalities"—factors outside the program itself that may govern its SSO or its "feel." Some of these factors may be due to marketplace realities, such as the need to present data in a standardized format; others may emerge from the need to develop software that is compatible with or makes the most efficient use of particular standards or hardware on which it is designed to run.

In the future, the pendulum of protection may swing back toward restricting a copyright holder's ability to prevent others from copying a program's "look." For developers of successful, path-breaking programs, the turn away from protecting the entire "look and feel" of a program may not be altogether good news. For those, however, who might choose to stand on the shoulders of software developers who have gone before, the more focused analysis of the protectibility of structural elements may create opportunities to develop new, improved, and compatible programs.

One of the most powerful forces for rethinking how broadly the industry wishes (or is able) to protect the "look and feel" of software was a 1992 decision rendered by the influential federal appeals court in New York, which has had a striking judicial following in the rest of the United States and also in the United Kingdom and Canada. This decision, *Computer Associates International, Inc. v. Altai, Inc.,*[11] rejected what some had argued was the all-too-straightforward formulation in the *Whelan* decision.

The defendant, Altai, had developed software to schedule jobs on an IBM mainframe computer, but then modified it to add an interface that permitted the software to run under three operating systems. Altai's programmer was a former employee of the plaintiff, Computer Associates, who had taken with him source code from his erstwhile employer (in violation of his employment agreement) and had used that code to create the interface modification for Altai. When the president of Altai learned of the copying, a new version of the program was prepared by employees who had no access to the Computer Associates code. The suit was brought on the question of whether the Altai modification, even after it was rewritten to remove copied code, infringed the plaintiff's copyrights. The appeals court developed and applied a three-part test to conclude that the plaintiff's copyrights were not infringed.

First, the court dissected the program to isolate its various levels of abstraction.

Second, it applied a filter to examine the program's components and determine which of them had been dictated by efficiency considerations and hence were unprotectible. The result of the court's inquiry here seems, curiously, to be that the more efficient the programmer might be—the more closely the structure approaches the program's idea or process—the less the program is protected. Should less efficient structures be adopted for the purpose of introducing protectible expression into the program? If the answer were "yes," the decision would, to say the least, create perverse incentives for developers. Apart from elements dictated by efficiency, elements dictated by externalities (including programming practices and structural elements taken from public-domain material) are to be filtered out. Not much of the program may be left after the application of this abstraction-filtration test.

In the third step, the court compared the post-filtration "kernel" of protectible expression with the allegedly infringing program. Here, the goals were to determine whether the defendant had copied any of that core expression and to determine the relative importance of the copied portion to the program as a whole. The court concluded in *Altai* that it needed to use expert testimony to evaluate whether the two programs were substantially similar.

It is obvious that in *Altai* the court was not at all shy about disturbing what had become almost settled expectations. In fact, the court expressly invited Congress to revisit the advisability of applying copyright principles to computer software. In suggesting that making decisions in cases involving the copyrightability of software is akin to fitting a square peg into a round hole, the court provided some support for those who argue that copyright may not be well suited to protecting computer programs. Of course, there also are those who believe that the court's decision, in raising anew the questions of the suitability of copyright for software, deviated a bit too sharply from the text and the spirit of Congress' statutory direction.

Hence, we seem to have come almost full circle to a situation that existed in the late 1970s. Might we even see a CONTU II? Or, less dramatically, do *Altai* and the many cases that have followed it represent nothing more than the latest, and welcome, manifestations of our great tradition of common law, which continually refines the law in applying hoary legal doctrines to new technologies? Thus, then, will some of tomorrow's great litigation issues be joined.

Moving toward Interoperable Environments: Rights to Decompile Programs

Most of us do not have the time or patience to learn or remember lots of commands or interfaces—what the F10 key will do in various programs, for example. It is for this reason that some programmers are developing software that is compatible and interoperable with the programs of other companies. Users want specialized calendaring or word processing programs to operate in an environment to which they are accustomed. To make this happen, however, requires examining the program that establishes the environment in order to ensure that the program being developed will be interoperable with it. To "examine," however, requires that the developer have access to the underlying program so that he or she understands how it operates and therefore is able to produce an appropriate interface between the two programs. Copyright's newest frontier is the terrain between permissible access for purposes of examination and naked copying—a frontier on which battles are now raging. Most frequently, the litigation has large companies, which generally refuse to give any quarter, poised against smaller software houses, which are designing compatible or competitive programs.

Litigation over the so-called rights of decompilation is not unlike the movement of banners on the field of combat, by which an observer can try to discern the ebb and flow of battle. As the law evolves, it may be signaling whether the user-driven trend toward standardization and interoperability will endure in the face of arguments for safeguarding the unfettered right of companies to prevent others from enhancing or competing with their products.

Decompilation is also called "reverse engineering." Decompiling software means analyzing a program at the level of machine language and object code and then translating it into a form that programmers can understand. Such translations are effected by using devices that read the object code and download it into a computer. The object code is then translated into assembly language. This process is relatively time consuming, but, of course, no more so than the development of the program being decompiled.

Decompilation may implicate several rights that the copyright law grants to the author of the original program. First, the decompiler will have to make one or more intermediate copies of the program that is being studied.[12] In addition, the decompiler's enhanced program may be considered a derivative work. Many proponents of maximum copyright protection have argued that decompilation's principal purpose is to encourage the development of cheaper commercial substitutes for the original programs. The contrarians here (including smaller software houses, academics, and various observers) contend that decompilation can result in complementary software that makes use of a common interface—for printers, for example. Supporters of decompilation believe such a process is needed to encourage innovative software-development efforts in the United States.

The statute books of the United States, unlike a recent directive of the European Community (described below), contain no express language that would grant developers the right to decompile software. The legal issue presented to American courts is rather circumscribed yet has considerable consequences for the evolution of computer software technology: Is decompilation permissible as a "fair use" (or is it otherwise justifiable) under the copyright law?

The fair-use doctrine of the copyright law is a defense against copyright infringement and is characterized as providing courts with an equitable rule of reason in judging such claims.[13] It should come as no surprise, therefore, that there has been widespread disagreement in all segments of the copyright community as to the scope and the proper application of the doctrine. Suffice it to say that fair use is a necessary check on the absolute rights that the law generally accords copyright holders. Fair use is intended to encompass, and to protect, such uses of copyrighted materials as research and study. The doctrine is absolutely integral to the intellectual-property bargain, because it encourages the public to use copyrighted material to produce yet other works for the benefit of all.

The mid 1980s brought a series of inconclusive decisions on the legality of reverse engineering. In 1992 and 1993, however, two influential courts recognized decompilation for the purposes of understanding how certain software functions, in order to develop compatible programs, as a legitimate fair use. These cases did not involve the traditional software houses; instead, the litigants were the major players in the videogame business: Atari, Nintendo, Sega, and Accolade.

In *Sega Enterprises Ltd. v. Accolade, Inc.*[14] the appeals court decided that the defendant's use was fair, owing in large part to the importance of having access to Sega's (the plaintiff's) programs. The judges implicitly questioned the bases of the premise of the copyright law that a literary work is a literary work is a literary work. Like their colleagues who rendered the appellate decision in the *Altai* case, they found that computer programs are "utilitarian articles" and, accordingly, should receive "a lower degree of protection than more traditional literary works." [15]

Beyond reopening the debate as to whether CONTU's findings were correct, the judges who decided the *Sega* case expressly recognized that permitting decompilation would increase the number of independently designed video games. This result, they stated, would mean a laudable "growth in creative expression," which would redound to the benefit of the public.[16] The court also tried to balance the intellectual-property rights of original creators with the needs of those who wish to produce compatible programs. In doing so, it criticized Sega's attempt to control the market by exercising monopoly control over video games that would run on Sega consoles.

The *Sega* decision represents a strong commitment to affording programmers access to basic technologies and, therefore, to the goal of industry standardization. As can be imagined, critics of the decision are legion. They claim that the court's grant of expansive authority to decompile virtually propels proprietary standards, which may have been developed at considerable expense, into the public domain. Now almost anyone can develop video games that will operate on Sega or Nintendo consoles. What incentive do those companies (or their successors) have to invent and market technologically innovative systems? Is there, however, any empirical support for the argument that decompilation might devastate incentives to invest in technology?

Conversely, do video games that are independently created but are designed to run on the consoles of other companies compete in a way that violates the spirit of the copyright law? And is it fair to argue that all such newly developed programs are ready substitutes for the decompiled software, and that decompilation should therefore be considered commercial piracy?

The fundamental goal for future developers (and their lawyers) should not be to argue narrowly over the scope of the fair-use doctrine or over whether decompilation rights should be permitted or proscribed. Rather, it should be to understand both the purposes underlying and the economic and social results of decompilation activity. Even more broadly, it should be to develop a policy consensus, within the industry and involving Congress, as to the desirability of encouraging compatibility and interoperability among programs.

Following—But Not Quite—in the Footsteps of the United States

Japan, Europe, and Australia, along with other industrialized countries, also have been caught up in the web of arguments embodied in the CONTU Final Report as well as in the litigation over "look and feel" and the debate over the permissibility and scope of decompilation. Following the lead of the United States, they have, in general, opted for protecting software under a copyright framework. Moreover, the United States, Japan, and Europe seem to have shown substantial and growing support for the patentability of computer-program-related inventions. Mathematical algorithms or programs are generally excluded from protection, but program-controlled processes may be patented. In Japan, thousands of patent applications for computer-program-related inventions are filed each year.

The Japanese are continuing to explore the contours of the rather ample protection that their law now grants to computer programs. In particular, in mid 1993 they announced that they would be considering the possibility of amending the copyright law to permit some reverse engineering of computer programs. This step was being taken, of course, in the wake of the decompilation-related decisions in the United States (described above) and the European Community's computer software directive (discussed below).

The announcement from Japan has caused substantial concern on the part of larger American computer program producers. The Business Software Alliance estimates that U.S. software companies hold 55 percent of the market for prepackaged personal computer software in Japan. They fear an erosion of protection for their works in Japan and in other countries that might follow Japan's lead. They expended resources to energize the U.S. government to exert pressure on Japan to block any amending legislation that would weaken legal protection for U.S. software. Following intense pressure from the U.S. government, the Japanese announced at the end of May 1994 that they would not be recommending any changes to the law to permit reverse engineering, and that the situation merited further consideration at some unspecified future time.

Europeans, too, have been keenly aware that the future health and competitiveness of Europe depends on the development of a competitive software industry. Integral to that goal was the development of a scheme that would provide effective and harmonized protection of software throughout the European Community. To that end, in 1988 the Commission of the European Communities published a "Green Paper on Copyright and the Challenge of Technology." The Commission proposed a directive that would apply copyright protection to computer programs, but it asked for the public's views on whether access protocols and program interfaces should be excluded from the scope of protection.

The Commission adopted a directive on legal protection for computer programs after a fierce intra-industry debate over whether decompilation should be permitted. Although the Europeans generally followed in CONTU's footsteps, the directive embodies a compromise that permits some decompilation to achieve interoperability.

The approach, while essentially reaffirming U.S. law and policy, expressly recognizes the value of paring back software developers' monopoly rights. The Commission struck the bargain in a way that is just a bit more favorable to the broader public-policy goals of access to information that are inherent in intellectual-property law.

Notwithstanding confident assertions by developers that copyright law is well suited to protect computer software, inquiring minds outside the Northern Hemisphere also have ventured to take a second look at just how nicely copyright is accommodating itself to new technological developments. The Australians, in particular, are stressing the importance of striking the right balance between "adequate protection" and "the need to provide the community with reasonable access to intellectual property and the benefits which it confers."[17] A draft proposal would permit program decompilation to allow developers to create interoperable, independently created programs, and to curtail protection for "look and feel." Like their American, Japanese, and European counterparts, however, the Australians are recognizing that it is not easy to achieve the delicate balance required by copyright law.

We can expect that the international trend toward convergence of protection among the most developed countries will continue. It will be fueled, in part, by the multinational reach of software houses and by the inevitable realization of courts, expert committees, and legislative bodies that national differences in approach can impede the development of technology. Implementation of multinational trade regimes, such as the North American Free Trade Agreement and the Uruguay Round of the General Agreement on Tariffs and Trade, is another key element in stimulating a worldwide consensus on protection. By contrast, any counterpoised force that would facilitate or encourage divergences among countries or regions would be detrimental to the interests of the software industry.

Who Owns the Rights?

Whether you are a developer or a user of software, perhaps the most important fact is who has the legal right to control the exploitation or any other use of the software. Over the next decade, practical and legal questions over who has proprietary ownership of software will continue to vex the business community. Why are such questions likely to be important? Software houses, of course, must know with certainty who has the right to exploit their products commercially. Users need to be assured that, when they buy or take out a license on software, the licensor has good title, or else take their chances on being sued for infringing the intellectual-property rights of the real owner (or at least a claimant).

Under prevailing copyright laws, ownership is tied to "authorship." Authors can freely negotiate to assign or sell their rights, of course. Patents are issued to inventors, who, too, can contractually relinquish or transfer their rights. Today, and for the foreseeable future, these seemingly simple and straightforward principles can be difficult to apply in practice.

The most fascinating aspect of the problem of authorship is that, of course, intellectual property is the creation of the thought processes or artistic ambitions of human beings. Individuals write poems, direct motion pictures, compose music, paint, and create computer software. The "boy genius" software developer working in his garage represents what we believe is the quintessence of Yankee ingenuity. Yet, at least as applied to intellectual property, the law also recognizes the present reality that most commercial software is created by teams of individuals working in businesses or at universities. Emerging from the tension between individual initiative, innovation, and creativity and the desire (even need) to have institutions commercialize intellectual property are some of the most complex problems of the future. A particularly intriguing manifestation of this dialectic between human and institutional authorship of intellectual property is the constellation of issues surrounding the question of "authorship" of computer programs generated by computers.

Whither the Young Developer?

Johann Sebastian Bach's monumental Mass in B Minor is unquestionably among the most profoundly moving of all choral works. During his extraordinary career, Bach, like many other musicians of his century, served in several successive positions, including court organist at Weimar, Capellmeister to the court of Anhalt-Cöthen, and cantor at St. Thomas's School in Leipzig. The final version of the B Minor Mass, composed while Bach was at Leipzig, is a collection of materials composed especially for the Mass and earlier works. Almost one-third of the completed Mass is music Bach borrowed from himself; one section, the Osanna, was first performed as part of an entirely secular cantata honoring King-Elector Augustus III. Who can be said to have "owned" the rights to the Mass—which of Bach's patrons or several employers? Might the different sections be owned by different persons, depending on the dates of their composition or of their inspiration? These issues do not seem to have preoccupied Bach, though his music was and is of inestimable spiritual, if not economic, value.

Silicon Valley programmers also move around a lot. Now, this mobility confronts us, as it did not challenge Bach and his contemporaries, with the provocative question as to who owns the creative impulses of the human mind. Once human thoughts are fixed on paper or on disk, the copyright law kicks in. Then, as we have seen, the law endows the author, the author's employer, or some other contractual party with legal rights to the fruits of the author's creation.

Who owns a software developer's not-yet-written-down thoughts when she takes a job at another software house? The answer, we would have thought, ought to be firmly grounded in human anatomy, if not in principles of natural law: each of us has the exclusive rights to the workings of his or her own brain.

Enter the laws of trade secrets, which protect confidential business or other proprietary information against unauthorized use or disclosure. In the United States these laws may vary among the states, although about half of the states have adopted the Uniform Trade Secrets Act. Japan has a specific law protecting trade secrets, which are also protected in a few European countries but not generally elsewhere. All this will change, however, because the Uruguay Round agreement contains provisions that require signatories to afford legal protection to trade secrets.

Trade-secrets laws apply to formulas, processes, or programs, such as computer software, that would afford a competitive advantage to one business over its competitors. They protect secret features of software, and they operate—in a belt-and-suspenders way—simultaneously with the protections of the copyright and patent laws. The key to protection under these laws is that the information is confidential and is not generally known to competitors or to the public. What could be more secret than the inner, undisclosed thoughts of human beings?

The law of trade secrets does, however, empower businesses to maintain control over how their former employees can use information to which they may have had access. A company's brightest software engineer may have developed or been exposed to proprietary programming processes or features that gave the company a real edge over its competitors. It will have taken all kinds of security measures to maintain the secrecy of that commercially valuable information. Indeed, under prevailing law, even the release of software, where the trade secret is embedded in the object code, does not destroy the secret nature of the information.[18]

Employers have gone to court to obtain injunctions against their former employees' using the trade secrets to which they may have had access, or may themselves have developed, during the course of their employment. In some cases, the fact that an employee had authorized access to his employer's information may be a good defense to a charge that he misappropriated a trade secret. As a result, downstream employers have to take particular pains to ask a new employee where and how he developed the ideas or codes that are reflected in the software that he creates, particularly if that software competes with the software of his former employer. The facts in the *Altai* case, where a programmer had used source code from his previous employer in coding a program for his new employer, demonstrate some of the dangers lurking for companies who pick up talented software programmers from their competition. In no small part, Altai's being hauled into court was a direct result of the bad acts of its new employee.

These situations—whether they arise in courts or in the software laboratory—raise profoundly difficult questions. How can we distinguish independently generated thinking, which belongs solely to the human being, from thoughts that result from information obtained from one's colleagues or one's employer? Courts and businesses are continuing to wrestle with these problems. No obvious solutions present themselves.

In the years ahead, software development will become an even more valuable component of the global economy. With more and more software developers and with even greater job mobility, billions of dollars' worth of potential trade secrets are at stake. To ensure that such valuable proprietary information is protected software houses resort to employment contracts.

Employment contracts or other legal obligations between an employee and a new employer are far from a panacea, however. (The fact that Computer Associates had had an employment agreement with someone who then went to work for Altai did not stop him from purloining the source code, in violation of the contract!) In an action to enforce the contract, the employer and the erstwhile employee will still haggle over just what pieces of knowledge that the individual absorbed in his old job he is forbidden to use in his subsequent jobs. What information was well known in the industry or should otherwise not be regarded as a trade secret? What information was properly marked as secret corporate lore? What knowledge was the product of the employee's own intelligence? The challenges presented by drafting and enforcing a judicial order that can so precisely parse human thought demonstrate that, at bottom, "intellectual property" is very much the personal property of a human's intellect.

Authorship across Borders: Electronic Networks

Assume that three software engineers—an independent contractor to a company in the United States, an employee of an affiliated company in France, and an employee of an entirely separate company in Taiwan—

are working collectively on an interactive electronic network to develop software for the operation of robots. Who will own the rights to the software?

The short answer, of course, is that contractual arrangements among the venture partners should determine this question. Did the partners intend that the three engineers create what is called a "joint work?" Joint works, such as songs that combine lyrics and music, are created where the authors intend that their contributions become inseparable parts of a whole. But whose intentions would control? The complication here is that there are differences in how the three countries' laws allocate rights between the individuals and the institutions for which they are working.

An independent contractor in the United States would, barring a written assignment, have ownership rights to software he has created. In Taiwan, however, it now appears that an employee who creates software within the scope of his employment is considered the author of the software, at least if there is no written employment contract to the contrary.[19] So, a contract among the American, French, and Taiwanese companies will not control who has the rights to the software. The Taiwanese law will operate to protect the Taiwanese engineer, who will have personal rights in the software. In the absence of a contract with that engineer, he could be able to block the commercialization of the software that he has created jointly with his American and French colleagues. The U.S. company will certainly be surprised when it learns that it cannot stop the Taiwanese engineer from licensing his rights to one of its competitors, which intends to sell the software outside the United States!

The French software engineer, moreover, could have yet another type of claim to the software. The U.S. company may feel secure because it has ensured that its French affiliate has a work-for-hire agreement with its employee. The laws of France and Taiwan, however, along with those of most other European countries and Canada, will give the engineer so-called moral rights. These moral rights, which are independent of any copyright or other contractual rights, safeguard the author's right to preserve the integrity of his work, to be associated with the work, and, in general, to prevent the distortion or mutilation of the work. Moral rights may provide a basis for bringing suit to prohibit modification of a computer program or of its output.

The moral rights of the French and Taiwanese engineers could pose a hidden danger for the U.S. company, which had thought that it owned all rights to exploit the robotics software. The company might find that it needs to adapt the software for particular applications or markets. And, ordinarily, it would be able to do so. The engineers, however, may well be successful in exercising their moral rights to block any such modification. To be sure, the U.S. company is hardly disturbing the integrity of an artist's work—slashing the Mona Lisa, for example. Nevertheless, French courts could prevent it from changing the software, without paying the French engineer or obtaining a waiver from him, by deciding that it was distorting the work that he had helped to create.[20]

The greater the number of countries, companies, and people in a consortium or an enterprise, the greater the uncertainty as to who owns rights to the software that they develop. In all this, the only thing that may be certain is the need for more international software lawyers.

Patent Protection for Computer Software: Strategy for Tomorrow's Battleground

Traditionally, patent protection for computer software has taken a back seat to copyright. Throughout the 1980s and the early 1990s, however, many software developers (particularly those with the most significant resources) have moved aggressively to take out patents on their programs. They have been encouraged to do so by the Supreme Court and the U.S. Patent and Trademark Office, which have gradually broadened the scope of computer-related inventions as patentable subject matter.

It is often said that patents and copyrights augment one another. But how and why? Simply put, patent laws, much more than copyright, afford developers enormous strategic advantages over their competitors, whether they be domestic or foreign. The use of the patent laws in this strategic fashion, it cannot be disputed, has profound implications for the structure of the software industry, and indeed for U.S. competitiveness worldwide. Although these consequences spring directly from the nature of the intellectual-property bargain, only recently has there been a focus on the real impact of developers' ability to exercise monopoly patent rights.

The hypothetical example of the bicycle (itself an invention now long in the public domain) demonstrates the power of a patent. The owner of a patent on the bicycle could prevent anyone from making another bicycle, even one that improved significantly on or differed from the patented invention. Depending on the scope of the claims, the patent owner might be able to block any other manufacture of a two-wheeled, self-powered machine for locomotion, or of any of its critical components. Another developer of handlebars or pedals that improved on the original might not be able to manufacture them (let alone the entire bicycle) without a license from the patent holder.

Although the grant of a patent does result in disclosure of the invention to the public, a patent on basic technology is likely to constitute a fairly effective blockade to technological development. Just one example from corporate America is Polaroid's efforts to use its patents to block Kodak from being in the instant-photography business. For this reason, patents on basic types of software, such as operating systems, common user interfaces, and applications programs that are industry standards, give their owners extraordinary leverage.

In applying for a software patent, the applicant can include not just the source code but also a diagram or a flow chart of the software. If issued, the patent therefore might protect not just the expression but also any program that performs the functional steps or carries out the processes described in the claims.

Given the power of patents, we should not be astonished that developers are obtaining them as part of a portfolio that they will then use to implement both offensive and defensive strategies. Here, then, is the battleground of the next decade:

When issued a patent in a particular country, a developer can use its rights offensively to block anyone else from producing or selling in that territory a product that is based on its software. Injunctions can be issued to prevent infringements. Would-be competitors will have to expend substantial resources in developing a competing software product that is designed around the claims of the patent. The comparative certainty of the protection afforded by a patent can be a highly important business tool in planning whether and how to exploit the software. In lieu of blocking competitive manufacture, software developers may choose to license their products to reap significant royalties in order to recoup the costs of past and future development efforts.

Patents can also be used to shape industrial arrangements and structure. Patents and cross-licenses can be used in a strategic sense to force or facilitate joint software-development efforts or other ventures. Two companies with complementary technologies may decide that it makes sense to allow each or both to use their software to create a suite of products or to ensure the interoperability of their software.

Today, companies are reviewing and developing large and usually undervalued patent portfolios to implement a wealth of strategies that can best be described as defensive. A company with a patent on a basic software technology may choose to lie relatively low. One of its competitors might expend substantial resources on developing a program for which it then tries to obtain a patent. The program of this competitor, however, might fall within the claims of one of the patents in the first company's portfolio. In this situation, the competitor is not only likely to fail to prevent the first company from making or selling its basic software technology; it may be forced to enter into a cross-licensing agreement to market the second program at all. At the very least, a hefty patent portfolio can be an effective defensive tool with which to ward off litigation.

Big companies increasingly will enter into comprehensive cross-licensing arrangements that will enable them to design and develop software with complete freedom. This is a strategy that IBM has pursued with other developers having significant patent assets. Of course, developers that are not parties to these agreements are simply frozen out.

A clever strategy, which relies on the intellectual-property bargain inherent in the patent laws, makes use of the fact of disclosure that accompanies the issuance of a patent. When a patent is issued, the claimed invention is made known to the public and, therefore, becomes "prior art."[21] A subsequent developer of software that is similar to the patented software might find that it is unable to obtain a patent because its work would not be regarded as "novel" or "non-obvious." Rather, the software technology may, as a result of the publication of the first patent, be widely known. Once a software developer becomes aware of another company's competitive efforts, it might rush to the Patent and Trademark Office to obtain a patent on its software, thereby disclosing it (if the patent is granted) and potentially making it impossible for the competitor to qualify for a patent.

Patents create or reinforce dominance. A software patent filed and granted in the United States and in other countries will strengthen significantly the competitive position of its owner. Even for smaller companies, obtaining or suing to enforce software patents is one way to survive in an increasingly cut-throat sector. For these reasons, the U.S. software industry has been a vociferous proponent of maintaining and enhancing patent protection for software as an incentive that (it argues) is necessary to stimulate technological innovation and development. To enable U.S. companies to obtain patents for computer software-related inventions abroad, the industry has urged and will continue to pressure the U.S. government to negotiate with the United States' trading partners. The objective of this is to ensure that the scope of patentable subject matter includes software and that U.S. patent applications are processed fairly. In this joint industry-government effort, few dissent from the proposition that "continued patentability of computer-program related technology" is "important for the United States' worldwide competitiveness." [22]

A small but contentious group of critics of granting patents for software has emerged, including industry guru and Lotus Development Corporation founder Mitch Kapor and the League for Programming Freedom. They have voiced the concern that patents are being granted for fundamental concepts and that software patents could impair technological ingenuity in the United States. These and others highlight another major problem for the industry: that it can be extremely difficult to search for prior art in the area of software patents. The result? Even when a patent is granted, the patentee is at risk of being sandbagged by the presence of prior art, including patents previously issued. (The Patent and Trademark Office announced in December 1994 that it was reexamining a patent that had been granted to Compton's NewMedia in response to criticism from the multimedia industry that that patent, which had been first submitted for review in October 1989, covered basic steps in searching and retrieving data that had been industry practice for years. The reexamination will focus on the existence of prior art, and less on the more sensitive business issue of whether all CD-ROM publishers would have to pay royalties to the patent's co-owners, Encyclopaedia Britannica and Compton's.)

The Advisory Commission to the Patent and Trademark Office was created to answer some of these concerns. As we have seen, it did note these objections. Nonetheless, it came down foursquare on the side of those who would maintain, if not enhance, the patentability of computer software. It did recommend, however, several steps to improve access to prior art and the examination of patent applications.

The January-February 1994 hearings on software patents conducted by the Patent and Trademark Office elicited the broadest spectrum of views on these matters. Critics of today's system urged better databases to search for prior art and publication of patent applications for software before issuance (to avoid submarine patents); several parties concluded that patent protection is too expensive and that the industry should rely on copyright and trade secret laws. Supporters of software patents acknowledged that the process of reviewing and issuing software patents is not flawless, but that patentability promotes competition and the ability of U.S. companies to sell software in markets outside the United States.

Which is it, then? Do patents, in increasing protection for software, strengthen the competitiveness of U.S. companies? Or will patents for software eventually handicap American industry in its race to maintain its commanding technological lead in the digital age?

Concluding Observations

Peering even further into the future, what can we predict about the legal issues that will shape the rights of creators and users of computer software? It is not dodging the question to emphasize that much will depend on how the software industry evolves in the years ahead.

It borders on a truism to note that technology itself, particularly in the software industry, races far ahead of courts, and even further ahead of legislative bodies and their enactments. As we have seen, CONTU was a much-delayed and much-debated reaction to a series of technological developments that had emerged decades earlier. Judicial decisions that recognized the protectibility of "look and feel" or the legitimacy of decompilation followed, by definition, in the wake of the very industry practices that had given rise to the litigation.

Multimedia Works: Multiple Challenges

At least two technological developments will challenge legal doctrine and, perhaps, settled expectations. One is the emergence of multimedia works and technologies on a national information highway. Such multimedia works will force both lawyers and the law to be almost as innovative as the creators in obtaining the necessary rights and in selling and licensing the end products.

From an engineering perspective, as some in the Clinton administration have suggested in support of their agenda for a national information infrastructure, it may be true that bits are bits. The copyright law, however, for better or worse, distinguishes among various kinds of intellectual property. Each category of work has different rights attached to it, either as a result of the statute itself or as a result of varying doctrinal strands in the case law. For example, the owners of a diskette embodying a computer program have a statutory right to make an archival backup copy, whereas no similar right is accorded owners of other kinds of literary works (such as novels). And the principles of fair use produce different results when they are applied to the sound sampling of sound recordings than to the decompilation of software.

Perhaps even more significant, the various copyright industries distribute and license their works and receive their compensation in highly distinctive ways. Computer programs may be sold through shrink-wrap licenses or through highly sophisticated custom-software-development agreements. Both types of contracts are efforts to preserve rights and control the consumer's use. Books, records, and videotapes, by contrast, are sold (or rented) as commodities. A songwriter's principal compensation is derived from performance licenses issued to radio stations and from royalties paid by record companies on album sales.

What is the significance of these differences for multimedia works? If they are treated as computer programs, then do the principles of decompilation apply in a way that might not be the case with respect to the pure audio, video, or textual components of such works? Multimedia works are more likely to be regarded as audio-visual works and, therefore, as less utilitarian than software. Will, however, the software elements of the work be subject to less protection, or more rigorous scrutiny, than the audio and visual components? Although these questions pose some challenges for intellectual-property law, undoubtedly the multimedia industry will resolve them, as well as a plethora of others, in the years ahead.

Artificial Intelligence: Questioning Copyrightability and Non-Human Authorship

AI is an area where only a few commentators have addressed the scope and the type of intellectual property protection that might be available to inventors. Some of these commentators have suggested drolly that there is nothing special or unusual about the questions AI presents for intellectual-property law and lawyers. Notwithstanding these views, how best to protect the latest manifestation of AI—neural networks, which attempt to emulate the functioning of the human brain—seems to be of more than passing interest.

In light of the enormous growth in the neural network industry, the importance of neural network research and applications, and the efforts made to develop neural networks, it seems clear that a strong legal regime for the protection of neural networks will have to be developed or applied. But what kind of intellectual-property rights should be available to developers of neural networks, and to which elements of such networks? And who should own rights to works generated entirely by computers or by computer-computer interaction?

As to the first of these issues, there seems to be an emerging consensus (not without some dissent) that existing intellectual-property law, perhaps with some doctrinal modifications, is sufficient to meet the challenges posed by neural networks. At least 200 patents have been issued for neural network technology over the last three decades. Although there remain some skeptics, patents seem as appropriate to protect neural networks as they are for other kinds of computer programs. Nonetheless, neural networks are not exactly the paradigmatic technology for which the patent law was designed. A patent, for example, protects an inventions or a process that essentially has not changed from the state it was in when the application was filed. How, then, should a patent protect a trained neural network, which may have been trained by a large number of possible inputs, when the network in that state cannot have been claimed or disclosed at the time of the application? As to copyright, copyright registrations recently were granted for a neural network weight matrix. The internal weights, which are learned by a neural network, may be regarded as a type of computer program used by a neural computer. This is because neural weights, like symbolic programming systems, are used to bring about a certain result. In continuing the analogy to more conventional computer programs, then, these weights might be regarded as a form of expression that is protected by copyright.

As to the second of these issues, the weights produced by neural networks, as well as other programs generated solely by computers, are bereft of human authors. Does this disqualify them from being protected by copyright? They are not, after all, "original works of authorship," as the copyright statute would seem to require. Neural network weight values, for example, are entirely removed from human creation. They signify nothing to humans. They constitute expression that has meaning only for the network. In these aspects, however, perhaps they are not so different from most object code programs.

The possibility of machine authorship does raise some questions, not all of which are due to the language or the requirements of either the copyright statute or the "authors and inventors" clause of the U.S. Constitution.[23] More fundamentally, to what extent should policy makers, in the United States and elsewhere, conclude that it verges on the oxymoronic to accord intellectual-property protection to works not created by the human intellect?

It is hardly in the realm of theory or speculation to point out that computers are capable of generating works through processes that are singularly removed from humans. Suggestions have been made along the way that ownership of such computer-generated works might lie variously with the developer, the owner, or the operator of the computer, or that rights should be allocated contractually or judicially among them. These solutions all generally presuppose that a human author can and must be identified. They assume that some person is proximate to or readily associated with a computer and the works that it generates. That paradigm, however, might not reflect tomorrow's reality.

As computers become more sophisticated, and as neural networks are trained and in turn train other networks, the human component of or relationship to what they produce will, at least in some situations, become increasingly remote and will border on the irrelevant. What will happen, in the not-too-distant future, when several computers, each with its own

owner and programmer, are linked together in vast multinational networks in a collective effort to produce programs that operate interactively
with and on those machines and that themselves generate new works?
How readily will we be able to isolate or identify the programs eligible
for copyright that might result, let alone ascertain and assign rights to
discrete human authors? Finally, how comfortable will we be in making
the great leap to according legal rights of ownership to a machine?

Neural networks are here today, however, and they may raise issues
even more complex than those raised by the authorship of conventional
programs generated by computers. To the extent that neural networks
attempt to replicate the human brain's processes, will their results be
copyrightable? In the end, will we find that the actual processes of the
human brain, when discovered and written down by an individual, fall
within the monopoly rights of the laws of intellectual property? Herein
lie some of the formidable challenges that, sooner rather than later, will
confront computer programmers, their lawyers, courts, and legislators.

Industry Structure and Its Impact on the Law

In response to the emerging revisionist view that copyright law overpro-
tects their rights, IBM, Digital, Corporation, Apple, Lotus, Computer Associates, Nintendo, and Sega contend that only by exercising their legal
monopolies can they earn the economic rewards (and get the incentives)
to which they are entitled. In American courts and in policy battles in
Europe and elsewhere, these major American players have targeted other
principal industry participants, such as Microsoft and Borland, as well as
a range of less-well-known U.S. companies and Japanese and European
concerns, who are skeptical of allowing the larger players to develop and
control *de facto* standards. The battle between Lotus and Borland over
spreadsheet programs is a harbinger of future conflicts between dominant
vendors and others, who favor interoperable or open systems products.
Of course, over time these companies that are developing interoperable
programs also have a strong interest in protecting the software that they
develop.

The tension between these two sets of interests is fundamental to copyright law. Historically, the holders of rights have attempted to block
others, whether competitors or innovators, from making use of their

copyrighted material. In the motion picture, publishing, and music fields, proprietors often have succeeded in preventing such unauthorized downstream uses. The applicable legal precepts for those industries are now well established.

In the still-evolving software industry, by contrast, the number of players continues to increase, and real questions have been raised as to the proper breadth of a developer's monopoly rights and the guiding legal principles. Those issues are far from settled. The industry's further maturity will affect the shape and texture of the litigation to come. If the global industry continues to have two tiers of businesses, with differing strategies, it seems likely that litigation over their respective rights will continue to flourish. A similar result can be predicted if new, small players continue to come into the market to serve niche or now-unserved customers.

The next decade, by contrast, might see a consolidation of the industry. Smaller houses might establish business partnerships with, or even be acquired by, their larger brethren. Should such a consolidation occur, litigation among the fewer remaining players might well subside. One characteristic of more established copyright-related sectors that have become quite concentrated, such as the motion picture, recording, and book-publishing industries, is that there is relatively little infringement litigation among the principal players. If the software industry ends up following this course, litigation between companies might eventually be supplanted by wary competition and intra-industry cooperation.

Protection for Software: Revisiting the Consensus?

The irony in the relationship between the convergence of protection for software internationally and the more recent evolution of U.S. law should not be lost on American businesspeople and policy makers. The United States has had great success in forging a consensus on the desirability of obtaining maximum protection for software in the NAFTA, in the Uruguay Round, and in various national arenas. Just as it has done so, however, U.S. courts and commentators are questioning some of the very principles that the United States has managed to internationalize. How ironic it would be if this process of internationalization now were to preclude a reexamination of those principles at home.

The precise interplay between the domestic creation of software and the international variances in levels of protection is still not well understood, though that relationship is of considerable significance. In the context of intensifying litigation in the United States, it may be time for Congress to ask a CONTU II to reexamine some of the thorny litigation issues on which this chapter has touched, particularly in light of international legal developments.

The prospect of an unfettered constitutional convention that might revisit the most cherished principles of the United States' founding document produces considerable anxiety. Similarly, any reopening of matters that CONTU assertedly resolved will be resisted strenuously by some of the most powerful segments of the American software industry. In view of the importance of protecting their intellectual property, their reluctance to endorse a CONTU II is understandable. Nonetheless, continued litigation, whether between big software developers or between them and smaller software houses, contributes to a business and development climate of substantial uncertainty. Such uncertainty serves neither individual corporate interests nor broader national goals.

From this wider perspective, it is clear that the issues that a CONTU II could address are critically important to continued American ingenuity in an industry in which the United States' worldwide success is unrivaled. Achieving a public-policy consensus on the contours of legal protection for computer software makes good sense. There is no better time than the present to start talking about how we should do so.

Notes

1. DiagSoft, Inc., Customer License Agreement for QAPLUS (1990–93).

2. *Baker v. Selden,* 101 U.S. 99, 100 (1879).

3. *Baker v. Selden,* 101 U.S. 99 (1880); *White-Smith Music Publishing Co. v. Apollo Co.,* 209 U.S. 1 (1908).

4. Pub. L. No. 101–650, § 702(a), 104 Stat. 5133, 5133 (1990) (codified at 17 U.S.C. § 101 (1988)).

5. National Commission on New Technological Uses of Copyrighted Works, *Final Report on New Technological Uses of Copyrighted Works* (1979).

6. Computer Software Copyright Act, Pub. L. No. 96–517, 94 Stat. 3028 (1980) (codified at 17 U.S.C. §§ 101 and 117 (1988)).

7. The Advisory Commission on Patent Law Reform, "A Report to the Secretary of Commerce" (Aug. 1992).

8. 797 F.2d 1222 (3d Cir. 1986), *cert. denied*, 479 U.S. 1031 (1987).

9. *Lotus Development Corp. v. Borland International, Inc.*, 799 F. Supp. 203 (D. Mass. 1992) (granting partial summary judgment to Lotus on claim Borland had copied user interface).

10. *Lotus Development Corp. v. Borland International, Inc.*, 831 F. Supp. 223 (D. Mass. 1993) (issuing permanent injunction against Borland's infringement on grounds, in part, that significant differences in other spreadsheet programs demonstrated that Borland would not be limited in choosing an interface design).

11. 982 F.2d 693 (2d Cir. 1992).

12. To be fair, reverse engineering may not require decompilation or the making of an intermediate copy. Programmers can review a program's documentation, which may have been published, or observe the program's operation. These methods of learning about a program, however, are unlikely to be as helpful or as instructive as decompilation.

13. 17 U.S.C. § 107.

14. 977 F.2d 1510 (9th Cir. 1992), *amended*, 193 U.S. App. LEXIS 78 (9th Cir. 1993) (holding that acts of decompilation, including intermediate copying to create games that would operate on Sega's game console, was a fair use).

15. *Sega*, 977 F.2d at 1526.

16. *Id.* at 1523.

17. Copyright Law Review Committee, "Draft Report on Computer Software Protection" 3 (1993) (draft to the Attorney-General, circulated for public comment).

18. Conversely, it may be difficult or legally impossible to maintain as a trade secret the user-interfaces of an applications program, such as tiled screens or icons. Of course, other kinds of protections, such as copyright, trademark or trade dress protection might be available for such elements of a program.

19. See Copyright Law of the Republic of China, May 14, 1928, art. 11 (amended June 12, 1992).

20. See *Bodin v. AGOSPAP*, P.I.B.D. 1993, III-227 (Trib. gr. instance de Paris Jan. 20, 1993), appeal filed Mar. 15, 1993 (holding that software engineer has moral right to block modification of software by company for which he had developed program under a work-for-hire agreement).

21. Many large companies disclose inventions even without taking out patents on them. IBM may choose to publish an invention in its Technical Disclosure Bulletin instead of pursuing a patent.

22. *Advisory Commission Report, supra* note 7, at 156.

23. U.S. Constitution, art. I, § 8, cl. 8.

Knowledge and the New Magnitudes of Connection

Derek Leebaert
William B. Welty

The coordination of knowledge work is the largest and most pervasive challenge to all forms of administration in this century. Just as chemistry passed from the gentleman's laboratory to the factory floor, so software has gone from scientist's tool to becoming the framework of the corporation. Up to this point in the Industrial Age, it made sense to radically differentiate workers and management. Little but effort was expected of workers. Yet, as the skill component of jobs increases, the value that once could be added only by certified "managers," or within "developed" countries, is entering into processes and initiatives worldwide.

Companies have responded to this upheaval in at least three basic ways. First, they may move offshore to pursue lower labor costs, as with international demands for Indian biochemistry, Jamaican data-processing shops, and Mexican assembly plants. Second, they can keep endlessly "downsizing" (or "rightsizing," as this phenomenon is more hopefully called). Third, they may alter the way they function on the basis of knowledge, which almost certainly entails a good deal of both the above—and more.

The only choice for U.S. enterprises is the last. The United States is still in the lead of the Knowledge Age—although these are still very early days—because of the fecundity of its ideas, the speed with which those ideas can be disseminated, the flexibility of so much of its population, and the efficiency with which all these factors can result in high-quality goods and services. So to search the globe for lower labor costs cannot be the whole story. And constant attempts to "downsize" are often undertaken in a spirit of mere mechanical squeezing. This may result in bursts of productivity, but it can also lead to trends of longer, more intense work for lesser reward.

To compete on the basis of steady improvement of knowledge, however, requires the imaginative employment of different tools and structures than characterized most work before the 1990s. Exhaustive attention has been devoted in business and government to what new structures are most efficient. The preceding chapters discuss many of the tools that can extend this efficiency into the new century.

Once we look at how these tools are actually used, we encounter the early-1990s mantra of "reengineering," a term that represents the ill-defined family of processes that can prepare Knowledge Age institutions for new life. Although the term implicitly appeals to the hard-won standing of real engineering (and derives from "retro-engineering"), it is unlikely that the processes under consideration were "engineered" to begin with. The term essentially means "rethinking" and deconstructing the corporate fabric to see how objectives are being met. A quarter-century ago, however, the same procedures, definitions, and terminology were simply called "institution building." What more or less saves the enthusiasm for "reengineering" from being just another business fad are the tools that are now brought to bear.

To present reengineering—even backed by the most productive technologies—as the essence of current change is still a mistake. Conditions confront us, not theories. The great forces that are upending institutions and concentrating minds—the aftermath of the great 1980s boom, the competitive capacities of Asia, and the first computer-literate generation's sense of information's power—have no need for doctrine. Such forces are what make process innovation necessary, feasible, and acceptable.

Challenging traditional organizational practices, as well as eliminating work that is not adding value, immediately spotlights every player left on the team. The familiar label "information worker" is so general as to be meaningless, lumping theoretical physicists with data-entry clerks. It is merely a category related by family resemblances, but with no single characteristic. Perhaps a better description of work activities comes from Labor Secretary Robert Reich, who uses three general classifications: routine production services, in-person services, and symbolic/analytic services. They all entail collaboration, learning (and unlearning), decision, creation, and the coordination of these elements.

The last classification can be called knowledge work. A knowledge worker addresses himself to adding value to information. This is not just a question of applying a particular skill. Instead, the role involves at least three functions: a knowledge worker may administer information, just as an accountant or a financial officer makes choices about information as it arrives. He might incorporate information and its fruits, as do engineers and researchers. Or the knowledge worker may construct information systems—which can mean anything from software to the management of information flow. People in this role understand that ongoing knowledge about their work is more important than simple application of a repetitive learned skill.

The United States still has a vastly higher proportion of its labor force engaged in knowledge work than any other country. We have tools for many of these functions: relatively powerful tools for learning, for decision support, for design, and for financial creativity. All these will be recast thoroughly very soon. But so far the tools for coordinating knowledge work have been limited, and the costs of coordination have been high.

To be competitive entails an endless balancing between human and material resources: it is an ongoing dialectic of improvement in work rather than an attempt to preserve jobs. Consider three phases of coordination through which enterprises have evolved: the movement of materials, of data, and of knowledge. The first was characterized by the general brute efficiency of mass production. Because Judge Gary dictatorially ran the J. P. Morgan steel interests (in Gary, Indiana and elsewhere) while never venturing from his New York law offices, it was said that he never saw a blast furnace until after he died. That easy waste of talent in the mills, as on Henry Ford's assembly lines, should be relegated to history.

Before World War II, few substantial businesses avoided such a command structure. Stanley Resor Sr.'s advertising firm, J. Walter Thompson, was rare in its abhorrence of titles and hierarchy. It was a service company which was intended to be constantly flexible. No one-color car salesmen need apply. A more characteristic successor to Gary and Ford, however, was IBM. Richard Watson's IBM World Trade made the moving of data rather than material an international event. In what today seems ironic for that downsizing colossus, IBM's innovation was not just information as product but also a certain decentralization as organizational gospel: the salesman was elevated to a missionary expert on his customer.

Now we are encountering a third phase: the movement of human commitments. This involves the subtlest coordination and negotiation, and also new ways of valuing time. The business processes of the steel industry, like those of Ford and even those of IBM, reflected an ancient approach to work. It was the approach of primitively assessed cause and effect, with hierarchies, commands, and strict measures of production. With the exceptions of Detroit's star designers such as Harley Earl and IBM's research wizards in Yorktown Heights, the people in these companies were not really knowledge workers. (See figure 1.)

Between cause and effect falls coordination. Knowledge workers must innovate. Ford brought specified materials to one end of the assembly line and got specified cars from the other; IBM helped turn loose data into cards or printouts. However, we will be less and less able to predict what specific innovations knowledge workers will come up with. All sorts of surprises can emerge until they are finished with their tasks.

We are moving into a world in which the cooperation that underlies management has come to undercut management's traditional authority. Work becomes a matter of participation instead of submission. This is very different from the movement of materials and of data. It can be a result of technological transformation, as well as of a new and chastened awareness that central authority can impede innovation.

We emphasize the importance of three-dimensional and interactive coordination rather than of simple, linear collaboration. We stress the need to organize work processes so as to create the harmonious integration that will yield the most effective results. In business this means coordinating the "conversations" (speculations, negotiations, promises) among knowledge workers. These lead to their commitment to purposeful activities—activities that seek steadily to transcend the processes with which they started.

In the early days of electronic emancipation, organizations sent data to electronic bases in South Dakota or Nebraska. Space became unreal. Now we are able to work in real time.

The 1990s keep showing a hunger to recast the rigidities of corporate life. But enthusiasm is one thing; applying the software is another. The ongoing boost given to organizational productivity by information

Criteria	Industrial Age	Transition Age	Knowledge Age
ACTIONS	Sequential and slow	Sequential, faster	Fast
DECISIONS	Made by top management	Made by top management	Collaboration of specialists
SPECIALIZED KNOWLEDGE	Staff specialists	Line management	Knowledge held in electronic repositories
INFORMATION	Middle management as conduit	Limited upward flow; photocopies down	Immediate access by all
DATA	Stored on paper; limited access	Stored on paper, wider access	Accessible anywhere, any time over the net
KEY RESOURCES			
INFRASTRUCTURE	Roads, trains, airports	Phone system	Digital networks
EDUCATION/TRAINING	None; knowledge not expected	Greater, since middle management gone	High; most decisions made by employees
PROCESS AIDS	Assembly line	Fax machines	E-mail, Groupware
KNOWLEDGE	Resides in small group— top managers & staff	Rapid self-teaching by employees	Continuous learning sponsored by company
SPEED	Slow: information flows not real-time	Faster: workers put in longer hours	Fast: real-time digital connections

Figure 1
Using information: decision making in the industrial age and in the knowledge age. Source: Volpe, Welty & Company.

technology is always ahead of its recognition by management. Productivity is camouflaged by being grafted onto familiar, undynamic approaches to work. To computerize the insurance-policy functions of Aetna, for example, is really to overlay a sliver of the information age onto enduring Industrial-Age processes: workers still perform step by step and by rote as they sift information in an endless chain of undynamized, easily monitored piecework. Now we want to bring such skills up to the level of real knowledge work. In such a transformation lie the great efficiencies and innovations. Coordination soon replaces the vertical command role of management. Businesses will be defined by their processes and outcomes, not by an organization chart with its present results. What steps in structure and technology must be taken to achieve this evolution?

The Knowledge Base

Only four times in U.S. history has there been a need to make huge national infrastructure commitments: once with the building of the intercontinental railroad net, once with national electrification, once with the creation of a telephone network, and once with the building of the interstate highway system. A high-bandwidth digital network is about to offer the fifth such opportunity. At its heart is the Internet, the federal-government-subsidized system that already links more than 20 million people in 100 countries. Whereas the continental size of America made earlier industrial undertakings unique to the country, this next challenge is planetary. Such a network, it is estimated, could create $321 billion of new wealth for the United States by 2007.

Knowledge workers will be empowered by a communications system that enables them to input, manipulate, transmit, store, and display voice, video, text, and graphics. Communications must be "W3"—whatever, whenever, wherever. And only digital systems pass this test.

The "Net"—of which the Internet is only a part—is an amalgam of electronic bulletin boards, on-line information services, and computer conference sessions connected via global telecommunications networks. Communication is now confined mainly to text, but the Net is gaining the ability to handle voice, video, and other media.

Access to the network by personal computers is producing a natural selection in which conscious, reflective knowledge work is fast pulling away from information routines. Equally important, the real-time and intercontinental outreach capacities of modern knowledge technology are permitting completely task-specific combinations of skills. This is the antithesis of corporate forms of organization which require (or at least tolerate) huge bureaucracies that merely maintain information.

The most important trend in communications is reflected in the law of reversal, named by Nicholas Negroponte of MIT's Media Lab: communications currently being transmitted over the air will move to wire, and communications currently being transmitted on wire will, in the future, occur over the air. The radio spectrum is scarce and finite, while fiber-optic cables are easy to make and limitless. So, for instance, voice conversations, which use relatively little bandwidth, should use cellular technologies. Television broadcasts, which use enormous bandwidth, should be transmitted over wire. The proliferation of cellular phones and cable television systems confirms Negroponte's 1991 prophecy.

The test of a network is how nearly seamlessly, invisibly, and reliably it meets its users' information needs. Many elements of the communications system are digital already, and bandwidth, data compression, and computer power dictate that more of them should be. But we have a poor sense of the connections between technologies as one breakthrough multiplies another. Where is this all heading?

A now-unusual way to reduce the costs of visual communications is to create virtual worlds in which all participants are modeled. In the extreme case, the representation of a video conference takes only a few hundred bytes of cuing information per second, while very expensive computers process three-dimensional models in real time to recreate reality from movement cues generated by the conferee on the other end. All transmitted images in the digital world are complex tradeoffs involving image quality, bandwidth cost, data-compression algorithms, and processing power. (Figure 2 shows the cost of computer power for virtual reality now and in the future.)

In the early 1990s, thirteen corporations formed a consortium (led by MCC) to accelerate the development of a national digital communications infrastructure. Called "First Cities," it was a response to the significant market demand for networked multimedia information and home entertainment products. Potential applications include multimedia teleconferencing, interactive games, entertainment on demand, shopping and

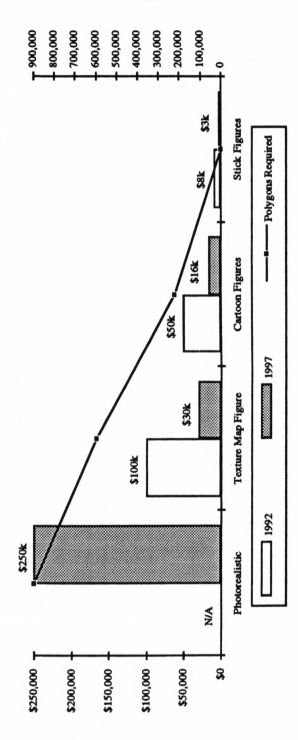

Figure 2
Polygons per second versus cost of achieving full motion, 1992 and (projected) 1997. Sources: Silicon Graphics, Inc.; SOFTIMAGE Inc.; Volpe, Welty & Company.

transaction services, and customized multimedia information—and, soon, education and health-care information. Most of the potential, however, is unknown—modernization means continually being alert to possibilities for which the technology was not designed (e.g., using computers in hybridizing cattle was not considered when computers were first being built to chart missile trajectories). Consider what happens when the level of assumption that can be built into our network becomes more sophisticated and comprehensive. The result is a wider range of combinations, subtler possibilities, and a greater chance of transcending the sterile given in favor of breedable possibilities.

The recent exemplary case of how fast a really compelling technology penetrates is the speed with which the question "Do you have a fax machine?" shifted to "What's your fax number?" Now digital connections between personal computers are being rapidly made, and there is ever more rapid growth in the connection of local-area networks, in electronic mail, and in remote-access connections to the Net—a prodigious opportunity for coordination. In 1995, 90 percent of the personal computers used by businesses are digitally connected to LANs. The challenge is to create a similarly ubiquitous digital-connection pattern among the nation's common carriers of communications. And what can we expect as software is delivered directly over the Internet?

The growth of video conferencing shows that people expect to be able to "image" to anyone, anywhere: doctors wanting to send high-resolution x-rays, virtual-reality cyberpunks flipping their 3-D animations or artificial worlds across the network, and so on. A two-hour digitally compressed movie will be delivered to the home in 10 seconds. But until the thrill of faster-than-real-time delivery becomes reality, the agony of slower-than-real-time standard-setting will plague us. The remaining physical problems on the Net derive from differences in protocols, formats, and conventions within and between the communications and computer industries.

On-line information systems are an essential part of any network. They are designed as institutional storage systems which are created and used by information entrepreneurs—information wells that are indispensable to the symbolic and analytic activities so central to the Knowledge Age. The real limitation will be in the capacity to attain information.

Information becomes real knowledge, as distinct from raw data, only when it and the instruments used to interrogate it are organized in congruent ways.

Information must not merely exist to be usable; its existence must be easily established, and it must be readily accessible. Thus, one of the Net's criteria must be community of services. All information entrepreneurs need access to on-line systems. All information users need access to something much better than a national electronic "yellow pages." To fuel the input the Net craves, we need an encouraging and reliable system of advertising, pricing, and payment for the owners of information.

Once we have direct access to all the data splashing through the Net, the less important functions in our offices tend to fold together. We can question ever greater data banks directly without calling in the staff vice-president to cross-reference sources. All this can be compared with the impact of writing upon the world. At one time, most data which were marked to endure had to be turned into memorable verse. This undoubtedly brought much mumbo jumbo and sloganeering as well as the *Iliad* and *Mahabharata*. Similarly, the Net is calling forth ever greater techniques for drowning reason in data and for blinding us with science.

Clearing and reclearing critical paths of relevance through the growth of raw information becomes indispensable. This makes the process of sharing information as important as identifying and classifying it in the first place. So our system becomes an architectural device as well as a self-inquiring file and a document organizer. It can take us anywhere in the global city.

The potential of these new arrangements of people, infrastructure, process, and space will still be only a function of our capacity to search, access, sort, and recombine the information which the Internet offers. Any filter that allows only the information you want to issue from your computer—to define in advance what you need—is contrary to the true values of the Knowledge Age. You want to have the power to make new connections between seemingly unrelated information.

Many insights are in fact transplantable answers to other questions. Filters hinder us from seeing such connections. As we ask larger questions, the answers can have shattering effects in other categories. In fact, we have a poor sense of the connectivities of technologies themselves as one breakthrough multiplies another.

The network will be made most effective by the translation of speech to text and by the simpler sibling of that process, the translation of text to speech. We already have text-to-speech capacity, and the problem of speech-to-text is becoming tractable. Several firms produce cost-effective software for a few applications. Designers face many problems, but most of them are on three fronts: contextual understanding of similar words (two, too, to), where does one word end and the next begin (Tupelo, Mississippi, or Two-pillow miss is hippy?), and the ability to identify phonetically differentiated sounds ("you all" versus "yawl"). Continuous speech recognition—which may be the most important step toward creating the Very Large Knowledge Base—is also the most important technology needed to complete the full use of digital communications networks.

So what does the system of the future look like? In *Neuromancer*, William Gibson writes of "a custom cyberspace deck that projected the disembodied consciousness into the consensual hallucination that was the matrix." The characteristics of this portable device are input, manipulation, transmit, store, output, and display against the communication forms of audio, video, and graphics (still and animated, text, and numbers). (See figure 3.)

Knowledge Workers

Activity can be replicated endlessly in layer upon unnecessary layer; purpose requires reimaging and rewilling, and probably short-circuiting. Technical issues relentlessly dictate ever greater interlocking of disciplines. So activities must constantly be resolved into their component bundles of implications and possibility if they are to offer extraordinary challenges to establishing context, sequence, and profit. One result is that nearly everyone in the Knowledge Age is usually out of date even on matters that truly concern them.

Each level of technology involves reconceptualizing the "therefores" of the processes we are working with. (Every executive is a computer user, therefore. . . .) With these levels building upon themselves exponentially, constant reconceptualization is necessary not just for success but for survival. Moreover, every level of conceptual improvement must ground itself on an improvement in information gathering. All this requires ceaseless coordination.

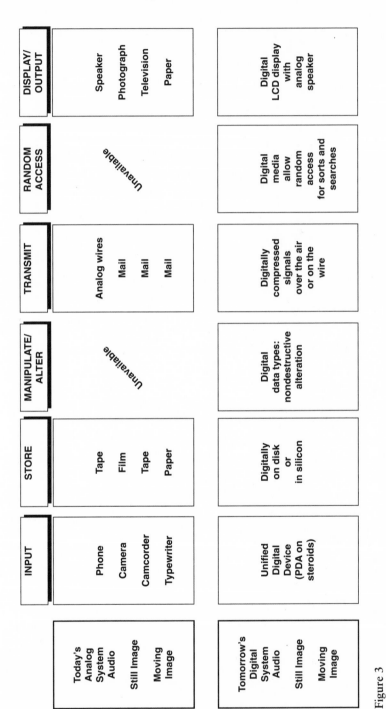

Figure 3
Communications in the future: comparison of digital and analog systems. Source: Volpe, Welty & Company.

Along the way, some see a paradox. The higher skills, lifelong learning, and employee involvement of a work force for the Knowledge Age are endlessly extolled. But at the same time, this era's demand for organizational dynamism and maximum company flexibility—even for "virtual corporations"—means contingent, temporary employment. There is apparently no reciprocal commitment from the company to providing job security for, or even long-term relations with, so-called knowledge workers.

We do not see a contradiction. Knowledge work represents a higher degree of efficiency and a higher level of employment. Too many people working inefficiently becomes catastrophic, as the collapsing state industries of Eastern Europe and Russia dramatically show. Instead of a lifetime relationship with a corporation, knowledge work implies a greater degree of being in charge of oneself—of combining and recombining one's talents. Only the simplest activities can from now on be seen as "lifetime"—i.e., not subject to initiative.

If we raise the individuality and the quality of the input, we can expect work to have more combinations and to be more transient. No one expects a physicist to be doing the same thing for 40 years: why should that be expected of workers in Gary or in Detroit? They will work much more like someone, such as the physicist, whose employment rests in his capacity to learn (e.g., to stay on top of his profession as it races ahead). No job or worker can be taken for granted in the Knowledge Age. Judge Gary and Henry Ford bought their workers in bulk. Modern work implies the rebirth of the skilled craftsman dealing with his employer of the moment.

Along the way, more and more paradoxes will be seen in business as well as in life. Paradox is the classic facet of modernism. When we encounter the new, our range of choices is increased while we juxtapose them with ever greater transformations and possibilities. "The world will be a lot more rewarding for some," says a General Mills senior vice-president, "but for everyone it will be a lot riskier."[1] One adjustment to such a bustling meritocracy is the spread of "pay for performance" (or variable pay), in which nearly all levels of workers share in the company's risks as well as its rewards—thereby also inducing them to pull forward together as the company decentralizes. Another adjustment is the increasingly effective training through which temporary-employment firms boost the value of their workers. "Manpower, Norrell, and Kelly have done more to train inner-city residents than all the government training programs combined," says the National Planning Association's chief economist.[2] And all these adjustments require vast coordination.

The greatest challenge facing managers in the developed world, according to the management expert Peter Drucker, is raising the productivity of knowledge workers. This is a highly painful task in the developed nations, because it entails acknowledging the liquidation of so many jobs, but it is unavoidable.

Awareness is discomfort. The more we know, the more we know we could do better. The more that is known, the more likely someone will do better than us. Let everyone in the organization be uncomfortable. In the mid 1990s, we can expect to be discomforted by knowing that our skills are likely out of date. We can also expect difficulty in demonstrating the precise value which we and our knowledge tools are bringing to the organization.

Sixty years ago, the great economist Sir Dennis Robertson described his profession. "An economist," he said, "is someone who, when told that a bulldozer can do the work of fifty men with shovels, asks how much work can be done by one man with fifty shovels." Robertson had three points: that the economic notion of achievement can be strikingly un-future-oriented; that addressing the accounting and assessing side of innovation can be easily muddled; and that we often assume that a given task remains the same even though the tool changes, whereas instead the task has to be seen as the way to an objective and not as the objective itself.

Economists may not be particularly good at discerning transformation and measuring productivity. The development of a new pool of knowledge is rarely found to give a direct return. Thomas Jefferson, not Adam Smith, foresaw that the balloon meant intercontinental flight rather than the equivalent of bungee jumping. Arthur C. Clarke, not John Maynard Keynes or Milton Friedman, had the technological vision of the communication satellites that now uphold global markets.

The notion of productivity was formulated for manufacturing and extractive industries around the turn of the last century. A given iron ore field yielded X tons per man-hour; X number of men in a factory working

X number of man-hours were required to make one locomotive, or 10 million pins. "Man-hours" is redolent of another term that entered the idiom at the same time: "horsepower." Time-and-motion studies were unpleasantly close to treating the human being as a machine tool. They were popular, philistine, and ultimately destructive. But what happens when work is continually changing, and when no basket of goods is ever identical to its successors (even a month let alone a generation apart)? How, for instance, do we quantify the productivity of a particular addition to the Internet? We can no longer easily assume that we know how to measure adequately the ratio of human output.

Productivity is a function of very determinable factors. Yet how these factors affect and combine with each other is far harder to establish. And when feedback becomes rapid and powerful (thanks to ever more worthwhile software), measurement becomes truly tricky. This is apparent not only in "service" functions, such as inventory management, but also in thinking about the production of "durable" and "nondurable" goods. Such a distinction is particularly dated because almost everything manufactured with even halfway decent concern for quality will become at least obsolescent before it wears out.

Something is always becoming obsolete in the Knowledge Age. Consider the building of computer operating systems, which followed switchboards; of faxes, which followed telephones; of copiers, which followed printing presses. All we can say with some assurance is that the speed of economic and social change means that any crucial product is not just improved, it is reexamined. The telephone is no longer something for the boss to use to bark orders; now it is a channel by which the boss can be buried in data. Achieving real productivity from information systems depends on understanding how the specific company works—its cellular physiology—rather than on planning and strategies (or programming) imposed from above, whatever "above" may now mean.

Information work (as distinct from knowledge work) is still painfully measurable. Controversy surrounds the monitoring of data workers who use computer terminals. Measuring work in the Knowledge Age, however, focuses less on the amount of work and more on its quality.

It is the sifting and organization of knowledge that challenges us. Meeting this challenge depends on improvements in coordination. That, in turn, depends on tools which make most of record-keeping and of the tracking of purely mechanical processes, which compress costs of time and distance, increase mutual understanding, and promote freer access to information. Agreed-upon conventions, such as an active pricing system for financial securities or a red octagonal STOP sign, are a primary instrument of reducing coordination costs. But beyond that we encounter much more powerful improvements in communications hardware and connection software operating over a digital network. They will permit the virtually automatic tracking, referencing, and retrieval of current coordination agreements.

The public is in as great a state of constant change as are the technologies which it encounters. People are more sophisticated than ever before in confronting whatever is being produced in goods and services. Constant demands for "more"—most dramatically "more" computer capabilities but also demands for "more" in the banking, entertainment, and other revolutions—mean that public initiatives are imposed on companies. This is very different from companies' having grand strategic visions of needs and markets.

Adam Smith stressed the importance of general education so that the judgment of talented people would not be overshadowed by the needs of the specialists. He thought he was talking merely about skilled craft specialists. He might as well have been talking about such specialists as, say, chief information officers. Companies are increasingly challenged to *institutionally* assimilate change. The problem is not one of redefining executive authority over how we use our knowledge tools but one of redefining the awareness of *everyone* in the organization so that such central executive positions are less important.

Ongoing, advanced innovation is in fact a complex harmony: it combines intensified specialism and continually-amplified integration. Adam Smith also taught us how it is easier for seventeen workers, operating stage by stage, to make a myriad of pins more swiftly than for one craftsman to make one single pin. Already a century ago, the ablest specialists who were engaged in, say, steamboat building could not be expected to understand all the processes involved in creating their product. Today, even the most extremely able specialist must ignorantly take for granted nearly all of the complexities that surround him. (For example, a physics professor at Caltech is likely to have little understanding of Traverse Technologies' communications protocol converters, which prepare the bill for his awards banquet at Pasadena's DoubleTree Inn.)

Life is reflecting a compounding need for both specialization and coordination. The need is met by software tools which replace conscious identification and decision by use of mechanical processes. It will astound our younger successors on the job how much was still being left to boring, fallible human decision in the mid 1990s. Each great discipline, almost by definition, requires more diverse efforts than anyone realizes. A modern technology, such as breathtaking breakthroughs in computing power, can reach its potential only by inventing a whole other number of disciplines to carry it, such as new horizons in software design.

After World War II, when television was still widely regarded as magic, the science fiction writer Robert Heinlein reflected on how a TV repairman's grandfather was liberated by the cotton gin. Now technologies elicit new capacities in the bored clerk just as so-called adaptive technologies (such as large-membrane keyboards or voice recognition) emancipate the disabled lawyer. This clerk and this lawyer then add their own energies and imaginations to the division of labor. Skills are rewarded which otherwise would have been unseen.

No end is in sight as to how ever more readily instant transactions are enhancing the individual's power to decide when and how to sell just about anything, while dispersing the location of the information and the processing power that enable these decisions. Technology dissolves particularity as we move ever closer to real-time interaction, both over great distances and over great bodies of data which we could not previously interrogate in the available time. Since knowledge is power, one of the most important functions for our new tools will be how to distribute that power.

Knowledge Organizations

At the level of the steam engine and the telegraph—or of Judge Gary's steel mills and Henry Ford's assembly lines—all worthwhile information pointed downward. The old description of the U.S. Army, "designed by geniuses to be run by idiots," is the classic formula for a quality, learning, changing, information-poor, employee-rich organization.

At that level, there is not a loop function with all sorts of mobilized talents jumping into the problem. These familiar machines and processes work in one way: people downstream are fundamentally passive to the invention whether it be a pin factory or whether it be a long-gallery coal mine worked by men lying on their sides. ("Passive," as the history of such mining shows, does not remotely imply "cowardly" or "feeble.")

It has become a business-school cliché to acknowledge that an organization of sufficient magnitude must be remaking itself all the time if it is to keep up with the world's complexities. Right into the early 1990s, IBM kept reorganizing itself, as it had been doing for at least two decades. But ultimately management and reorganization from the top can assert only the most general initiatives. Such top-down change does not meet George Patton's famous credo: trust the initiative of others to solve assigned problems and you'll be astounded by the resourcefulness which is evoked.

Management—in this case meaning administrative rationality—once rested on a sense of the near-duplicability of things and of people. Everyone remembers Henry Ford's remark about the customer's being able to get a car in any color so long as it was black. The more complex the technology, however, the more the participants in that technology become innovators themselves as *they* learn amid constant change. Acting more and more as individuals, they pass their insights up and out. When we scrutinize the dynamic organization, we see that ever more crucial specialty skills from these individuals are vital. In a time of compounding and accelerating change, with peaks of innovation crowding ever closer together, we see a shift in responsibility—in human commitments—with which many organizations and administrators have not caught up.

Management could safely be considered a science only in the period during which particular events converged. That period included the assembly line, the triumph of internal combustion, first-generation electronics, the displacement of coal, mass unionization, the consumer goods revolution, a culture disciplined by depression, and the organizational assumptions that introduced the concept of the corporation. But "all complex systems contain contradictions," says the Nobel economics laureate Kenneth Arrow. Notions of management as a science become dangerous as the emphasis shifts to coordination.

Every organization is distorted in getting things done the first time; the more innovation, the more distortion. So the capacity to adapt at full speed to process change is the critical differentiator amid worldwide competition. Global networks, after all, are creating a level communications field within, quite as much as between, organizations. In many ways it is the latter transformation that goes deepest to the heart of work relations. Yet organizations are changing far more slowly than their most important factor of production, the knowledge worker.

For instance, fewer than 30 percent of General Motors' employees are production workers, but GM (which first fully applied the military's hierarchical model to industry) continues to be organized as it was when 60 percent of its people were in production. The growing dispersion of knowledge and initiative, the immediacy of feedback, and the impossibility of god-like omniscient central authority are rapidly undermining such structures as they dictate new ones.

For a generation, there has been an enormous upper middle class in the United States operating on rather marginal skills. Getting a BA in English and then an MBA is not what we would call a transforming educational experience. The combination of hardware and advanced software has made it brutally possible to cut layer after layer out of management, to flatten organizations, and to make a huge part of the management of flow merely clerical if not merely mechanical. Not only do the consequences of this transformation hang over our heads and careers; they also hang over the institutions that service us, such as banks and schools.

In all of the Industrial Age until just about now, authority saw itself as controlling knowledge about processes, markets, competitors . . . everything above the shop floor, and most of that too. Knowledge was centralized and slow to change. Now it is dispersed, expanding, and changing faster than any controlling institution can assimilate. Previously, people moved to their work ("I've Been Moved"). Now work moves to them—if they know how to summon it or be open to it.

Business owners had immense leverage over employees when men and women rarely had to perform as knowledge workers. Work was the continuity. Workers were fungible—a relationship which is reversing itself ever further down the ladder. Good generals, surgeons, and bankers were always mobile and likely to be ahead of their employers. Now anyone with a personal computer can be mobile.

Instant communication offers the chance to maintain flexibility through coordination and to dispense with uniformity. Costs saved by dealing with an outside specialist whose charges are reduced by economies of scale must be weighed against the costs of the effort at connection. These costs are entailed by coordinating work with what is still thought of as an outside organization. But such costs of coordination will plunge over the rest of this decade as interdependent networks increase, as companies compete more on the basis of a large sense of knowledge resources, and as better network hardware enhances coordination.

Consider T*HQ, a small company in the entertainment software business with $40 million in annual revenue. It doesn't develop, manufacture, package, advertise, market, or sell anything. Such functions it hires out. It doesn't even create characters. Those again are licensed from others. The service it offers is almost purely coordination. And declining coordination costs seem extremely likely to lead to much greater outsourcing of just this kind—and of subtler forms yet unimagined. Each firm which T*HQ uses is a knowledge base concentrating on its own specialty—and so is T*HQ, with its profound knowledge of what entertainment characters it can license and profit from.

A recent American Electronics Association survey showed that, on average, members outsourced 22 percent of their value, with more than a third of the respondents indicating they were going further. High-speed digital networks, the growth of specialized knowledge bases, and software tools that diminish the cost of coordination will make it absurd to keep many functions in house when they can be performed so much more efficiently "elsewhere"—though the difference will be one of function rather than geography as entities become ever more virtual.

Business magazines increasingly profile manufacturing companies that started with little capital, minimal space, only a handful of employees, and a good piece of software. This new type of company is being dubbed a "soft factory." For example, New Mexico's Quatro Corporation has only a few employees who manufacture material testing equipment. Its principal value added lies not in parts or an assembly line but in software. Three transducer assemblies are clamped to the surface of, say, a car door, to find welding or bonding flaws inside. They run an algorithm that interprets sound waves resonating inside the tested part. Whatever a soft factory may be, it has a large component of knowledge in its finished products.

Change in commercial structure and processes might be most dramatic—because it is most apparent—in the transformation arising between more traditional kinds of factories and the "store." Wholesalers and retailers are being squeezed out of many product categories just as ruthlessly as middle management is being squeezed out of the corporation. Manufacturers and consumers deal directly with each other, just as "management" can interact intimately with "workers." Accelerated by these coordination technologies, the marketplace seeks out the most efficient and profitable commitments between and within companies.

Electronic data interchange (EDI) is an early manifestation of the tighter links both possible and necessary between customer and supplier. The rapid growth of this early form of life on the net, as Sterling Software demonstrates, clearly shows the freedom of outsourcing options conferred by lower coordination costs. In fact, transaction-processing service companies handling the data needs of other organizations were the first to carve out significant pieces of this kind of corporate activity, because data processing tasks offer virtually no barriers to switching.

As coordination costs come down in more areas of the economy, these companies, with their advantages of scale and experience, will prosper yet more. Even more intriguing is the electronic billing of transactions taking place on the network. There will be fewer intermediaries. This is because a major function of retailing is the acquisition and dissemination of knowledge, and because the total cost of acquiring knowledge is decreasing. For instance, a credit card transaction processor that owns or co-ventures with an on-line information service can become a formidable low-cost distributor of goods and services.

Transaction costs will fall as they are made more nearly between the buyer and the manufacturer, in many cases eliminating all layers of distribution. Once the consumer can inexpensively access an adequate degree of specialized information, much of the retailer's function as a knowledgeable intermediary is lost. People who use Apple computers, for example, are on average more knowledgeable about their machines than people who use Microsoft-based systems. It should be no surprise, then, that nearly 80 percent of Macintosh software is bought through the mail—a much higher percentage than in the Microsoft world.

Moreover, the philosophy of interaction among network partners is changing. Perhaps the best example is the work of Fernando Flores of

Action Technologies, who has developed a model of general human inter-action flowing out of linguistic theory. Previous systems approached work by using an input/process/output model; Action Technologies formulates its approach as request/agree/perform/accept. The difference between the two models is the role played by the customer. The Action Technologies approach starts with a customer's request and ends only when the customer accepts the work that was agreed upon.

Tighter links are promoted between customer and supplier, and rework is minimized because the customer is able to voice clarifying requests and criticisms much earlier in the process.

Software products to design and automate business processes will flourish in the rest of this decade, helping push decisions to the people who do the work and ensuring open and immediate communication. Everyone doing the work is expected to know the entire value-adding role of the firm, as well as his or her role in the process.

The engaging but imprecise term "groupware" is often bandied about. Perhaps it would be clearer to speak of computer-supported cooperative work (CSCW). It places specific computing systems in a secondary role, behind collaboration between human beings or between machines, or between humans and machines. Remember the prime goals of knowledge organizations: to improve communications between people, reduce decision time, improve decision quality, move faster into new markets, rework and create products faster, reduce teamwork overhead while raising performance, and thereby improve overall customer satisfaction.

As division of labor increases, thereby increasing the numbers of knowledge specialists, the number of transactions increases. This all produces more and more paths in all directions. Formal intervening steps, which more often than not are choke points, have to diminish. Monitoring by some higher authority becomes inefficient, if not impossible.

A really adaptive organization responds to opportunity. This usually means accessing more information by improving flow and storage—and above all by improving use. Knowledge is channeled through the minimal number of checkpoints and assertions of authority. But checkpoints (perhaps mechanical) there must be. Passivity to information subverts the pursuit of relevance.

The technology aspects break into four categories, best expressed in Paul Wilson's book *Computer-Supported Cooperative Work:*

• communication systems, such as video conferencing and electronic mail, which enable widely dispersed groups to see, hear, and send messages to each other
• facilities, such as remote screen sharing, which enable people to work on the same electronic space
• shared information facilities, such as multi-user databases, which enable people to work on common bodies of information much more swiftly
• support facilities to augment group work processes.

Conversations can flourish with ever greater ease, as between engineers working at two different plants (or homes or conference sites) with tools for computer-aided design or manufacturing. This dissolves the formal constraints of work time as well as work space. It is said that Thomas Hobbes carried a notebook attached to his walking stick lest he lose some passing thought forever. Four centuries later, he would be smothered in hand-held products. Inevitably, these devices will be linked so that creativity can flourish at all hours and places.

Today, collaboration is still severely constricted. CSCW gives it wings, making intense cooperative contact possible in a range of times and places. The existence of tools so capable of enhancing human performance will bring into existence organizations that can live effortlessly with the acceleration of transaction time. Lotus Notes is the preeminent commercial example of a tool that fits today's prime battleground of corporate competition—namely knowledge and speed. CSCW work is to the Knowledge Age what mass production was to the Industrial Age, and organizations similarly need to recast themselves in order to meet mounting standards of performance.

A company's technical documentation, patents, policy guidelines, rules, case studies, and employee experience are usually its most undervalued assets. This is because they are the least efficiently used. Until recently, most of these repositories were inaccessible to procedural and database technologies. But new developments in artificial intelligence and multimedia technologies are beginning to awaken and deploy such cobwebbed treasures, essentially streamlining asset turnover. The best use of professional capacities comes from their being accessibly pooled, not doled out one-on-one-on-one.

Of course, Newton attained the greatest single intellectual feat of man by working alone in candlelight with a quill pen. Leibniz could add to the wonders of knowledge while traveling in solitary coaches along the washboard roads of the Holy Roman Empire. What even they could not achieve was the effortless mobilization of lesser intellects. And that is the hope of an ever more nearly seamless world of knowledge.

Companies such as Andersen Consulting and McKinsey are building such knowledge repositories as they try to concentrate what were previously their almost impalpable prime resources. They have no alternative. This is a practical refutation of the criticism that such firms use the acumen of a senior person at the start of an engagement and then have the tasks fulfilled by junior associates. Such pooling should involve object-oriented databases, expert systems, smart forms, e-mail, multimedia, and sophisticated natural language query mechanisms. On today's e-mail systems, for example, the most frequent question starts with "Does anybody know. . . ." Tomorrow's knowledge repositories will carry this random querying to an entirely different level.

And one result is the birth of the temporary corporation. It is created to handle a short-term opportunity, to contract the required skill of temporary workers to get to market quickly, and to dissolve back into foam on the knowledge ocean once its function is discharged. New models of profit sharing will arise. Investors often rail that corporations reinvest income in new ventures when their original opportunity has been exhausted. In the future, investors will be able to figure out how to finance entities that exist for only a moment in time, and to reliquefy them as a matter of course with no entrenched management to stand in the way.

If large corporations such as Apple, Amgen, Genentech, and Novell end up holding their high ground for a mere 20 years, that may well be reckoned as a triumph. No one, for instance, expects great software or biotech companies to replicate themselves like salmon; we expect them to ripen and wither like roses. Their sudden rise is a salutary index of the fluidity of talent—probably the less fixed the better. Software companies may be most susceptible to this effervescence. Microsoft, which in a decade equaled the value of IBM, will leave no rusting ingot mills beside the Monongahela.

Conclusion

New processes will accelerate decentralization as knowledge-based competition induces changes in work, in organizations, and in life itself. Those who have the most familiarity with the new technologies are also those with the most leverage over their working conditions. Communications systems, software for coordination, and personal craftsman-like independence will let such people live almost anywhere. First we worked with PCs, then with PCs on the LAN, then with the WAN, and now on the remote-access network. Once you live on the remote-access network, you can indeed live anywhere and work anytime. In due course, skilled manual workers may operate their machines from half a continent away.

Telluride, Colorado, is one of several unofficial testing grounds which cater to people who, aided by modern communications, are able to work just about anywhere they want. Workers bring their jobs with them. Through a project called InfoZone, largely funded by telecommunications companies and state and local governments, Telluride residents can get direct links to the Internet and other networks.

Companies in Western states are in fact far more avid to adopt telecommuting than those in any other region. Some 10 million Americans have set up shop at home, and nearly a quarter of them telecommute. Receptivity to these new arrangements is spreading, for many reasons. The California Highway Department predicts that by the year 2000 commuting times will have become unacceptable. Powerful process software will make telecommuting a popular choice, and will be matched by company incentives to work elsewhere—especially if discounts in telecommuting tariffs help stimulate use of the currently underutilized residential part of the network. Remote offices in booming "edge cities," such as Walnut Creek, Framingham, and Tyson's Corner, are now connected to headquarters by LANs and WANs. With life on the net, there is simply no need for any offices to be considered remote.

The principles of the division of labor have not been repealed, and the growth in new knowledge means an increasing specialization in work. Outsourcing is nothing more than the economic recognition that specialization occurs and that ever more tasks can be done cheaper, faster, and better by specialists whom it would be uneconomic to employ oneself. To harvest the full complex of economic possibilities on the network, we must reduce coordination costs. And the combination of digital communications systems with changes in software process tools will drive such costs down sharply.

Falling coordination overheads will allow easier collaboration, ultimately meaning that steadily more of the value in the computer-communications complex is in the connection and not in the computation. The United States still lacks an end-to-end bandwidth digital communications infrastructure, many of the software tools which will transform organizations from hierarchical to horizontal, and, most important, an education system which can benefit fully from computer and communications technologies. But the country's pivotal strengths remain the adaptability of its people and a market economy which encourages entrepreneurs—as well as an overall belief that capitalism is an act of creative destruction.

Certainly there can be too much "creative destruction," as when the idealogues of deregulation rightly targeted monstrously overprotected airlines but did so without working out airport economics. Yet by and large it is now taken for granted that big corporations need not last, and there is something exhilarating in watching a corporate Austria-Hungary like IBM devolve.

The prime short-term "creative destruction" of the knowledge revolution is in knowledge jobs themselves. We have not come anywhere near the kind of expert system that can cut down a tree and get it to a sawmill, or that can build a car. But systems are at our fingertips which can book a hotel reservation or can meet a payroll with only the smallest intervention. Information clerks are being cut back in a way that, say, ambulance drivers are not. It is important to understand that the disjuncture at this stage is not between knowledge workers and non-knowledge workers. It is between the next generation of knowledge sophistication and today's huge mass of service slots (the greater part of them information slots). The latter, moreover, have been relatively unproductive during the last few decades.

Coordination, however, provides the mediating conditions which can bring about the most efficient techniques as well as the best attitudes for success. We are mostly the objects of technologies: they tend to act upon us more than we act upon them. Occasionally we are also the initiators in working with technologies. Then we have to understand how to ensure that corporate rather than artistic ends are met. As if software development (perhaps best explained in Frederick Brooks' classic *The Mythical Man-Month*), there is waste in great but questionably relevant artistry.

The "corporate end" of all our work, however, is not just getting a leg up on the competition. It is also the creation of new offers. A corporate research task, for instance, is necessarily focused. But without becoming artistic for its own sake, we are increasingly better equipped to ensure that such a research task can also be open-ended: it might raise a host of questions, including the financing of fundamental research, the profits from our work at the third remove, or, say, the question of how fundamental inquiry links to practical ends (as we see them at the moment).

Companies of all sorts will increasingly resemble advertising agencies or law firms, with continuous, nearly random recombinations of talent and with the senior players only as good as their (very recent) last achievement. Stanley Resor's model, after all, was a set of fluid activities rather than of organizational charts. The most creative advertising agencies must maintain themselves as free-floating, highly coordinated combinations of talent.

New York's Young and Rubicam, for instance, has implemented automated workflow processes into its daily business. It has automated the paper-and-time-intensive process of project traffic control, using Action Technologies' ActionWorkflow Management System as implemented in Lotus Notes. Competitiveness increasingly means raising productivity— and without increasing the burdens upon the workers in place. Nowhere is this need felt more acutely than in advertising, where clients have cut their spending while demanding the same quality and creativity. A firm such as Y&R uses workflow tools to boost productivity amid decreasing resources. At the same time, it can reduce charges for the overtime and rush jobs characteristic of that industry. In other businesses, ranging from hotels to hospitals to casinos and grain elevators, a small software firm such as Traverse Technologies can speed the flow of knowledge throughout an enterprise by using "middleware" interfaces to dynamize what were previously marooned sources of vital information.

As any organization becomes more complex, it faces the insufficiency of its earlier efforts at coordination. The U.S. Army, for instance, is both a command institution and a set of proud subcultures. It can carry out its most demanding missions only by relying on a great deal of necessarily local initiative. If so naturally hierarchical and authoritarian an institution as the Army can live like this (and, to a striking degree, like it), it is hard to believe that, say, automobile manufacturers cannot.

Loss of hierarchy can come quite as much by experience as by intention. Who really *knows* enough about a process to stand at its peak? Does *anyone* know enough about a truly complex undertaking to manage it from start to finish? As the number of transactions increases, more and more paths are formed in all directions. Formal intervening steps—which more often than not are choke points—are forced to diminish. Monitoring by some higher authority becomes steadily more inefficient.

By the early 1990s, two decades of oil cartelization, great-power entanglements, sclerotic economic management, foreign competition, and perhaps simple unpreparedness had undercut the U.S. economy's supremacy and its all-too-carefree postwar momentum. But one thing defies the assertion that the relative loss of headway in the world economy translates into an absolute mediocrity or a decline in living standards, and that is simple observation. From the banker's office to the classroom to the factory to the operating theater, the passive-technical world of ledgers, lecture halls, assembly lines, and scalpels is giving way to the world of machines which are helping to push their users forward. And all this is due to our barely awakened capacity to direct these machines and to make things new.

Up to now, the most advanced technologies could bring basic news instantly but still lagged badly where detailed information was concerned. The triumph over distance was striking, yet it was less complete than it seemed at first glance. Now, a genuine real-time planetary network for trading information, discussing designs, or making decisions is becoming accessible to more and more of us. Telecommuting, long-distance teaching, and new tools for coordination are all parts of this network. The sense of having to wait, and equally of having time before a distant continent makes its impact upon our lives, is dissolving as we watch.

The earlier problem was merely to hold things together amid gradual change, given the amount of distance and delay involved. The sad comment about how "seas roll and months pass between the order and the execution" was still true in essence if not literal numbers; there was too much that could not be bridged by the cable or the executive jet. The world in which there is little difference in information terms between "down the corridor" and "across the Pacific" is enforcing not merely new consciousnesses but new and unconsidered attitudes. It is dissolving hundreds of matters which institutions and their participants too long took for granted.

Notes

1. Quoted in *Fortune*, November 1, 1993, p. 84.
2. Quoted in *Washington Post*, October 23, 1993.

About the Authors

Scott Brown is Manager of Advanced Systems Development at Novell. Previously he was a director of engineering programs, a senior strategic planner, and a director of product development and support at Tandem and a designer of network architecture at Burroughs. A co-author of "A Multi-Dimensional Look at the Future of On-Line Technology," which appears in *Technology 2001*, he holds a B.S. in computer science from Utah State University and an M.B.A. from Santa Clara University.

Peter F. Conklin is Digital Equipment Corporation's director of systems development. He previously directed all hardware and software development in Digital's AXP Program. The first software engineer on the VMS project (in 1975), he also ran the VAX architecture team and was (in 1982) the first person to sponsor UNIX in Digital's product strategy. Author of many articles on these matters, he holds an A.B. in mathematics from Harvard University.

Jeffrey P. Cunard is a partner at Debevoise & Plimpton, a New York law firm, where he directs the telecommunications practice. A co-author of two books (*The Telecom Mosaic* and *From Telecommunications to Electronic Services*) and of many articles, he is a graduate of the University of California at Los Angeles and of the Yale Law School.

Gustave Essig is the founder of UniNet Communications, a computer-integrated-telephony company. His earlier work in technology financing involved him with the banking, oil, and biotechnology industries. He holds a degree in analytical philosophy from Princeton University, where he received the Dickinson Prize for his writings on the mechanisms of language.

Edward A. Feigenbaum is a professor of computer science at Stanford University, where he is also scientific co-director of the Knowledge System Laboratory and software study director of the Computer Industry Project. Author of many books and articles, he has served on numerous professional and government boards. He is a past president of the American Association for Artificial Intelligence. The first recipient of the Feigenbaum Prize, awarded by the World Congress of Expert Systems, he holds degrees from Carnegie-Mellon University.

Denos C. Gazis, a director at the IBM Research Center in Yorktown Heights, N.Y., previously directed the General Sciences Department and served in a variety of other senior research posts at IBM. A consultant for the Congressional Office of Technology Assessment, he has also been a visiting professor at Yale. He has written several books and many articles on traffic science and the vibrations of solids. The author of "Brief Time, Long March: The Forward Drive of Computer Technology," which appears in *Technology 2001,* he holds a Ph.D. in engineering sciences from Columbia University, an M.S. from Stanford, and first degrees from the Polytechnic in Athens.

Joshua Lederberg received the Nobel Prize in Physiology of Medicine for pioneering the field of bacterial genetics with the discovery of genetic recombination in bacteria, and for subsequent research on bacterial genetics. He is University Professor at Rockefeller University, which is devoted to biomedical research. Before coming to Rockefeller University in 1978, he was a professor of genetics at the University of Wisconsin and then at Stanford University School of Medicine. At Stanford he was also Professor of Computer Science. While working on artificial intelligence in biochemistry and medicine, in collaboration with E. A. Feigenbaum and B. G. Buchanan, he was already deeply involved in the use of data networks for scientific communication.

Derek Leebaert teaches Management of Technology at Georgetown University's Graduate School of Business and is an investor in the software and biochemistry industries. He also consults for industry and government. Formerly chief economist for the Computer and Business Equipment Manufacturers Association and a postdoctoral fellow at Harvard University's Center for Science and International Affairs, he was a founding editor of the *Journal of Policy Analysis and Management* and of *The International Economy.* He holds a D.Phil. in economics from Oxford University.

Deborah K. Louis is the director of customer operations in the Worldwide Operations Division of Lotus Development Corporation. She previously worked in manufacturing (at Wang Laboratories) and in management consulting. A member of the Software Manufacturing Association, she holds a B.A. from Occidental College.

L. Alexander Morrow is the general manager of cross-product architecture at Lotus Development Corporation, where he guides the implementation of standards across Lotus products and is also responsible for the exploration of advanced technologies. Previously at IBM (most recently as a manager of systems architecture and development for technical computer systems), he is among the founders of the Open Software Foundation. A recipient of the Association for Computing Machinery's Outstanding Contribution Award, he holds a B.A. in mathematics from Trinity College.

Eric Newcomer is a member of Digital Equipment Corporation's Production System Program Office. DEC's primary representative to the SPIRIT Consortium (U.K.), he was previously the representative to the MIA Consortium (Japan). He holds a B.A. from Antioch College.

Timothy O'Brien, a consultant for Intel, is also a contributing editor to the Seybold Office Computing Group. A former West Coast bureau chief for *Network*

World, he is a founder and a former president of the Account Data Group. He holds a B.A. from Stanford University.

David Vaskevitch is Microsoft's director of enterprise computing. A founder and a former chief technologist of Microsoft Consulting Services and a former director of U.S. marketing at Microsoft, he holds a B.S. in mathematics, computer science, and philosophy and an M.Sc. in computer science from the University of Toronto.

William B. Welty is a general partner in Volpe, Welty & Co. Formerly a senior vice-president and a member of the management committee at Hambrecht & Quist, and before that a member of Paine Webber's investment policy committee, he is the author of *Life on the Net: Business Competition in the Knowledge Age.* He holds degrees in engineering and business from Iowa State University.

David Williams directs Intel's Consumer Software Lab. Before joining Intel, he was chief strategist for Novell and then for Banyan Systems. He holds a B.S. in electrical engineering and computer science from California State University at Los Angeles.

Index

Action Technologies, 281–282, 287
Action Workflow Management System, 287
Agents, 7, 33–34, 142
Altai, Inc., 237
American Electronics Association, 280
American National Standards Institute, 84, 85–87
Anderson, Phil, 1
Anderson Consulting, 217–218, 284
API, 93, 147
APL, 9, 31
Applications
  deploying, 167–168
  rewriting, 60
Application software, 30
AppWare Loadable Modules, 165
Argotechnos, 21, 217
ARPANET, 82
Arrow, Kenneth, 278
Artificial intelligence, 16–17, 178
  copyrightability of, 255–257
  and visual programming, 174
Assembly language, 30
Assembly line, 50
Astounding Science Fiction, 13
Asynchronous Transfer Mode, 131
AT&T Corp., 80
Australia, software copyright law in, 243
Authorship
  and electronic networks, 247–249
  and ownership, 244–245

Bacon, Francis, 3
Banks
  and Business Process Reengineering, 55–57
  and customization, 71
BASIC, 9, 31
Benjamin, Robert I., 43
Berne Convention, 230–231
Bitzer, Don, 75
"Body shops," 220
Boeing Corp., 80
Boole, George, 186
Brain, 192–194, 198
Bright Air, Brilliant Fire (Edelman), 198, 199
Brooks, Fred, 34, 287
Bundling, 219–220
Business Process Reengineering, 50, 51
  and rewriting applications, 60
  self-managed teams and, 53
Business Software Alliance, 242

C, 31, 78
C++, 87
Cargill, Carl, 11
Carroll, Lewis, 177
Categorization, 198, 200
  functional, 200, 202–204, 206, 209–210
CBE, 88
Cellular automata, 8
Chomsky, Noam, 202
Clarke, Arthur C., 4, 17, 211, 274

Client/server, 58–60
COBOL, 78, 85–87
Cockton, Gilbert, 41
Cognitive latency, 137
Cognitive science, 200
Collaboration, computer-supported, 15, 128–139, 144–145, 148, 150–156
Communication
  anytime/anyplace, 138
  forms of, 73
  intelligent, 109
  intercomputer, 182
  process and, 73–74
  process orientation and, 50
  protocols for, 82
Community of services, 270
Component technology, 70–71
"Computer and the Brain" (von Neumann), 209
Computer Associates International, Inc. v. Altai, Inc., 237
Computer-Supported Cooperative Work (Wilson), 283
"Computing Machinery and Intelligence" (Turing), 186
Contingencies of Reinforcement (Skinner), 29
CONTU, 232, 259
CONTU II, 259
Cooperative work, computer-supported, 282–283
Coordination, 3, 286–287
  costs of, 279–280, 285–286
  phases of, 263–264
  technology of, 281
Copying, illegal, 221
Core competencies, 98
COSE, 88
C programming, language for, 86–87
C Programming Language (Kernighan and Ritchie), 86
Creativity, safeguarding, 228–230
Cross-licensing, 251
Customers, as partners, 113–115
CWIS, 143

DARPA, 82
Databases, 55
  access to, and CSC applications, 147–148
  free-text, 189
  games and, 76
Decision making, 50, 265
Decompilation, rights to, 238–240
Decomposition, functional, 62
Del Rey, Lester, 1, 3
Deregulation, 131
Digital Equipment Corp., 93
Distributed systems, 61–63
  factors inhibiting, 61–62
  of Japan's software, 218–219
Downsizing, 50, 58, 60
Drucker, Peter, 274

Earl, Harley, 264
Ease of use, 36, 89–90
Edelman, Gerald, 198–199
Education, software and, 24–25
Einstein, Albert, 190–191, 199, 201
Electronic data interchange, 281
Electronic Design News, 37
Electronic file cabinet, 141
Electronic mail, 72, 131–132
  as CSC application, 147–148
Electronic networks, authorship and, 247–249
Employees, self-reliant, 111–113
Employment, contingent/temporary, 273
Encapsulation, 161
Encyclopaedia Britannica, 253
Encyclosoft, 217
Engelbart, Doug, 75
End-to-end bandwidth digital communications, 286
Entailment, 206–207
ESPRIT, 192
European Community, and copyrights, 243
Examination, vs. copying, 239
Externalities, 236

Fair use, 240, 254
Feel, 234–238
Fifth Generation project, 192
First Cities consortium, 267–269
"Five Papers on WordNet" (Miller),
  201
Flores, Fernando, 281–282
Food of the Gods (Wells), 13, 105
Ford, Henry, 96–97
Formats and protocols, 93
FORTRAN, 9, 31
Fuzziness, source of, 202–203
Fuzzy logic, 173–174

Games, 38, 76
Gary, Judge, 263
Gates, Bill, 79
General Motors, 279
Gibson, William, 271
Globalization, 19
Granularity, 162
  and control, 164
"Green Paper on Copyright and the
  Challenge of Technology," 243
Groups without meetings, 116–118
Groupware, 282
GUI. *See* User interface

Heinlein, Robert, 277
Hersey, John, 232
Hierarchy, loss of, 288
"Highway," 79
Hopkins, Martin, 32
Human interface, 94–95
Hypermedia, 41
Hypertext, 40–41

Icons, 158, 180
Ideas and Opinions (Einstein), 190,
  199, 201
IEEE, 83
Indeo, 148–149
Information, access to, 57–58
Information systems, on-line, 269
Information technology, 42–43, 81,
  127–128
Information utility, 79

Information work, 275
InfoZone, 143–144, 285
Innovation, intensification of, 22–23
Intel, 148–149
Intellectual-property bargain, 229–230
Intelligent agents, in workflow pro-
  cesses, 140–142
Interaction, philosophy of, 281–282
Interchangeable parts, 96–97
Interface languages, 180
Internal weights, 256–257
Internalization, and software protec-
  tion, 258–259
Internet, 82–83, 266, 270
Internet Activities Board, 82, 83
Interoperability, 92, 93
Interoperable computer devices, and
  copyright, 233
Interoperable environments, 238–242
ISDN, 97, 131
ISO, 82

Jacquard loom, 6, 21
Japan
  copyright changes in, 242
  software industry in, 19–20, 215–225
Japan Lotus, 217
JCL, 34
Johnson, Harry, 22
Johnson, William R., 78
Just-in-time business, 128–129
  and CSC applications, 151
JUST Systems, 217
  illegal copying in, 221

Kapor, Mitchell, 79, 252
Kay, Alan, 45
Knowledge, 205
  artificial, 195–197
  categories of, 205
  cognitive, 194, 195
  forms of, 195–197
  linguistic, 195–197
  units of, 203, 205
Knowledge base, 266–271
Knowledge organizations, 277–284
Knowledge repositories, 283–284

Knowledge representation
  categorical, 208
  functional, 204–208
  as missing link, 192–197
  natural language and, 190–191
Knowledge revolution, 286
Knowledge work, 263
Knowledge workers, 271–277

Lakoff, George, 200
Languages, and computing environments, 30–32
League for Programming Freedom, 252
Legal protection, debates over, 232–234
Local-area networks, 269
Local customization, 52, 54
Local flexibility, 58
Look, 234–238
Lotus Notes, 72, 136, 283
Lotus 1-2-3, 33, 235–236
Lowenberg, Richard, 143

Malone, Thomas W., 43
Management, 22, 50. *See also* Total Quality Management
Man-hours, 275
Mann, Thomas, 127
Marketing, as bottleneck, 169–172
Markoff, John, 7–8
Mathematical logic, as computer base, 189
Medawar, Peter, 45
MediaMail, 166–167
Merger, doctrine of, 236
Messaging, 131–132, 147–148
MIA Consortium, 92–95
Middleware, 287
Millar, Victor E., 43
Miller, George, 201
Minsky, Marvin, 201
MITI, 217–218
Moore, Gordon, 2
Motif, 88
MS-Windows, 87, 88
Multimedia, 35–37, 133, 223–224
  servers for, 136

Multimedia works, challenges to, 254–255
Multitasking, 35
Mythical Man-Month (Brooks), 287

NAFTA, 244, 258
Naming service architecture, 146
National Commission on New Technological Uses of Copyrighted Works. *See* CONTU
National Research Council, 42
Natural language, 177–178
  beginnings of, 195
  as primary medium of communication, 199
  syntax of, 202
Naturalware, 211
Negroponte, Nicholas, 267
Networking, open, 82
Networks, 145–148
  semantic, 201–202
Network Management Forum, 95
Neural networks, legal protection of, 255
Neuromancer (Gibson), 271
"New hard," 223
NewMedia, 252
Nielsen, J., 41
Nintendo, 215–216, 224
Nippon Telegraph and Telephone, 80, 91
NuSopht, 166–167

Object-oriented design, 154
Objects, 144, 157, 161, 162–163, 166–167
Obsolescence, 275
Office of future, 70–74
Operating systems, 30, 34–37
Organizations, and processes, 65
OSI, 82–83
Outsourcing, 285
Ownership, and authorship, 244–245

Palette, 158
PARC, 87
Partners, with shared goals, 118–121
PASCAL, 31

Patent laws, strategic advantages of, 249–252
Patent portfolios, 251
Patton, George, 278
Pay for performance, 273
Perelman, L. J., 24–25
Personal digital assistants, 155
Petrotechnical Open Software Corp., 154–155
Piel, Gerard, 13
Piracy, 228
Planetary network, 288–289
"Plug and play" approach, 133, 217
Portability, 92–94
Porter, Michael E., 43
POSIX, 83
Power spiral, 149–150
Power Visualizing System, 39
Prairie School, 121
Prior art, 251, 252
Processes, 63–66
  communication and, 73–74
  concept of, 72–73
  distributed, 64
  and distributed systems, 66
Processing, 72
Process orientation
  communication and, 50
  problems solved by, 67–68
Productivity, 274–275
  improving, 43, 44
Programmers
  classes of, 165–166
  need for, 20
Programming
  environmental movement in, 32
  two-dimensional, 32–33
Programming languages, limited functionality of, 191
PROLOGUE, 31–32

Quatro Corp., 280
Query By Example, 33
Queues, 51
QUICKTRAN, 9, 31
Quillian, M. Ross, 201

Reengineering, 262
Re-Engineering the Corporation (Hammer and Champy), 51
Reference implementation approach, 83, 88
Regulations, need for, 81
Reich, Robert, 262
Relevance, definition of, 46
Remote access network, 285
Remote Task Invocation, 93
Resor, Stanley, Sr., 263, 287
Reversal, law of, 267
Reverse engineering, 239
  legality of, 240
Rights, moral, 248–249
RISC, 32, 37–38
Ritchie, Dennis, 86
Robertson, Sir Dennis, 274

Sapir-Whorf Hypothesis, 199
Schank, Roger, 201
Scheduling, with personal computer, 134–139
Scientific method, Einstein on, 190–191
Second, measurement of, 11–12
Sega Enterprises, Ltd. v. Accolade, Inc., 240–242
Seiden, Philip, 8
Selection, coordination, or arrangement (SCA), 234
Servers, 68
  role of, 53–58
  software for, 75
Simulation, 167
Simon, Herbert, 9
Smith, Adam, 276
SMTP, 147
Soft factory, 280
Speech recognition
  continuous, 271
  and visual programming, 174
SPIRIT, 95–98
SQL, 78
Standardization
  benefits of, 78–79
  process of, 85–90

Standards
  conflict over, 10–11
  de facto, 84
  de jure, 84–85
  developing new, 80–85
  generation of, 12–13
  multiple, 88–89
  need for, 77
  for open networks, 82
  reference implementation approach
    to, 83, 88
STDL, 93–94
Stone, David, 79
Strachey, John, 9
Structure, sequence, and organization
  (SSO), 234–235
Subsidiaries, Japanese, 218
Swift, Jonathan, 7
Systems analysts, need for, 20
Systems, open, 81, 83

Teams, self-managed, 54, 57–58,
  67–68
Technology 2001, 4, 17, 45
Telluride, 143–144
Telluride Institute, 143–144
Temporary corporation, 284
They Call It Software, 29
T*HQ, 280
Total Quality Management, 55, 57
TP monitor, 93–94
Trade secrets, laws of, 246
Transactions, 51, 62
  atomicity of, 63
  costs of, 281
  definition of, 63–64, 92–93
  monitoring, 282
  and processes, 65
Transaction processing
  lack of standards in, 92–93
  systems for, 62
Turing, Alan, 184–185, 186
Turing Test, 186–187
Two-phase commit, 63, 68
TxRPC, 94

Uniform customer file, 56
Uniform Trade Secrets Act, 246
Universal Turing Machine, 184, 187
  multifunctionality of, 189
UNIX, 37–38
Uruguay Round, of GATT, 230–231,
  244, 246, 258
User interfaces, 30, 40–42, 180
  common, 92
  graphical (GUI), 41–42, 60, 160, 181
Users, challenges for, 90–98

Version control, 167–168
Very Large Knowledge Base, 16, 271
Video conferencing, 135
Virtual community, 143–144
Virtual reality, 38–40
  cost of, 267
Virtual system, 34–35
Visual AppBuilder, 165
Visualization, 39–40
Visual programming, 160–166
  and software development, 169, 173
von Neumann, John, 5, 184, 209

Watson, Richard, 253–264
Weitzner, Daniel, 79
Wells, H. G., 13, 105
*Whelan Associates, Inc. v. Jaslow Labo-
  ratories, Inc.,* 235
Wilson, Paul, 283
Windowing, 87–88
Women, Fire, and Dangerous Things
  (Lakoff), 200
Work activities, classifications of,
  262–263
Workflow, 140
Workflow processes, intelligent agents
  in, 140–143
Workgroup computing, 115

X-Windows system, 87, 88

Yates, Joanne, 43

Zloof, Moshe, 33